Give Us This Day

Copyright 1986, Leroy Brownlow
Gift Edition: ISBN 0-915720-23-X
Trade Edition: ISBN 0-915720-89-2
Leather Edition: ISBN 0-915720-24-8

Brownlow Publishing Company, Inc.
6309 Airport Freeway, Fort Worth, Texas 76117

Give Us This Day

A Devotional Guide for Daily Living

LEROY BROWNLOW

Other Brownlow Gift Books

Introduction

Give Us This Day was written for all ages and all peoples in every situation and condition of life. This book is for my grandsons, for my family and your family, for the young, for those in middle life and for those in their golden years.

All of us need strength. And there is no more effective way to get it than on a daily basis. For life is a growth, which is a daily process. This volume is my third book of daily meditations, the first two being *Today Is Mine* and *Living With the Psalms.*

Each person is what he thinks, and as he reads he thinks. Thus it is exceedingly imperative that each has a little time everyday for uplifting meditation.

An effort has been made to make this volume profound, readable in simple language, interesting, and at times humorous, and most of all — helpful. An attempt has been made to present the deep meaning and ever possibility of life, to give lines that penetrate the heart for practical benefits. May these daily messages furnish guidance in times of difficulty, counsel in moments of perplexity, rest for the weary, courage for the threatened, cheer for the despondent, comfort for the afflicted, power for the struggling, cure for the blues, hope for the faint-hearted, and vision for all to see the fuller, more exhilarating and more jubilant life.

Inasmuch as humanity's needs are ever present and basically the same, this book — except in minor points — should always be up to date. Its suggestiveness and helpfulness should be as relevant tomorrow as today.

Now the hope is cherished that you and all readers may find these pages, day by day, the stepping stones to higher ground.

Leroy Brownlow

I Will Start Afresh

Add ye year to year. Isaiah 29:1

Happy New Year!

The old one is behind us. Forever! Some things God gives often, but He gives time only once. The flowers of spring return again and again. The trees burst into a new foliage year after year. But time does not come twice to anyone.

We enter the new year with high hopes. Every new year holds a brighter hope than the last, and we are ever ready to shake off bad habits and to give life a new start and a new effort. Such thinking has possibilities, for every improvement begins with a thought. This was the power that turned the feet of the ancient Psalmist who said, "I thought on my ways, and turned my feet unto thy testimonies" (Psalms 119:59). The trouble has been we have allowed some conflicting thoughts to grab us and change the direction of our feet.

• *So our first resolution is to keep our thoughts working for us.* No person is better, bigger or stronger than his or her thoughts.

• *Second, let us be grateful for the many blessings of last year.* We are not worthy of more, if we are ungrateful for what we have.

• *Third, may we determine to be sympathetic toward all less fortunate persons than ourselves.* Having a heart is a big accomplishment.

• *Fourth, let us resolve to place the best reasonable construction on the words and deeds of others.*

• *Fifth let us build life on the good foundation of loving God and our fellowman.*

Give Us This Day

Let me go, for the day breaketh. Genesis 32:26

In what is commonly called *The Lord's Prayer* we are taught to pray, "Give us this day." It is a sacred gift. Definitely a gift. Sacred because it is God-given. It is a gift worthy of petition and we pray for its continuance.

Ralph Waldo Emerson said:

A Day is a miniature Eternity.

This day is a whole world within itself. It can make a world of difference in the life God has given each of us. In these twenty-four hours one can plot a course that will shape one's life and destiny. In these 1440 minutes there are blessings to be received: bread to sustain life (but much more), opportunities to be used, challenges to be accepted, internal peace to quiet nerves, joy to give buoyancy, vision to look ahead, ability to struggle, time to make amends, and will power to make dreams come true. Today — too much cannot be said in its behalf. Without it, the tent has been folded and the pilgrim has gone home. With it, the world beckons.

Today — let me grab it, seize it, use it, live it, enjoy its every second. It is more valuable than money — no amount of money will buy another today. Treasure it as if your entire life depended upon it, and it very well could.

This day is nothing unless appreciated, used and enjoyed. What are books, health, wealth, travel, security, if we have not today?

Too much value cannot be placed on today, for it comes only once. Salute it at dawn and hold on to it until tomorrow turns into another day.

Resolved to Have a Better Year

Behold, now is the accepted time. II Corinthians 6:2

When Thorwaldsen was asked, "Which is your greatest statue?" he replied, "The next one."

It has been said that Cromwell wrote in his Bible, "If I cease to become better, I shall cease to be good." Even the best may be bettered. Indeed, it must be bettered if it is not to become worse. Nothing remains static very long. It is meant for us to advance on our past. Whatever we gain each year is not meant to be a level on which to stop but a plateau on which to ascend. This means that we need to resolve and plan to go on to better things and greener pastures. For this reason, good resolutions are more than a duty — they are a necessity.

Let us thoughtfully meditate on the following lines:

I will start afresh each new day from petty littleness freed;
I will cease to stand complaining of my ruthless neighbor's greed;
I will cease to sit repining while my duty's call is clear;
I will waste no moment whining, and my heart shall know no
fear.

I will not be swayed by envy when my rival's strength is shown;
I will not deny his merit, but I'll try to prove my own;
I will try to see its beauty spread before me, rain or shine;
I will cease to preach your duty and be more concerned with
mine.

As we travel the new year path, let us keep a sharp look out for sign posts. The bypaths are plainly marked, *Ruin, Misery, Death.* The right path reads, *Happiness, Peace, Success.* Look forward to the journey. Neither turn to the right hand nor the left. Keep going!

Look to This Day

*For Moses had said, Consecrate yourselves today to the Lord,
even every man upon his son, and upon his brother; that he may
bestow upon you a blessing this day. Exodus 32:29*

Most people miss the best of today, because they plan to get
the best tomorrow. And then when tomorrow comes it is no
better than today. So all their tomorrows become only dusty
dreams. But by saluting the dawn you make today your blessing and tomorrow your hope.

> *Look to this Day*
> *For it is life, the very breath of life.*
> *In its brief course lie all the verities and*
> *Realities of your existence;*
> > *The Bliss of Growth*
> > *The Glory of Action*
> > *The Splendors of Beauty;*
> *For yesterday is already a dream*
> *And tomorrow is only a vision.*
> *But today, well lived,*
> *Makes every yesterday a dream of happiness*
> *And every tomorrow a vision of hope.*
> *Look well, therefore, to this day!*

From the Sanskrit

It is the stuff of which real living is made!

How to Be Happy This Year

I must walk today, and tomorrow, and the day following.
                                          Luke 13:33

• *Learn to forget.* Bury the miseries of the dead past. Let them stay buried. If God forgets, why shouldn't you? The only use of bygones is to prepare us to meet bycomes. One of the secrets of success and happiness is letting go that which absorbs our energies and hinders our progress.

• *Make your conscience a source of peace and joy.* Conscience is the voice of approval or condemnation in the soul. Do what you believe is right and the voice will approve and give you an appreciation of self.

• *Cultivate contentment.* Every discontented person is unhappy. Furthermore, it decreases his or her level of efficiency. Many people are unhappy beause they spend their time looking at other people and thinking how happy they could be if they were in their place. The truth is, those people are looking at you and thinking the same thing. Blessed is the person who can say, "I have learned, in whatsoever state I am, therewith to be content" (Philippians 4:11).

• *Be helpful.* To be happy we must be helpful. Happiness cannot be obtained without giving it away. When you lift another's burden, you lighten your own.

• *Be trustful.* All that I *have seen* teaches me to trust God for all that I *cannot see.* If God can control the universe, He can help me and will — not always as I wish but always in my eventual welfare. Do not permit the ghosts of doubt to move into your heart; if you do, you are setting yourself up for anxieties and fears — for bad days ahead when you could have good ones.

Brave Enough to Wrestle a Bear

Be strong and of a good courage, fear not, nor be afraid of them: for the Lord thy God, he it is that doth go with thee; he will not fail thee, nor forsake thee. Deuteronomy 31:6

Our little town was too small to have a picture show, and at that time there were no radios or televisions. This made it very inviting for tent shows to come at intervals for a one or two night stand.

I recall that one of the traveling shows had a big bear trained to wrestle. The show people would put gloves on the bear's paws and feet and a guard over his head. This was to protect the man who wrestled him from being cut and chewed to pieces. If any man ever prayed in his life it was when he stepped into the ring to battle that bear.

To draw a crowd, they wanted a well known man of the community to wrestle the bear. My father accepted the challenge. I shall never forget it. The match was some contest, and my father came away unhurt.

The next day at school I was so proud. It was thrilling to hear them say, "Heh, your daddy did well wrestling the bear."

A few years passed and he got older and I got grown. He became a Christian and I admired him more than ever.

Everybody appreciates bravery. Wrestling a bear, however, is just one kind of heroism. During the last eight years of his life he was painfully ill, but day by day he showed a new kind of courage, more valiant than meeting the bear.

Though their bravery is unsung, multitudes are going through trials and hardships — physical, mental, social, economic — that make them heroes in their own rights.

Never Say *FAIL*

Behold, we count them happy which endure. James 5:11

John and Mary are climbing to the top. Happy, too. The reasons are obvious. They miss a step occasionally, but they won't say *fail*.

Among the millions of youth destined to reach a bright future there is no such word as — *fail*.

The ability of man to dignify and elevate his life is found in his refusal to utter one word — *fail*.

Never say *fail*. If at first you don't succeed, try, try, again.

If our poor performance is not in our stars (and it's not), why quit? We can change ourselves and keep on struggling.

> *Keep pushing — 'tis wiser*
> *Than sitting aside,*
> *And dreaming and sighing,*
> *And waiting the tide.*
> *In life's earnest battle*
> *They only prevail*
> *Who daily march onward*
> *And never say fail!*
>
> *In life's early morning,*
> *In manhood's firm pride,*
> *Let this be your motto*
> *Your footsteps to guide;*
> *In storm and in sunshine,*
> *Whatever assail,*
> *We'll onward and conquer,*
> *And never say fail!*

A Determined Burro

Yea, thou shalt be steadfast, and shalt not fear. Job 11:15

A city man spent his vacation on a cattle ranch and learned some very interesting lessons. He rode with the cowboys on a roundup. It was thrilling, and even more — it was a school within itself.

There was one wild steer over in the breaks that didn't want to be driven to the corral. He wouldn't drive. Neither would he be pulled; when roped, he would lie down and twist and roll. He was the wildest, meanest thing that ever walked on four hoofs. Whirling, turning, charging, ever watching with blood-stained glassy eyes, breathing out a vapor of murder, he was saying he wouldn't be tamed. However, the old cowboys knew better. They knew what to do. They tied that unbroken beast close to a little Mexican burro. When they turned them loose that big angry animal threw that pint-sized burro ten ways to the veterinarian. And he kept doing it. But everytime that burro got up he got up one step closer home. He wanted to go home.

About ten days later the steer and burro arrived at the corral. And that steer was the tamest thing anyone had seen. Persistence and steadfastness had won.

Sometimes it's not how big we are but how steadfast we are that gets us to where we wish to go. The grit to continue when the going gets rough has a way of coming out on top.

It is fatal to enter any endeavor of struggle without the will to win it. Persevering people begin their success at the very point where others end in failure.

Hearken to Logic

Hear now my reasoning, and hearken to the pleadings of my lips. Job 13:6

A teacher asked her pupils this question, "Which is more helpful to us — the moon or the sun?"

Jimmy replied, "The moon."

"Why?" asked the teacher.

Jimmy answered, "The moon gives us light at night when we need it. But the sun gives us light only in the daytime when we don't need it."

We laugh at the child's reasoning, but it's no laughing matter that some of us adults don't do much better.

Logic is a process used for cutting down our mistakes. Whatever characteristics we have, logic should be one of them. We do so many foolish things because we either don't use logic or it is faulty. We should not throw to the wind such logic as:

"A man that hath friends must show himself friendly" (Proverbs 18:24). "A gift in secret pacifieth anger: and a reward in the bosom, strong wrath" (Proverbs 21:14). "Confidence in an unfaithful man in time of trouble is like a broken tooth, and a foot out of joint" (Proverbs 25:19) "Where no wood is, there the fire goeth out: so where there is no talebearer, the strife ceaseth" (Proverbs 26:20). "Where there is no vision, the people perish" (Proverbs 29:18). "Wherefore by their fruits ye shall know them" (Matthew 7:29). "For whatsoever a man soweth, that shall he also reap" (Galatians 6:7).

Each of these statements is common sense reasoning that is unquestionably right.

Be Considerate

So I returned, and considered all the oppressions that are done under the sun: and behold the tears of such as were oppressed, and they had no comforter.   Ecclesiastes 4:1

There are many oppressions, hardships and burdens of every kind. Whatever our fellow man's oppression may be, we should be considerate and compassionate in dealing with him. Unless we have walked in his steps we don't know what he has been through.

DO NOT JUDGE TOO HARD

Pray do not find fault with the man that limps
    Or stumbles along the road, unless you have
        worn the shoes he wears,
Or struggled beneath his load.

There may be tacks in his shoes that hurt,
        though hidden from view,
    Or the burdens he bears placed on your back —
Might cause you to stumble, too.

You may be strong, but still the blows that were his,
    If dealt to you in the selfsame way at the
        selfsame time —
Might cause you to stagger, too.

We should be considerate of each other for all of us belong to the same family, having been made of the same clay. But there is a relationship in addition to blood. Human need and pity relate us all to each other; our needs vary, but all have them.

One of the principles of Christianity is sympathy: "Rejoice with them that do rejoice, and weep with them that weep" (Romans 12:15).

Touch Means Much

And Jesus, moved with compassion, put forth his hand, and touched him. Mark 1:41

There is an interesting and helpful story to learn from a five-year-old girl. She had a fascinating interest in the story of "The Three Little Pigs." Understandably, she requested her father to read that story night after night.

While it became boring to the father, it continued to be gripping to the daughter. Seeking relief, the father simply made a tape of the story, and when the daughter asked for it, he simply switched on the recording.

This worked for three nights and then the next evening the child handed the storybook to her father.

"Now sweetheart," he said, "you know how to turn on the recorder."

"Yes," said the little girl, "but I can't sit on its lap."

Aloofness makes cool strangers of us all, but touch has a magnetic pull that unites and makes us friends. Even beasts respond to the touch of a loving hand. How much more does man!

Touch speaks a message that words cannot utter. Learn the art of it for the most effective communication.

And Then Some

And whosoever shall compel thee to go a mile, go with him twain. Matthew 5:41

An executive once stated the secret of every successful person he had ever known was in three little words: "And then some."

This is the second mile philosophy.

It is following in the steps of God who does not think in terms of least amounts but rather does "exceeding abundantly above all that we ask or think" (Ephesians 3:20).

Our world is a competitive one. To get ahead you can't stop at the minimum. It is absolutely necessary to give more, outdo and outlast others — do your duty "and then some." Anyone who works with the view, "I'm going to do the least I can to hold a job," is not going to get promoted. In merchandising it is better to give an ounce than to take an ounce, and to give a pint of gasoline than to short the customer a pint. In school you will receive no awards if you are satisfied just to pass.

If it's your philosophy that you are not going to do anything for anybody you don't have to do, then mankind will never overflow your basket. But — "Give and it shall be given unto you; good measure, pressed down, and shaken together, and running over, shall men give into your bosom" (Luke 6:38). The giver in the verse is man. Give to him and he shall give to you good measure and running over.

Duty — "and then some!" Therein is success!

Two Burdens No One Can Bear

Sufficient unto the day is the evil thereof. Matthew 6:34

There are two burdens no one can bear — yesterday's and tomorrow's. No person gives way beneath the burdens of to-day. It's the ones of yesterday and the ones of tomorrow that break us. Too much for any human to bear. The wolves that howled at you yesterday are already gone; and the roaring lions you see for tomorrow may be only friendly kittens.

• *One way* to eliminate worry from your life is to forget the things which are behind. This was the psychology the apostle Paul followed in his own life. He said:

> *Forgetting those things which are behind, and reaching forth unto those things which are before, I press toward the mark.*
>
> Philippians 3:13,14

Dragging a lengthening chain of regrets from the dead past is like the life of a prisoner with a ball and chain around his ankle.

• *Another way* to prevent ulcer-creating apprehension is to live in the present rather than the future. Fear is the dread of trouble to come and a feeling of inability to handle it. But if I admit no evil which I cannot surmount, with God's help, then I shall not be afraid as each day dawns. As Gertrude Bower Webster has written,

> *When storms swoop down, and torrents roar,*
> *And troubles crowd your day,*
> *Be robust, brave, and undismayed*
>   *For troubles pass away.*
>
> *All ills are transients that afflict*
>   *And cumber life's brief way,*
> *They flee before eternal things*
>   *That never pass away.*

A Dog Named Sunshine

How long wilt thou forget me, O Lord? for ever? how long wilt thou hide thy face from me? Psalms 13:1

To the majority, life presents problems that often perplex and discourage. Then it is easy to question your lot and the God that supports you. Many of the Psalms of the Bible give utterance to this feeling.

My soul is also sore vexed: but thou, O Lord, how long?
Psalms 6:3

Several years ago I visited an old woodcutter in his one-room cabin. His face bore the lines of hardship, and the contents of his cabin signaled privation. His life had consisted of only bare necessities. No comfort or luxury had ever entered his door, except maybe one — his dog. It was a big dog he called *Sunshine.*

In all of his loneliness, privation and suffering he had been able to find a little sunshine, even if it was only a dog. Here is an example for us.

In the course of our conversation, he stated that he had been through the wringer of disappointment, suffering and sorrow; and that for a short time his faith weakened, and it was then that he questioned God's care for him, but not any more. He further stated that time had given the events a different perspective and he was now a better and more sensitive man because of what had happened to him.

Indeed, some pages in life's book are hard to understand, but we do know that pain can sweeten and ennoble human character. That is the reason the Apostle Paul could say, "We also rejoice in our sufferings." (Romans 5:5). And this we further know — what looks topsy-turvy to us is clear and un-toppled before the eyes of Him whom we serve.

Dream a Little

I must also see Rome. Acts 19:21

For a man 1900 years ago — in Paul's state and that far away as distance was measured in that day — to dream of going to Rome was considered mere fantasy by most people.

We can learn from Paul. No one should ever stop reaching for new lands to conquer and for new goals to reach. To rise above earth's common ground you must dream a little. Dream of a star and hitch yourself to it.

The world is filled with dreamers, but the ones who really profit from it are the ones who dream when they are awake.

Those who dream by day are cognizant of many things which escape those who dream only by night.

Edgar Allan Poe

The dreamers are the lonely pioneers of human progress. Our society is blessed by the fortunate visions of its open-eyed dreamers.

Humanity cannot afford to forget its dreamers. It must not let their ideas wither and die. For every great reality was once only a dream. Dreams are the seeds of realities. Illustrious accomplishments rise from little dreams just as mighty oaks sprout from little acorns.

Don't quit dreaming. As long as you dream you are alive. Cease to dream and life loses its zest and ebbs away.

Maybe in your own soul there is a vision that is beginning to stir. Not a material one. A spiritual one. A vision of a fuller life that will glorify your Maker. The dream you have of yourself — that you will become.

What Makes a Strong Nation?

And God said, Let us make man in our image, after our likeness: and let them have dominion over the fish of the sea, and over the fowl of the air, and over the cattle, and over all the earth, and over every creeping thing that creepeth upon the earth. Genesis 1:26

As seen from the above passage, man was created and designed by a wise Creator to rule over creation — not to be held in any form of bondage.

Unquestionably, among all races and nations there are various degrees of talent, but equality gives each the right to develop his own endowment.

Hugh Black has forcefully stated that America must not fail on the proposition of equal opportunity:

"Faith in the people rests on the belief — in spite of ignorance and folly and mob passion, and all the rest of the indictment which we know so well — that the average man is honest and fair and wants to do right. I do not see how you can be a real democrat on any other basis.

"We make an appeal too often to the baser side of man, to prejudice and self interest. The better side of man is the stronger side, if we would believe it seriously and apply the faith unflinchingly . . . .

"America is a great political adventure, dedicated to the incredible proposition that men are born equal. I know all the criticism of that in fact and logic, but if America fails here she fails entirely."

Be Strong and Prevail

Be ye strong therefore, and let not your hands be weak: for your work shall be rewarded. II Chronicles 15:7

BE STRONG

Be strong!
We are not here to play, to dream, to drift;
We have hard work to do, and loads to lift;
Shun not the struggle — face it; 'tis God's gift.

Be strong!
Say not, "The days are evil. Who's to blame?"
And fold the hands and acquiesce — oh, shame!
Stand up, speak out, and bravely, in God's name.

Be strong!
It matters not how deep entrenched the wrong,
How hard the battle goes, the day how long;
Faint not — fight on! Tomorrow comes the song.

Maltbie Davenport Babcock

When I, barely seventeen, went away to college my mother said, "Son, be strong." Three words, but they carry a world of instruction and warning.

Be strong enough to know you're weak.
Be strong enough to be your own person.
Be strong in resisting temptation.
Be strong in wholesome associations.
Be strong in worthy friendships.
Be strong in honor.
Be strong in the defense of right.
Be strong in the pursuit of truth.
Be strong in respect of the elderly.
Be strong in facing difficulties.
Be strong in Bible reading.
Be strong in prayer.
Yes! Be strong! Be strong! Be strong!

Sow in Tears and Reap in Joy

She weepeth sore in the night, and her tears are on her cheeks. Lamentations 1:2

Life on this earth consists of sorrows and joys, tears and smiles. There is a time for each. Solomon said, "A time to weep, and a time to laugh." When the time comes for either, let us give ourselves to it. Shakespeare said, "If you have tears, prepare to shed them now."

Those who weep are cognizant of many things which escape the ones who only smile; and they receive a deeper blessing, though it's grievous, than those who have never known the depth of such sorrow. As John Cheney once said, "The soul would have no rainbows had the eyes no tears."

There are four things for which we can be thankful concerning tears:

First, we do have emotions that can be stirred. We're not robots. "Mine eye is consumed because of grief" (Psalms 6:7).

Second, God sees our tears. "Thus saith the Lord . . . I have heard thy prayer, I have seen thy tears: behold I will heal thee" (II Kings 20:5).

Third, after sorrows and tears come joys and smiles. "They that sow in tears shall reap in joy" (Psalms 126:5).

Fourth, we have the assurance that in another land on a faraway strand *"God shall wipe away all tears* from their eyes; and there shall be no more death, neither sorrow, nor crying" (Revelation 21:4).

If the Lion Eats Daddy

There is a way which seemeth right unto a man; but the end thereof are the ways of death. Proverbs 14:12

A father took his little boy to the zoo where they saw the lions in the cage. Greatly impressed with the lion's ferocity, the child said, "Daddy, if the lion gets out and eats you up, which bus do I take to get home?"

While it seems a little incongruous, facing the possibility of a crisis, the child's thoughts turned to home.

It should be a part of the vital training of every youth to come home. Home is a place of refuge to which you return. And our boys and girls need a curfew. It is more evident every day that the street with its establishments is not a place of safety.

Home should be one of the first and most sacred thoughts of the child. Blessed is the child who has this feeling and carries it with him or her through childhood, through youth and through life. All need a magnetic pull back to the rallying point of home. There we bind our wounds, dry our tears, bend our knees, and read the Scriptures, rewind our energy, renew our quest and rekindle our hope.

> *'Mid pleasures and palaces though we may roam,*
> *Be it ever so humble, there's no place like home.*

Some young people with their contempt for the old standards and proven ways, seeking a life of no restraint of thrills and spills, catch a bus going to disaster, disappointment, dismay, failure, misery — even to prison.

Wherever you wish to go, take the bus that's going there. Not all buses go to the same place.

Revive Us Again

Though I walk in the midst of trouble, thou wilt revive me.
Psalms 138:7

The long-winded preacher preached and preached. After about an hour of shouting and whispering and pounding the podium, he stopped and asked, "What hymn shall we sing?"

One elderly brother appropriately responded, "Revive Us Again."

It nearly broke up the service.

The other day we were faced with a common problem. The battery was too weak to turn the motor on the van. It needed reviving. When it was recharged, it worked well.

So many times we need to be recharged. The possibilities are there but need rekindled. This is why churches have revivals; why schools have pep rallies; the reason political parties have conventions; and the reason the individual needs motivational helps.

Revival — this is something everybody and everything needs at times. Human spirits lag and need renewing. Enthusiasm runs down and needs winding up.

Because of this universal need we occasionally sing in the worship services the renowned hymn, *Revive Us Again*. Even the Psalmist at times was in need of spiritual revival. He openly admitted it: "But as for me, my feet were almost gone; my steps had well-nigh slipped." (Psalms 73:2). And then he told us how long it lasted and what reawakened him: "Until I went into the sanctuary of God" (verse 17) — a near approach to God. Bringing it down to date, going to church can revive us.

Let Your Light Shine

Let your light so shine before men, that they may see your good works, and glorify your Father which is in heaven.
Matthew 5:16

Man once used the candle for light. It was hailed as a revolutionary discovery and a big improvement over the burning stick and torch. However, it flickered, gave off odor, and the least puff of wind would blow it out.

Then came the kerosene lamp. It was applauded as the big jump of progress in the field of illumination. But it had problems. The bowl had to be filled with kerosene. The wick had to be trimmed and sometimes did not reach the fluid. The globe became smoky and had to be cleaned.

Another improvement was the Coleman gasoline lamp or lantern. We had one when I was a boy and one of my jobs was to keep it going. It required gasoline, mantles, and had to be kept pumped up.

Best of all, thanks to Mr. Edison, is the incandescent light. When connected to the power house and the globe is good, it's a very efficient light.

What kind of light are you? Just a *candle* that quivers and emits odor? Or just a *kerosene light* with a short wick and a smoky globe? Or just a *gasoline light* that won't shine at all unless someone is there to keep you pumped up all the time? Or an *incandescent light,* connected to the great source of light, that shines and shines and shines?

One of the greatest compliments ever paid mortal man was given by the Apostle Paul to the Philippians, expressed in these words, "Ye shine as lights in the world" (Philippians 2:15). A darkened world needs your light. Shine on! Shine on!

The High Cost of Free Advice

Whoso keepeth his mouth and his tongue, keepeth his soul from troubles. Proverbs 21:23

There are some shortages in the world. But there is one thing in overflowing abundance — advice. Furthermore, it's free, unless you take it; then you may find it very costly.

So much of the free (?) advice goes like this:

• *"Why don't you get a new car?"* But the advisor doesn't know of your finances, your obligations, your job security, your plans for the future, your priorities, etc. So it's advice from no knowledge.

• *"You should get a new suit, or new dress, or a new hairstyle, or new shoes."* But the advisor is not aware of your plans, problems or preferences.

• *"You should paint your house."* Again the self-appointed counselor lacks all the personal information you possess.

Many, many more examples could be cited. But why? It is better to stop it by asking, "Who is this that darkeneth counsel by words without knowledge?" (Job 38:2).

While I have been a counselor for many years, I freely say that it is not wise to give advice unless it is asked. Even Jesus taught against teaching or counseling those who don't want it. He called it casting "pearls before swine," who may later turn and rend you (Matthew 7:6).

There are exceptions, of course, to nearly all rules, including this one on giving advice. There are some friends and relatives with whom you are close enough to offer a little counsel, provided you don't appear superior or dictatorial. But generally speaking, refrain from it unless asked.

Turning Clouds Inside Out

But as for you, ye thought evil against me; but God meant it unto good, to bring to pass, as it is this day, to save much people alive. Genesis 50:20

Joseph's brethren did him an awful injustice, but it turned out to be a cloud with a silver lining. It became the means whereby he rose to the second highest office in Egypt, and thus enabled him to save the multitudes from seven years of famine, including his own people.

When one's plans are frustrated and he is saddled with pressing burdens, there is always the possibility of his becoming bitter and rebellious. Disgruntlement so often follows disappointment. The scoffer usually is a person whose expectations and hopes have been dashed. He saw the cloud, but not its silver lining. It is highly imperative, therefore, that we turn our clouds inside out that we see bigger hopes and brighter dreams.

> *The inner side of every cloud is bright and shining;*
> *I therefore turn my clouds about*
> *And always wear them inside out*
> *To show the lining.*
> Ellen Thorncroft Fowler

One of the most trying tests of life is how we meet adverse circumstances. I like the way the great Paganini met it. When his favorite violin was broken, he accepted the loss as a challenge and got another one. He said, "I will show them the music is in me and not in any instrument."

It is much easier to put back together the broken pieces of a dream when you learn to say, as Paul said, "My God shall supply all your (my) needs"; and when you have the grit to say, as Paul said, "I can do all things through Christ which strengtheneth me."

The World As Some See It

Behold, your house is left unto you desolate. Matthew 23:38

THE CENTER OF THINGS — the place where I am.

GOOD IDEAS — those that agree with mine.

BAD IDEAS — those that oppose mine.

SINFUL PLEASURES — the things others like to do.

INNOCENT PLEASURES — the things I like to do.

A SENSIBLE PERSON — one who heeds what I say.

BENEVOLENCE — everyone giving handouts to me.

HUMILITY — everyone bowing to my whims.

PATIENCE — everyone bearing with me.

COOPERATION — everyone working with me.

HOSPITALITY — everyone entertaining me.

ENCOURAGEMENT — everyone bragging on me.

UNITY — everyone going along with me.

SYMPATHY — everyone identifying with me.

MEEKNESS — everyone stepping aside for me.

A CONTENTIOUS PERSON — one who disagrees with me.

VISITATION — everyone coming to visit me.

Such a person can't see because he has too much "I" in his eye. This blinds him to the better and fuller life. It leaves his own little house desolate.

Handling Annoyances

And her adversary also provoked her sore, for to make her fret. I Samuel 1:6

A minister was asked if a man who was taking trumpet lessons on Sunday would go to heaven. The preacher's short reply with hidden meaning was, "I suppose so, but it's doubtful if the man next door will."

A person needs to smoothly and victoriously handle the annoyances. There are many things to ruffle one and grate on his nerves.

Just had a flat. The postman put the long-awaited check in a box down the street. The paper boy failed to throw your paper. You are ready to cook breakfast and you're out of coffee. The neighbor's cat spends too much time in your yard. The car ran out of gasoline. The children next door knock the ball through your window. You had bought tickets to go see your sister. The day comes and the airline is on strike.

What do you do about it?

First, accept the fact that life has annoyances as well as buoyances.

Second, decide that you are bigger than any annoyance that confronts you. That you can handle it.

Third, if the irritation is stressing you, count to ten; if it's still seeking to explode, keep on counting.

Fourth, through soul searching, meditation and determination, grow into a calmer person with a longer fuse. One of the qualifications of a bishop or elder is "not soon angry." This is an ideal to which all should strive.

Like the Gentle Rain From Heaven

For he shall have judgment without mercy, that hath showed no mercy; and mercy rejoiceth against judgment. James 2:13

In ages past, a king called his servants to give an account. One owed ten thousand pieces of money. Unable to pay, he pleaded for mercy, promising to pay. The king had compassion and forgave him.

Then that servant went out and found a fellow servant who owed him only a hundred pieces of money, and he took him by the throat and said, "Pay up." The debtor, not having the payment, pleaded for leniency, promising to pay. Now the very one who had asked for mercy and received it was unwilling to grant it to another. He ordered the poor man to be cast into prison till he paid.

When the news got back to the king, he was wroth, and reminded that cruel servant of the grace he had received but that he was unwilling to grant it in a much smaller amount to another. The king then commanded the unmerciful servant to be sent to the tormentors till he paid.

This is a good and apt story. I know it is. For it was given by Jesus Christ.

Unmerited clemency will do more than severity. Mercy purifies the soul, but vengeance lets it rot with rancor.

Humanity is too imperfect not to be in dire need of mercy.

Shakespeare stated that mercy twice blesses, him that gives and him that takes. This should make it free and unrestrained.

> The quality of mercy is not strained;
> It droppeth as the gentle rain from heaven
> Upon the place beneath: it is twice blest;
> It blesseth him that gives and him that takes.

Get Away From the Crowd and Think

I thought on my ways, and turned my feet unto thy testimonies. Psalms 119:59

A renowned example of seeking some solitude is Jesus. "And in the morning, rising up a great while before day, he went out, and departed into a solitary place, and there prayed" (Mark 1:35).

Solitude lends itself to many blessings, including prayer, self-examination, a reflection of one's past and present, and the formation of plans for the future. Free from the distractions of a fast-moving, hard-pressing world, we should ask: From whence have I come? Where am I now? Where am I going?

In a talk to young men, Robert Burdette said: "Get away from the crowd for awhile, and think. Stand on one side and let the world run by, while you get acquainted with yourself and see what kind of a fellow you are.

"Ask yourself hard questions about yourself. Ascertain if you are really the manner of man you say you are; and if you are always honest; if you always tell the whole, perfect truth in business details; if your life is as good and upright at twelve o'clock at night as it is at noon; if you are as good a temperance man on a fishing excursion as you are on a Sunday school picnic; if you are as good when you go out of town as you are at home; if, in short, you are really the sort of man your father hopes you are and your sweetheart believes you are.

"Get on intimate terms with yourself, my boy, and, believe me, every time you come out of one of those soul-searching sessions you will be a stronger, better, purer man."

The Stuff of Which Life Is Made

So teach us to number our days, that we may apply our hearts unto wisdom. Psalms 90:12

Since time is brief and uncertain, it behooves us all to live in the present and appropriate our days to the fullest. For the person who squanders time wastes the very thing out of which life is made. Thus by killing time one commits suicide tick by tick.

THE CLOCK OF LIFE

The clock of life is wound but once
And no man has the power
To tell just where the hand will stop —
At late or early hour.

Now is the only time you own!
Live, love, toil with a will;
Place no faith in "tomorrow" for
The clock may then be still.

Time deals kindly with those who use it rightly; and harshly with those who use it wrongly. Just a minute of time is a minute of life and is not to be scorned.

JUST A MINUTE

I have only just a minute,
Just sixty seconds in it;
Forced upon me — can't refuse it,
I must suffer if I lose it,
Give account if I abuse it;
Just a tiny little minute,
But eternity is in it.

Time works wonders — so use it.

Peace, Perfect Peace

To be spiritually minded is life and peace. Romans 8:6

• *Be thankful for life,* because it gives us the opportunity to work and to play and to live and to look into the heavens. "He giveth to all life, and breath, and all things" (Acts 17:25).

• *Affirm that our faith is stronger than our difficulties* and that we will conquer them. "This is the victory that overcometh the world, even our faith" (I John 5:4).

• *Constantly keep our goal before us.* Never give up our dreams. "I press toward the mark" (Philippians 3:14).

• *Live unselfishly, thinking of others.* The self-centered person can never get enough of himself or herself or the favors of others to find peace. "Look not every man on his own things, but every man also on the things of others" (Philippians 2:4).

• *Be satisfied with our possessions.* Then what you have, you have — not what you have has you. "There is a sore evil which I have seen under the sun, namely, riches kept for the owners thereof to their heart" (Ecclesiastes 5:13).

• *Stamp out negative thoughts with positive thoughts.* No person gets up the Mount of Happiness in reverse gear. "Whatsoever things are true, honest, just, pure, lovely, of good report; if there be any virtue, and if there be any praise, think on these things" (Philippians 4:8).

• *Put our trust in God,* in good times and bad, fully confident that we are in the hollow of His hand. "The Lord is my rock, and my fortress, and my deliverer; my God, my strength, in whom I will trust" (Psalms 18:2).

What Do You See?

Hear now this, O foolish people, and without understanding;
which have eyes, and see not; which have ears and hear not.
Jeremiah 5:21

Poor Henry — he never beheld anything but defeat, failure and disaster. Most of his years were spent in reverse. He wore the invisible crown of pessimism — or was it invisible? Perhaps more people saw that cloud of gloom encircling his head than he thought. For he had a way of showing it. He came in late at the club meeting and abruptly spoke out, "I don't know what you're talking about, but I can see it's wrong."

One thing that determines what we see is the kind of eye glasses we wear. If our glasses are blue, the world looks blue; if brown, the world appears brown; if green, the world seems green. Sometimes it's our glasses — not the world — that needs attention.

This is the difference betwen an optimist and a pessimist: An optimist sees an opportunity in every difficulty. A pessimist sees a difficulty in every opportunity. They look through different glasses.

But history — and your own past — teaches the brighter view. Sometimes it just takes awhile for it to develop. Moses was eighty years old before he was prepared to become the great leader of God's people. Maybe you, too, are now training for a greater service, and the best is yet to come. By looking for something better, we're more apt to find it. For what a person finds depends largely on what he looks for.

There is ever a sun somewhere, my dear,
Though the skies are dark, in time it'll break here.

Grandpa Was Not Fooled

But strong meat belongeth to them that are of full age, even those who by reason of use have their senses exercised to discern both good and evil. Hebrews 5:14

Grandpa had some very interesting stories to tell. All made sense. All had a point.

One of them concerned his inspection of a farm for sale. After arriving at the farmer's house and the customary greetings, they began to walk over the place. After the owner learned that Grandpa was a preacher he thought a naive lamb, ready for the fleecing, had come his way.

While walking through some bottom land, bordered by a little river, Grandpa noticed some mud and debris up waist high on the trees. This prompted him to ask, "Does this river ever overflow and flood this land?"

"Oh no, never," replied the farmer.

"Well, what's the mud and debris doing on the trees?" inquired Grandpa.

"What mud? What mud? You mean that mud over there on those trees? That was caused by the hogs. They get muddy and rub up against the trees."

They continued their inspection, circling back toward the house. Then the anxious farmer said, "Parson, you think you might like to buy my farm?"

"No, I guess not," answered Grandpa, "but I tell you what — I really would like to get a start of those hogs."

Be discerning, for not everything that's told is right. You can swap hats, but don't swap heads. Keep yours and use it.

Things Could Be Worse

*And now I exhort you to be of good cheer: for there shall be
no loss of any man's life among you, but of the ship.* Acts 17:22

Paul and 275 others (276 total) were caught in the midst of
a tempest at sea. There was neither sun nor stars for many
days. The situation was so desperate, in an effort to lighten
the ship they cast out the tackling and the wheat into the sea.
For fourteen days they fasted. The ship was wrecked, but all
the passengers and crew were saved. The calamity was severe
and frightening, but it could have been worse — there could
have been no survivors.

Nearly every reverse, mishap or disaster could be worse.

An old story is very illustrative: A doctor called a man and
said, "I have the reports on your tests. I wish you would come
to the office. I would like to talk to you." In thirty minutes
the patient was there. The doctor said, "I have bad news and
worse news. The bad news is you're going to live only twenty-
four hours." The patient interrupted, "Doctor, that's terrible.
That's awful. Only twenty-four hours to live. What could be
worse than that?" The doctor replied, "I tried to call you
yesterday."

May God give us the grace to see that our trials, backsets,
failures and disasters could be worse, and to be thankful that
we are as well off as we are.

Life could be worse. So, instead of sighing over how hard
circumstances are, take a look around you and see the blessings that bloom on every hand. A new day shall dawn and
its daylight hours shall let you see that things are so different
from what you saw in the midnight hours.

He Could Laugh at Himself

Suffer me that I may speak; and after that I have spoken, mock on. Job 21:3

A preacher friend of mine had a world of friends. Not because of superior ability as a pulpit man, but because of his blessed talent in getting along with people. One of his remarkable traits was his freeness in laughing at his own quirks. He could stand criticisms. Even better, he could joke about them.

Here is one of the stories he used to tell: After a Sunday sermon a man said, "Brother, you have a special talent; come to think of it, three talents: I believe you can stand the stillest, speak the longest, and say the least of any man I ever heard."

He could laugh at himself. To stand ten feet tall after you've been cut down is a major accomplishment.

The preacher's amusement in repeating the criticism shows that he was not possessed with a feeling of insecurity that demanded every one's plaudits. However, some people have to have such. They won't even admit to themselves that they may be weak on any point.

When we acknowledge our pecularities and weaknesses, then people love us and want to help us. But when someone dares to suggest that we might be wrong, it is our feigned perfection and bristling up that alienates and makes enemies.

There is a kind of greatness that doesn't depend upon superior fortune. It's our superior touchableness. Not being too sensitive, we haven't built a barrier that cuts off accessibility to us and closeness with us.

Try It Again

And he took his staff in his hand, and chose him five smooth stones out of the brook, and put them in a shepherd's bag which he had, even in a scrip; and his sling was in his hand: and he drew near to the Philistine. I Samuel 17:40

David, in going to fight the giant Goliath, picked five smooth stones. If the first failed, he could try again. This took courage.

THREE KINDS OF COURAGE

There's the courage that nerves you in starting to climb
  The mount of success rising sheer;
And when you've slipped back there's the courage sublime
  That keeps you from shedding a tear.

These two kinds of courage, I give you my word,
  Are worthy of tribute — but then,
You'll not reach the summit unless you've the third —
  The courage to try-it-again.

Roy Farrell Greene

Try-it-again is the stuff of which success is made.

The farmer's crop was hailed out. Did he quit? No. He planted again. The cowboy mounted the bucking bronc. He got thrown, but he tried him again. The baseball player struck out. He didn't quit. When his turn came, he went to bat again. A man seeking employment got turned down. But the world didn't end. He applied elsewhere.

It is comforting that God lets us try again. This is evident from the Prayer of Example. The prayer includes, "Forgive us our debts, as we forgive our debtors." However, we are not to pray this only once in a lifetime but often, indicating that we have erred, failed, and are in need of forgiveness. He forgives and lets us start again.

He Felt the Need of Prayer

Be careful for nothing; but in every thing by prayer and supplication with thanksgiving let your requests be made known unto God. Philippians 4:6

A tear-stained, emotionally bereft man came into my office. His mother had died the day before, and her funeral was to be conducted the next day. Aware of all this, my heart went out to him. In broken speech he said, "My mother lies cold in death and I can't even pray."

I assured him: "It's not hard, it's only a natural outpouring of the heart. First, address it to God as Jesus showed us when He prayed, 'Our Father which art in heaven.' Second, use hallowed expressions, for prayer is no place for flippant language. Jesus prayed, 'Hallowed be thy name.' Third, just express your feelings openly, freely and sincerely. You can be absolutely yourself, free from all pretensions and shams, for you couldn't fool God if you wished. You can thank Him for past and present blessings and pray for future help. Fourth, in closing, you can pray in Jesus' name, for He said, 'If ye shall ask anything in my name, I will do it' (John 14:14)."

On this basis and in this framework we prayed. It dried his tears and soothed his aching heart. He left a fortified man. He came with worry and left with assurance.

Prayer is a simple exercise of turning your thoughts heavenward. And God's ears that hear are more efficient than man's lips that pray.

Sooner or later, every person will find prayer an urgent necessity. For he will find his night too dark and his burdens too heavy. And how supportive it is to know: "The effectual fervent prayer of a righteous man availeth much" (James 5:16).

Saying the Wrong Thing

A word fitly spoken is like apples of gold in pictures of silver. Proverbs 25:11

Two men who had not seen each other in four or five years met at a sales meeting in another state.

"How is your wife?" one of them asked his old friend.

"She's in heaven," was the reply.

"Oh, I'm sorry." Then he realized that didn't sound right, so he added, "I mean, I'm glad." Now that sounded even worse. He finally blurted out with, "Well, I'm surprised."

The choice of words is a masterful art, so much so that colleges give degrees in it. A word can cut more than a sword or heal more than an ointment. Thus, "a word spoken in due season, how good is it!" (Proverbs 15:23).

Speaking the right word at the right time can change the world. Job expressed it this way, "How forcible are right words!" (Job 6:25).

Hot words inflame human relationships, but cool words never scald a tongue or burn a listener.

Words! Words! Words! Sometimes they come by the gallon while the thoughts come by the spoonful.

For words to be fitly spoken they must come from fitly thinking. Therefore, think before you speak; and if you do, sometimes you may not speak at all.

And if your mouth should misfire, be careful about reloading.

Abide With Me

And, lo, I am with you alway, even unto the end of the world. Matthew 28:20

Francis Lyte was born at Kelso, Ireland, 1793. His father died when he was a child, and he went with his mother to live in Dublin. There he was educated. At age twenty-two he answered the call for ministerial services.

In 1819 he went to Lymington where he overtaxed his strength and began to develop tuberculosis. Hoping to regain his health, he accepted the fisherman's parish of Brixhamon-Sea. But the tuberculosis continued to develop.

In the late summer of 1847 his doctors decided that he should give up all work and spend the winters in southern France, for he was slowly getting weaker. Thus arrangements were quickly made. The last Sunday came and in emotional language he bid his congregation farewell. Among the simple fisher-folk there was scarcely a dry eye. Later he strolled into the garden and sat down on a bank overlooking Tarbay, the sea below, the sky above, some clouds of night in the distance. He asked to leave something to help humanity. Then he went indoors, suffering the anguish of leaving a people he loved, and wrote:

> Abide with me; fast falls the eventide;
> The darkness deepens, Lord, with me abide;
> When other helpers fail, and comforts flee,
> Help of the helpless, O abide with me!
>
> Swift to its close ebbs out life's little day;
> Earth's joys grow dim, its glories pass away;
> Change and decay in all around I see;
> O Thou who changest not, abide with me!

The next morning he left for France and died there less than three months later, but the hymn he wrote will never die.

He Wondered Why He Was Disliked

A lying tongue hateth those that are afflicted by it; and a flattering mouth worketh ruin. Proverbs 26:28

A bothered man with a personal problem came to me for counselling. He stated that a fellow worker didn't like him and that it was very visible. He then explained, "I've never done him a wrong in my life. Not by word. Not by deed. I can't see why he dislikes me."

"Let me ask you a question," I stated. "Has he ever done you any special wrong?"

"Yes. Two years ago he lied on me and blocked my getting a promotion on the job. He wanted it but didn't get it."

"Now that's it," I continued. "He hates you not because of what you've done to him, but because of what he's done to you. After lying on you, his mind got busy and started making you into an awful creature that deserves the worst. This was done to try to justify the wrong he perpetrated. Since he did you wrong, he thought you wouldn't like him; so his mind reacted, 'You don't like me, now I don't like you.' Of course, he could have apologized but didn't. He chose the course of multiplying evil. As hatred renews itself it gets worse."

No faculty of the human mind is so perverted and so persistent as hate. Hate can usually find something wrong. If only a little, it can enlarge it. If non-existent, it can manufacture it.

I flinch at the thought of anyone's doing me wrong. Not that I can't take the punishment. I can. Not that I can't forgive. I can. It's because that person, unless he or she repents, will always be my enemy; and not because of what I've done to the person, but because of what that one has done to me.

Put Man Back Together

And God saw that the wickedness of man was great in the earth, and that every imagination of the thoughts of his heart was only evil continually. Genesis 6:5

We all remember the touching story of the father who noticed a map of the world in a daily newspaper. Thinking of a novel idea, he took this page of the paper and cut it into pieces, and told his young son to put the world together. The boy soon jubilantly said, "Dad, I've got it."

The father was amazed at how fast the job was completed. "So soon?" inquired the father. "How did you do it?"

The boy replied, "I turned the page over and there was a picture of a man. I just put the man together, and the world was right."

Here is a lesson for us: Put man together and the world will be right. Man has trouble with man (and there are a thousand ways for it to occur), because first of all he has trouble with himself. Our society is fragmented because man is fragmented, and hurts because man hurts. Man has ripped and torn himself up with selfishness, hate, envy, jealousy, laziness, irresponsibility, unforgiveness, dishonesty, untruthfulness, inconsideration, cruelty, vengeance, strife, covetousness, lust, pride and unthankfulness — not that all have split into such pieces of waywardness, but many have.

The only way we can put him back together is to rid him of what tore him apart in the first place. This can be done. The Ephesians did. The Apostle Paul said of them, "For ye were sometime darkness, but now are ye light in the Lord" (Ephesians 5:8). This revolutionary change occurred because they were redeemed (1:7), and Christ dwelt in their hearts by faith (3:17).

Reciprocal Living

*As we have therefore opportunity, let us do good unto all men,
especially unto them who are of the household of faith.*

Galatians 6:10

To receive a blessing and pass it on is like the running, pure water of a river. But to receive and hoard is like the dead, stagnant water of a pool that receives and keeps what it gets. In time the dead pool stinks; and so does the all-get-never-give person.

You have received a smile, pass it on; a kind word, pass it on; a helping hand, pass it on; a visit when ill, pass it on; encouragement when ready to faint, pass it on; a lift when you fell, pass it on; forgiveness when you blundered, pass it on; direction when you went astray, pass it on; sympathy when your heart was heavy, pass it on; and financial assistance when you were down and out, pass it on.

Life needs to be lived on a reciprocal basis.

Pass on more than empty words, for empty words feed with an empty spoon. Pass it on without fanfare. The glory-seeker takes ten steps to point attention to himself while he takes only one step to aid another. Pass it on freely, unselfishly, with no hook attached. Pass it on — not out of vanity but out of true commitment.

Have you had a kindness shown?
  Pass it on!
'Twas not given to you alone!
  Pass it on!
Let it travel down the years,
Let it wipe another's tears,
Till in Heaven the deed appears;
  Pass it on!

Henry Burton

What About the Box?

And be not conformed to this world: but be ye transformed by the renewing of your mind, that ye may prove what is that good, and acceptable, and perfect will of God. Romans 12:2

A certain soap-maker who ran out of superlatives to describe the perfection of his product came up with a novel and impressive way to attract customers. He stated: "As we couldn't improve our product, we improved the box."

We can't improve the gospel, but we can improve the box — ourselves. The gospel has no need to be improved or changed, though the methods of advocating it can be changed, and the box can be made anew with a more appealing appearance.

The gospel is carried in earthen boxes — humans. "But we have this treasure in earthen vessels" (II Corinthians 4:7). These vessels if defiled will be stumbling blocks — "that no man put a stumbling block or an occasion to fall in his brother's way" (Romans 14:13). In a reflection on the unattractiveness of a gospel container, a man once said to another, "I can't hear what you say, because I see what you do." The world is getting its idea of the preaching by observing the practicing.

The importance of the container is seen in all businesses. A more attractive building makes the merchandise it houses more salable. A finer and more elegant decor in a restaurant pleases the diners. Likewise, the gospel carried by those who live it is impressive. Example is a lesson all can read. What do they read in us?

A beautiful tribute is paid to Christian wives who influence their husbands by their righteous living — "that if any obey not the word, they also may without the word be won by the conversation [conduct] of the wives" (I Peter 3:1). It is the box that gets them interested in the contents.

Now That I Am Become a Man

*When I was a child, I spake as a child, I understood as a child,
I thought as a child: but when I became a man, I put away
childish things.* I Corinthians 13:11

The ability to handle the various affairs of life in an effective way is called maturity. The world's hard knocks are too much for babyish people. A mature person takes his job seriously, and does the best he can as long as he is on the job, regardless of pay. Maturity can't be bought with money. A mature person stays with a task until it's finished. It's hard to get a child to finish a job.

A mature person doesn't become frightened at every opposition or adversity. Children scare easily. A mature person is too big to act little. A child acts little because he is immature. A mature person doesn't enjoy feeling that he has been mistreated. A child does.

A mature person doesn't have to have his way about everything. The child says, "If you don't play my way, I'll pick up my marbles and go home." A mature person doesn't have to head the list and be first in everything. But a child that doesn't get to be first will often pout. A mature person is responsible. A child isn't.

A mature person is more discerning, can better distinguish fact from fancy. However, a child believes anything you tell him. A mature person is flexible and adaptable. But a child finds it difficult to change his plans. A mature person can take the stress and strain of life. A child will soon break under stress.

The best place to find help in maturing is the Bible. It talks about growing. It makes responsible people and gives them a whole new concept of living.

Lincoln's Speech Lives

The memory of the just is blessed: but the name of the wicked shall rot. Proverbs 10:7

President Abraham Lincoln's speech at the Gettysburg Battlefield, November 19, 1863, has been lauded as one of the greatest pieces of human literature. This is the address:

"Fourscore and seven years ago our fathers brought forth on this continent a new nation, conceived in liberty and dedicated to the proposition that all men are created equal. Now we are engaged in a great civil war, testing whether that nation, or any nation so conceived and so dedicated, can long endure.

"We are met on a great battlefield of that war. We have come to dedicate a portion of that field as a final resting place for those who here gave their lives that that nation might live. It is altogether fitting and proper that we should do this. But in a larger sense we cannot dedicate, we cannot consecrate, we cannot hallow this ground. The brave men, living and dead, who struggled here have consecrated it far above our power to add or detract.

"The world will little note nor long remember what we say here, but it can never forget what they did here. It is for us, the living, rather to be dedicated here to the unfinished work which they who fought here have thus far so nobly advanced. It is rather for us to be here dedicated to the great task remaining before us, that from these honored dead we take increased devotion to that cause for which they gave the last full measurement of devotion; that we here highly resolve that these dead shall not have died in vain, that this nation, under God, shall have a new birth of freedom, and that government of the people, by the people, and for the people shall not perish from the earth."

Give the Bug a Chance

They helped every one his neighbor; and every one said to his brother, Be of good courage. Isaiah 41:6

Abraham Lincoln, with that ready wit, deep insight, country style and homely sincerity, touched the hearts of millions of Americans who have given him a foremost place in their affections. He was so earthy and attendant to the little things of life as well as to the big things that build a worthy nation.

Mr. Lincoln was walking with a friend about Washington. When he saw a beetle that had gotten on its back, legs sprawling in air, and vainly trying to turn himself over, the President turned aside to help him. The friend expressed surprise that the burdened President should find time to assist a bug.

"Well," said Lincoln, "if I had left that bug struggling there on his back, I wouldn't have felt just right. I wanted to put him on his feet, and give him an equal chance with all the other bugs of his class."

The statement has great merit and practicality. It applies to helping not only bugs and nations, but men and women, boys and girls, upon their feet and giving them an equal chance with all others of their class.

> *When others' days are bleak*
> *Lift those fallen and those weak.*

In our age much is being said about the value of exercise in strengthening the heart, and there are many kinds. The best, however, is to reach down and lift people up.

The Bible says, "Bear ye one another's burdens" (Galatians 6:2) — it does not say, "Bear down on him."

Language of the Heart

Many waters cannot quench love, neither can the floods drown it. Song of Solomon 8:17

Valentine's Day is related to love.

Love is not fantasy. It is not a topic just for poets and philosophers. It is not just an idealistic longing for those who roam the silvery heavens. It is a state of the heart for *now* and *here*, and its need is as universal as man himself.

> It is the secret sympathy,
> The silver link, the silken tie,
> Which heart to heart and mind to mind
> In body and in soul can bind.
> > Sir Walter Scott

Love is the heart-beat topic that has been the thrilling theme of the sweetest eloquence through the centuries. The dearest words on this tuneful topic, however, have not been spoken by orators nor penned by poets. They have been uttered in broken, unrhythmic language, and lived in unlettered deeds by millions of unschooled people whose hearts overflowed with it. They knew the meaning of love. They learned it in the schoolroom of their own heart. It utters a heart language, and no one group has the exclusive possession of that kind of heart.

> Seas have their source, and so have shallow springs;
> And love is love, in beggars as in kings.
> > Sir Edward Dyer

Love is a powerful feeling that lets each speak it and demonstrate it in his own way, and that is the loveliest poetry and the grandest elocution. It is simple. As Shakespeare said, "All hearts in love use their own tongues."

Why Are We Here?

What is man, that thou art mindful of him? or the son of man, that thou visitest him? Thou madest him a little lower than the angels; thou crownest him with glory and honor, and didst set him over the works of thy hands. Hebrews 2:6,7

A mother while teaching her little boy on unselfishness concluded with: "We are in this world to help others."

After musing the matter, he asked her, "Well then, what are the others here for?"

The problems of many people stem from their not knowing why they are here. With no knowledge of why they are here or faith in the higher role of man, they have only a meager conception of the real meaning of life: its origin, its purposes, its opportunities, its potentials, its joys, it sorrows, its hopes, and its destiny.

We are here because *God put us here* and ordered man to multiply. We are the product of His command.

Also, we are here *to be free*, to occupy God's free earth, to breathe His free air, to stand up and be an ideal person and to live in keeping with our divine image.

Besides, we are here *to be in charge of God's creation*. May we be capable and worthy stewards.

Additionally, we are here *to give a hand* to the fallen; a word to the weary; a lift to the burdened; an example to the erring; drink to the thirsty; food to the hungry; and a light to those in darkness. Our humanity demands it.

Furthermore, we are here *to prepare ourselves* to live in a better world. This life is a school, and when school is out, we shall go home.

That Closed the Case

Unto me men gave ear, and waited, and kept silence at my counsel. Job 29:21

It is reputed that five women living in the same apartment house in Chicago got into a brawl of such severity that it resulted in their being hauled into court. When the case was called, they all rushed at the same time to the bench and began making bitter indictments of each other. Confusion had the floor.

The poor judge sat momentarily dumbfounded as accusations and counteraccusations filled the charged air. Struck with a thought, he suddenly rapped for order. When the verbal noise subsided and peaceful quiet prevailed, the magistrate gently said, "Now, I'll hear the oldest first."

That closed the case.

Have you ever noticed how quiet it becomes when the subject of age comes up? There should be other reasons, however, for silence at appropriate times.

Never talk:

- *If you have nothing to say.*
- *If your words come out heated.*
- *If it hurts another.*
- *If your words kindle strife.*
- *If it's a rumor.*
- *If it's untrue.*
- *If it does no good.*
- *If you don't know what you're talking about.*

Sometimes it shows more knowledge to say nothing. There is no wisdom like it. Even silence can have an eloquent tongue.

A Sort of Divinity

*Ointment and perfume rejoice the heart: so doth the sweetness
of a man's friend by hearty counsel.* Proverbs 27:9

Friendship is more precious than gold. There is no man so poor that he is not rich if he has a friend; and there is no man so rich that he is not poor without a friend.

Friendship is not fancy imaginations or vain words, but rather the golden strand linking lives forged from untarnished mettle. It is like the rope mountain climbers use to bind themselves for safety and progress.

Real friendship is abiding. Like love, it suffers long and is kind. It is not proud. It pursues the even tenor of its way, unaffrighted by ill-report, loyal in adversity, the shining jewel of happy days.

Friendship in sunshine or shadow is true. Wealth may crumble like some building shaken by an earthquake, but friendship still remains. Disaster and defeat may strike us and, like a storm, hide our star, and our ambitions turn to vanity on our lips; but friendship comes with a warmth and rekindles and fans into life the hope which had almost fled.

He or she is an antidote for despair, the panacea of hope, the tonic for depression.

Friendship is a gift, but it is also an acquirement.

It is a sort of Divinity which hovers over two hearts.

Daily Heroism

Be of good courage, and he shall strengthen your heart, all ye that hope in the Lord. Psalms 31:24

Heroes are found in many fields beside the battlefield. We see them in day-to-day living that keeps a forward pace — no turning from the goal, no holding back in fear. We see them as they seek better things and hope for the road's last turn to be the best.

Let me but live my life from year to year,
With forward face and unreluctant soul;
Not hurrying to, nor turning from the goal;
Not mourning for the things that disappear
In the dim past, nor holding back in fear
From what the future veils: but with a whole
And happy heart that pays its toll
To Youth and Age, and travels on with cheer.

So let the way wind up the hill or down,
O'er rough or smooth, the journey will be joy;
Still seeking what I sought when but a boy,
New friendship, high adventure, and a crown,
My heart will keep the courage of the quest,
And hope the road's last turn will be the best.

Henry Van Dyke

Live With Life

I know thy works, that thou are neither cold nor hot: I would thou wert cold or hot. So then because thou art lukewarm, and neither cold nor hot, I will spew thee out of my mouth. Reveleation 3:15,16

How sad! Many people are bored to frustration! But they weren't born bored. It is a state they have allowed to develop. Somewhere along life's way they lost their enthusiasm. Like the thought in the above Scripture, they are in the sad fix of being neither cold nor hot. The gusto for life is gone.

How glad! we are to be around people whose zeal spills all over us! One of my acquaintances who is physically weak and who has been through the wringer of trials has an eager spirit that flashes like a revolving beacon. Just to be around him five mintues will let you see that there is a man who enjoys himself. And that's not a bad definition of enthusiasm — the trait of simply enjoying oneself.

Enthusiasm is a generator of power. Power over self. Power over others. Napoleon said, "Men of imagination rule the world."

One of the secrets of success is enthusiasm. Without it no book is written, no church grows, no religion is propagated, no business flourishes, no battle is won, no empire is founded. The men and women of victory have been the ones who have kept the fires of fervency burning when other flames had burned into either the gray ashes of half-heartedness or despair.

The flame and warmth of wholeheartedness is a winning trait. You cannot kindle a fire in others unless it is burning within you.

The Buck Stops Here

So then every one of us shall give account of himself to God. Romans 14:12

The mother was away from home one evening, but she had planned for the meal to go on as usual. She appointed little Mary to sit in her place at the dinner table. You guessed it — the slightly older brother was not fond of the arrangement. In his dissatisfaction, he sneeringly said, "All right, now you're the mother tonight. How much is four times seven?"

Mary unhesitatingly and nonchantly replied, "I'm busy. Go ask your Daddy."

President Harry Truman had this plaque sitting on his desk, "The buck stops here."

Actually, the buck stops at each of us. We may try to pass it, but it won't pass. For the simple reason each is a responsible, accountable being. You just can't put the monkey on somebody else's back.

Responsibility is the price you pay to be a human being. Irresponsibility puts you in a jungle world. How dreadful! There irresponsible people walk with tigers they're afraid to stroke, and crawl with snakes where they keep their distance and dare not go to sleep. But responsible people fully accept their humanity and fully account for it.

As a human, every talent is a responsibility; every duty, an obligation; and every opportunity, a challenge. The very moment either duty or opportunity appears, that very moment man — different from animals — should arise with this assertion, "Here is where I come in."

Just being a person places on you accountability. You can't pass the buck.

Watch Where You Are Going

Nevertheless we made our prayer unto our God, and set a watch against them day and night, because of them. Nehemiah 4:9

A politician was speaking at a Fourth of July celebration with gripping and enchanting effectiveness. There were bugs — thousands of bugs — flying around the bright light over his head. Those bugs buzzed around him like jets, but he remained unperturbed and undistracted, and continued his speech with force and eloquence. Each time he inhaled, the audience thought surely he would suck in a bug. Finally the expected happened. He did. The people flinched. "What can he do?" they asked themselves. He swallowed hard, coughed a little, caught his breath and said, "That bug got what was coming to him, he should have watched where he was going."

Many an intellectual man at the height of his oratory has been a bug eater.

Diligent watch prevents misfortune. Watchfulness has been a part of man's life since time immemorial. Eternal vigilance is the price of freedom.

The condition upon which God hath given liberty to man is eternal vigilance, which condition if he break, servitude is at once the consequence of his crime and the punishment of his guilt.

John Philpot Curran

Constant vigilance is also the price of spiritual welfare. "Be watchful, and strengthen the things which remain, that are ready to die" (Revelation 3:2).

Discerning watchfulness is likewise the cost of doctrinal purity and a safeguard against the apostasy of the church. "Mark them which cause divisions and offenses contrary to the doctrine which ye have learned; and avoid them" (Romans 16:17). This requires watchfulness — and conviction.

The Father of Our Country

As the man is, so is his strength. Judges 8:21

It was a reflective experience to stand at the grave of George Washington. As I stood there I told myself that he is not dead. Truly, his beneficial works follow after him, though two centuries have passed. His struggles and sacrifices in behalf of freedom continue to live in a free and grateful people. His words, in times of peace and war, ring in the speeches of countless numbers.

While history says he lost more battles then he won, yet he won the last one. This is what really counts.

Though invisible, yet potent, he is a favorite for politicians to stand behind. They know that the very mention of his name in the midst of political turbulence has a winning appeal. It is magic. Hence, he is often quoted in public gatherings of every sort, at schools, clubs, businesses, political rallies and in the halls of congress.

Let us find direction and inspiration from the fact that Washington — patriotic, courageous, determined, modest, a simple man — stands today above fearful misgivings, selfish purposes, petty ambitions, turmoil of civil strife, and speaks to the scrambling throngs and bids us all to be manly, brave, thoughtful and considerate, not "like dumb driven cattle, but heroes in the strife." He is still saying:

> *Happily the Government of the United States, which gives to bigotry no sanction, to persecution no assistance, requires only that they who live under its protection should demean themselves as good citizens in giving it on all occasions their effectual support.*

The Buttons Are Behind Me and I'm in Front

But they hearkened not, nor inclined their ear, but walked in the counsels and in the imagination of their evil heart, and went backward, and not forward. Jeremiah 8:24

Little Naomi was trying to dress herself. After a long period she said, "Mother, will you help me? I guess you'll have to button my dress. The buttons are behind me and I'm in front."

Quite a predicament!

This amusing little story is a big enlightenment on many failures in all endeavors of life. Doing things backward. Going at it the wrong way. Misdirected effort. It tells us much.

Reminds me of the man who went deer hunting. He followed the deer tracks for a whole day before he discovered that he was following them backward.

Movement, activity, is not enough. Even the backslider is moving — down.

No matter how fast you're going, if it's in the opposite direciton you're not making progress.

Regardless of how hard you try, if it's the wrong way to do it you're not going to succeed.

We have seen individuals, businesses, and churches go backward and not forward. In most cases the reason was not so much a lack of effort as it was poor counsels and vain imaginations. In the majority of instances enough energy was expended to succeed, if it had been channeled into productive areas.

Half the way is to know the way.

Intertwined They Stand

Ye, being rooted and grounded in love, may be able to comprehend with all saints what is the breadth, and length, and depth and height. Ephesians 3:17,18

One of the wonders of the world is the Redwood Forest in California. Some of the trees are the oldest, largest, and tallest living things in all the world. Some of the trees are more than 300 feet tall and more than 2500 years old. Think of that! Their existence goes back hundreds of years into B.C. They have weathered the ravages of time, holding up against all the combatant elements. They stand tall in spite of the opposing forces.

Unknowledgeable people immediately jump to the conclusion that the redwoods have a very deep root system. To the contrary, it is shallow. What holds them? What supports them? They have a root system that intertwines and locks each to the trees inside it. They stand together — there is the secret. When wind and hail and upheaval threaten, neither stands alone but rather is strengthened and supported by the others. Each is needed for the support of the whole grove. The redwoods can truly say, "United we stand, divided we fall."

How true of us! We need the help of others. Even pigs in a litter lie close together to stay warm. Of course, man is grander and finer than a pig, but it is still a cold world out there for him if he's standing alone. One of the blessings of the church is its fellowship in which we have the intertwining of each other and of the Lord. Locked together we can withstand the storms of life. Unquestionably, "two are better than one" (Ecclesiastes 4:9).

Miserable Comforters

I have heard many such things: miserable comforters are ye all. Job 16:2

Poor Job was a man desperately in need of comfort. His children had been stricken in death, his property was destroyed, his body was afflicted with boils from head to toe, his irreverent wife gave tragic advice, and to cap it all, his friends were miserable comforters.

It is commendable to want to comfort the troubled, the perplexed, the suffering, the sorrowing. However, some just don't know how. In trying to help, they actually hurt; and in attempting to encourage, they truly discourage.

To do a first-rate job of comforting:

• *Avoid acting superior.* This was one of the disgusting faults of the Pharisees. A person with a hurt doesn't need to have his intelligence insulted.

• *Refrain from being judgmental.* Such a spirit is evident in the expression: "God is punishing you. You are getting what you deserve." But hardship is not necessarily rough treatment from God. It certainly wasn't in Job's case, even though his friends thought it was.

• *Never try to outdo the sufferer's woes.* For instance, "You don't have any real problems, let me tell you about mine."

• *Do not frighten.* For instance, "You haven't seen anything yet, just wait another two weeks."

• *Sympathize.* Enter into the sufferer's feelings and let him know that you are standing with him, ready to help. This lets another shoulder carry part of the load.

Today Is Your Day

Go to now, ye that say Today or tomorrow we will go into such
a city, and continue there a year, and buy and sell, and get
gain. James 4:13

One of the most tragic things about life is man's missing so much of it by being too much related to either the past or the future instead of the present. It robs us of the *now.*

We tend to put off living. While we dream of a magical rose garden — free from all thorns — across yonder hill, we neglect to enjoy the fragrant roses that bloom today so close, just outside our window.

Today is our day to act. When tomorrow arrives it will be today. When the far distant future gets here it will be today. So we don't have to deal directly with anything but today.

Rid yourself of self-pity, criticism and blame. Bury all excuses. Tomorrow is the fool's paradise. Today is ours. Take up every today, one by one, with clean hands and a pure heart and see what we can do with it.

Time — page writ, no returning line,
The vanished hour, no longer thine.
One hour alone is in thy hands,
The NOW on which the shadow stands.

It Could Have Been Different

My son, if sinners entice thee, consent thou not. If they say, Come with us, let us lay wait for blood, let us lurk privily for the innocent without cause: Let us swallow them up alive as the grave; and whole, as those who go down into the pit.
Proverbs 1:10-12

My phone rang one evening and a woman with whom I was not acquainted was the caller. It was evident she was emotionally disturbed. In broken, tearful speech she asked me if I would conduct the funeral for her son. I assured her I would, if I had no conflicting appointments.

Then she broken-heartedly said, "But he isn't dead yet." After a pause she continued, "He's to be electrocuted in the penitentiary just after midnight. Now will you still do it?"

"Yes, I shall still do it." I never ask for merit in serving human needs. God loves all.

That night I waked up about midnight — the fatal hour — and these thoughts weighed heavily on me: A young man who murdered a citizen while attempting to rob him will soon pay with his life. What happened? What wrong turns did he take? What shall I say?

The next morning I made a personal visit to the mother's home. I learned that she, a widow, had been compelled to go into a competitive, unsympathetic world to earn a living for her family. While she worked to support her children, there were evil forces up and down the streets and alleys working to destroy them. There had not been enough counteractive spiritual influences. At the most critical time when the family should have been in church they weren't.

As church attendance has gone down, the crime rate has gone up.

Use Your Head

Wisdom is the principal thing; therefore get wisdom: and with all thy getting get understanding. Exalt her, and she shall promote thee: she shall bring thee to honor, when thou dost embrace her. Proverbs 4:7,8

When my grandfather died my grandmother was left at age forty-one with six children at home. They lived on a farm of 140 acres, and from it their living had to come. No savings, no salary, no social security, no pension, no food stamps. It was up to her and the children and God. But actually that makes a winning team when they work together.

Grandmother was not bitter. Neither did she feel sorry for herself. Her philosophy was, "What is *is* and must be accepted." She was practical. She knew she had to play the game of life according to the hand that had been dealt her. It was more profitable to be thankful for what she had than to complain about what she didn't have. I can still hear her humming and singing as she went about her work.

She prospered and got along exceptionally well. After all the children had married she bought a home in town, although she kept the ownership of the farm. She had done so well that she was able to finance some farms for other people to buy.

One day a businessman asked her, "How is it that you have managed so well and accumulated what you have?"

Her simple explanation was startling: "Being I didn't go to school very much, I just had to use my head; so I figured that if I had more coming in than I had going out, it would leave me a surplus. And it worked." (She had some real humor.) She used her head. We call it wisdom.

Love Is Not Possessive

Love . . . seeketh not her own.
I Corinthians 13:4,5

Love grants freedom. It is not possessive. One of the most convincing manifestations of pure love is the freedom it grants another.

One woman in speaking of another said, "I can't afford to become a close friend of hers. She wouldn't let me have other friends. I would have to be with her constantly. She gives no freedom." Love doesn't draw a circle that small.

Demanding that your friend cut off all other friendships (even members of the family) and shower all the attention on us is not true love. It is only a distortion of love that reverts back to selfish childhood.

I am acquainted with a woman who nags and persecutes her husband when he goes fishing or golfing which is not often. She feels neglected. She harps on the idea that if he loved her, he wouldn't do it. Her love of self permits no latitude for him.

Then there is a case of a man who resents his wife's mixing in various social circles during the day. He says that she ought to be at home. He would imprison her.

But love is no browbeating, domineering quality. It is no choking process. It does not restrict all freedom and smother all dignity. It is rather a big soft kind of consideration that frees one to respond naturally to the lover. Also, it is more, much more:

> One heart, one mind, one soul, and one desire,
> A kindred fancy, and a sister fire
> Of thought and passion; these can love inspire;
> This makes a heaven of earth; for this is love.

When Neither Sun Nor Moon Shines

A friend loveth at all times, and a brother is born for adversity. Proverbs 17:17

There are many so-called friendships which are not born for adversity. Adversity is the stormy wind which separates the true from the pretended, the genuine from the feigned.

The Shadow once said to the Body: "Who is a friend like me? I follow you wherever you go. In sunlight or moonlight I never forsake you."

"That is true," answered the Body, "you do go with me in sunlight and in moonlight. But where are you when neither sun nor moon shines upon me?"

A true friend is one who is faithful when the storm rages and when the light of the sun or the moon is blotted out.

To be a friend one must: Be concerned. Be free of exploitation. Never pick a friend — to pieces. Learn to close one eye to faults. Never act superior. Keep your heart a little softer than your head. Be helpful.

When a friend makes a fool of himself, accept it as only a temporary deficiency.

Stick when adversity comes. See your friend through when others think he is through.

To have friends, *one must be a friend!*

Tragedy of Forgetting

Only take heed to thyself, and keep thy soul diligently, lest thou forget the things which thine eyes have seen, and lest they depart from thy heart all the days of thy life: but teach them to thy sons, and thy sons' sons. Deuteronomy 4:9

An older preacher, in praising the beauty and influence of motherhood, stated: "The happiest days of my life were spent in the arms of another man's wife — my mother."

A young preacher in the audience liked the novelty and force of the point. Thought it was a clever attention-grabber. In his next sermon he decided to use the shocking technique. Being young and inexperienced he was nervous. All went well until he got to the last of the story. He said, "The happiest days of my life were spent in the arms of another man's wife." Suddenly he suffered a memory blockage — he just couldn't remember the rest of it. He hesitated, backed up and started again: "The happiest days of my life were spent in the arms of another man's wife." Again he had forgotten the punch line. He paused, gulped and said, "For the love of me, I can't remember who she was."

All are threatened with the danger of forgetting matters much more important than the climax of a story. May I keep memory fresh and not forget:

The God who has given me a life, breath and all things.
Who I am and my duties in life.
My parents who sacrificed so much in my behalf.
The people who stood by me, held up my hands, and helped to make me what I am. So I say in the language of Rudyard Kipling:

> Lord God of Hosts, be with us yet,
> Lest we forget — lest we forget.

He's Still in There

*But he knoweth the way that I take: when he hath tried me, I
shall come forth as gold. My foot hath held his steps, his way
have I kept, and not declined.   Job 23:10,11*

The father had promised to take the children to the park on
Sunday afternoon. They could hardly wait. Yet they had a
problem. The father had lain down for a little rest and was
enjoying the relaxation so much that he began to play possum.
The youngsters tried to rouse him — begged him, pulled his
arm — to no avail. Finally the six-year-old daughter pried open
one of his eyelids, looked carefully, and said, "He's still in
there."

Tired, sleepy, but he was still in "the earthly house of this
tabernacle." Therein is hope.

Life is a race to be run — stay in there, refusing to be en-
cumbered with excess baggage that would weight you down.
It makes sense to "lay aside every weight, and the sin which
doth so easily beset us, and . . . run with patience the race
that is set before us" (Hebrews 12:1).

Life is a warfare to be fought — stay in there. "This charge
I commit unto thee . . . that thou . . . mightest war a good
warfare" (I Timothy 1:18). "Endure hardness as a good
solider." Keep up the fight. Much is at stake.

Life is a fruit to bear — stay in there. "Even so every good
tree bringeth forth good fruit; but a corrupt tree bringeth forth
evil fruit . . . Wherefore by their fruits ye shall know them"
(Matthew 7:17-20).

As long as you are in the flesh may others say of the race
you run, the warfare you wage and the fruit you bear, "He's
still in there."

Poor but Rich

There is that maketh himself rich, yet hath nothing: there is that maketh himself poor, yet hath great riches." Proverbs 13:7

A man poor in money — not poor, just poor in money — was brought into contact with a multimillionaire. The wizard of wealth worked hard every day at getting more money. In their conversation the man of little means said, "I'm richer than you are."

"What kind of mathematician are you to figure that?" asked the man nearly as rich as Fort Knox.

"Because I have as much money as I want," said the poor man, "but you don't."

No matter how big a fortune the lover of money amasses, he's never satisfied. The covetous person has a bottomless purse that can never be filled.

It is highly appropriate, therefore, that we identify The Richest People according to the Scriptures:

• *The rich in spirituality.* "Though he was rich, yet for your sakes he became poor, that ye through his poverty might be rich" (II Corinthians 8:9).

• *The rich in faith.* "Rich in faith, and heirs of the kingdom" (James 2:5).

• *The rich in good works.* *"That they be rich in good works"* (I Timothy 6:18).

• *Those who have a big bank account in heaven.* "Lay up for yourselves treasures in heaven" (Matthew 6:20).

Materials do not make one rich but busy, burdened and troubled. It is the heart that makes a person rich.

When Disaster Strikes

For thou knowest not what a day may bring forth.
Proverbs 27:1

The devastating quakes that struck Mexico City, the largest city in the world, and the surrounding area, in 1985, left a death toll of at least 10,000 and many more thousands injured and maimed. There is no way to assess the human suffering and misery. The lives crushed out. The injuries. The horror. The destruction. The chaos. The homeless. The orphans. The jobless. The threat of more quakes. The threat of disease. The bereavement. Tragedy immeasurable! Immeasurable!

How sobering! What a teacher of priorities! Many heroic stories came out of the catastrophe. One is that of a mother who gave her life to save her infant daughter who was only a few days old. Eight days after the quake when crumblings and debris were removed there lay a dead mother bent over her baby in protective form. The baby was alive. A mother's way!

This is only one of many brave and moving deeds.

The hearts of people throughout the world were touched. We take courage that mankind everywhere is sensitive and tender-hearted.

Relief efforts of food, medicine, and professional help poured in from all over the world. American engineers, French firefighters, British helicopter pilots, Canadian paramedics and many others rushed to the aid of the relief effort.

The response speaks well for the race. It is more than a humanitarian spririt. Man must be possessed with a spark of divinity. How great is man!

The Mouse Had a Church Day

Arise, go unto Nineveh, that great city, and preach unto it the preaching that I bid thee. Jonah 3:2

The audience had trouble holding back the giggles while the preacher was preaching. No, it was neither the preacher's wit nor boners. It was a mouse that climbed the lattice work of flowers next to the podium. After awhile the pulpiteer spotted the little four-legged nuisance which was proving to be a better attention-getter than he. Reacting with theological fervor but without mercy, he rolled his sermon manuscript into a club and whacked that mouse. But the mouse unharmed just ran away.

At this point one brother spoke out, "That sermon is too weak to slow even a mouse."

Then the audience gave way to those pent up feelings and broke into loud laughter.

If a sermon is not solid enough to affect a mouse, it has to be mighty soft and flimsy.

Paul told the young preacher Timothy to "Preach the word." That is solid. This is not to be interpreted to mean that preachers should tell people where to get off but rather where to get on. This is done by uncompromisingly preaching the Word without adding to it or taking from it, which has ever been a command of God (Deuteronomy 4:2).

Indeed, the pew often affects the pulpit. The audience may be too weak for a strong sermon. Paul dealt with the reality of the situation when he stated that some were too babyish and undeveloped for the meat of the Word and thus needed the milk of the Word instead. So sometimes we may have sermonettes because we have Christian-ettes for listeners.

Face Value

A merry heart maketh a cheerful countenance: but by sorrow of the heart the spirit is broken. Proverbs 15:13

Said in few words:

A smile has face value in every land.

Progress is built on smiles — not frowns.

There is magnetic power in a smile.

A smile is one of the very best relaxation exercises.

A person without a smiling face must not open a shop.

It is better to forget and smile than to remember and be sad.

A salesman has to smile — it comes with the territory.

A smile is one of the world's most cherished scenes.

Smile and you can go another mile.

A pleasant smile is sunshine in the house.

Nobody ever died of smiling.

Smiling is a tranquilizer with no ill effects.

Smile, if you are wise.

If you don't learn to smile at trouble, you are going to have more trouble — trouble that troubles trouble.

Do the Best You Can

Nevertheless the men rowed hard to bring it to the land; but they could not: for the sea wrought, and was tempestous against them. Jonah 1:13

Life is not always smooth sailing. Sometimes we have to sail in tempestous seas. When that time comes, row hard and do the best you can.

> For life is great to every man
> Who lives to do the best he can.

Rowing against boisterous winds in a turbulent sea tests character and builds muscle. If you are not able to handle your boat, a strong resolve lets you handle yourself, and that is the main victory and chief success.

Think not of failure. Think of success. Don't think *why* you can't. Think *how* you can. Some say, "It can't be done." But you say, "I will do it."

Be thankful if you are faced with a challenging problem or have a job harder than you like. Great character does not emerge from a life of ease, just as a skyscraper does not rise from a feather pillow.

About the only things that come to us without effort are sunshine, rain, air, flabbiness, wrinkles, gray hair, old age and death. Everything else we have to work for.

No effort, no result; little effort, little result; big effort, big result. That's how simple it is.

Ingenuity Finds the Way

*Then the king answered and said, Give her the living child, and
in no wise slay it: she is the mother thereof.* I Kings 3:27

In the context of the above Scripture each of two women
claimed to be the mother of a child. They asked Solomon to
decide which was the real mother. He commanded that the
child be split in two and each be given half. One exclaimed,
"Oh my lord, give her the child." Solomon then said, "Give
her the child . . . she is the mother." Solomon's ingenuity settled the matter and added to his fame.

• *Ingenuity solves the problem.* A young mother was greatly perturbed about her eight year old son. She was at her wit's
end. No matter how much she pleaded, exhorted or rebuked,
he went around with his shirt tail hanging out. Nothing she
said or did got through to him. However, her neighbor had
two boys, and she observed that their hair might be ruffled,
their faces and hands dirty, but one thing sure — they always
kept their shirt tail in. This difference in the boys alarmed her.
Finally the young mother asked her neighbor to tell her the
secret.

"Oh, it's easy," she answered, "I just sew a band of lace
around the bottom of all their shirts."

• *Ingenuity is the child of thought.* Thinking makes the
whole difference in people.

• *Ingenuity is the greatest time-saver of all.* It gets busy and
then we have inventions.

Don't be afraid to think. I never knew a person to kill
himself thinking. But I have known many who didn't think to
kill themselves by degrees.

If I Come Through in the Morning

Whereas ye know not what shall be on the morrow. For what is your life? It is even a vapor, that appeareth for a little time, and then vanisheth away.   James 4:14

My father had seen many doctors, and they said there was no hope, just a matter of time. Due to arteriosclerosis there was almost a complete blockage of the aorta. Because the blood was not getting to his foot, a portion had already been amputated.

But he learned of two heart specialists in Houston who had just begun to perform an unusual operation. They were taking the aorta from a dead person and transplanting it in the patient. So I took him to them.

The night before the surgery members of the family stayed with him even past the visiting hour. After having prayer, as we were getting ready to leave his room, he asked that I stay a little longer. He wanted to discuss some business and personal matters. Then when I was ready to depart, he took me by the hand and with a firm grip and an intensive look said, "Son, if I come through in the morning, it will be just wonderful; if I don't, it will still be all right."

While he never had much formal education, I consider his statement one of the most profound philosophies I have ever heard or read.

"If I come through in the morning, it will be just wonderful," for: Life is precious. It will give another opportunity for me. It will provide another day to achieve and to enjoy.

"If I don't, it will still be all right," for: There is another life. And death is the ending of this one and the beginning of the new one. He did come through and lived seven years.

Our Kind of a Man

Gird up now thy loins like a man; for I will demand of thee, and answer thou me. Job 38:3

Our kind of a man is:

• *A lover of liberty*, expressed by Patrick Henry: "As for me, give me liberty or give me death."

• *Uncompromising*, stated by Abraham Lincoln: "Important principles may and must be inflexible."

• *Truthful*, voiced by George Washington: "Father, I cannot tell a lie, I did it with my little hatchet."

• *Honest*, verbalized by Robert Burns: "An honest man's the noblest work of God."

• *A devotee ot enlightenment*, phrased by Thomas Jefferson: "Enlighten the people generally, and tyranny and oppressions of body and mind will vanish."

• *A lover of his children*, sobbed out by David: "Would God I had died for thee, O Absalom, my son, my son!"

• *Compassionate*, demonstrated by the Good Samaritan who aided the half dead man lying by the wayside.

• *A doer*, worded by Winston Churchill: "It is better to be making the news than talking it; to be an actor rather than a critic."

• *A servant of God*, spoken by Joshua: "As for me and my house, we will serve the Lord."

Truly, our kind of a man is no ordinary man — he is superior.

Only the Big Can Do It

Ye ought rather to forgive him, and comfort him, lest perhaps such a one should be swallowed up with overmuch sorrow.
II Corinthians 2:7

There is an old story about a convict who went before the governor of a state to get a pardon. The governor immediately recognized him as a steamboat mate under whom he had served as cabin boy. The ruler said, "I want you to promise you will never again take a stick and drive a sick boy out of his berth on a stormy night; because some day that boy may be governor, and you may want him to pardon you for another crime. I was that boy. Here is your pardon."

In addition to teaching the merciful spirit of forgiveness, the story also teaches the need to be good to children for you never know what they may grow up to become.

"Oh yes! I forgave her," said one woman feeling her big-heartedness, "but I was pretty cool to her for several days. I wanted her to know how I felt about it and how I resented it."

But forgiveness is not forgiveness when it disciplines and retaliates. Forgiveness cannot come from the surface. Neither will it stay at arm's length. Forgiveness must come from the heart, and as it comes it finds an eager, kind, sweet and compassionate way to help.

Another interesting story concerns a man who thought he was going to die. He expressed his forgiveness of a neighbor who, according to his view, had injured him. But he added, "If I get well the old grudge still holds."

The person who refuses to forgive needs forgiveness most of all. For "if ye forgive not men their trespasses, neither will your Father forgive your trespasses" (Matthew 6:15).

Experience Is the Best Teacher

*I have been young, and now am old; yet have I not seen the
righteous forsaken, nor his seed begging bread.* Psalms 37:25

The writer had learned from experience. One of the advantages in being old is experience, which has no substitute.

A city boy went to visit his country cousin. Being from what he thought was a privileged state — tall buildings, concrete slabs, traffic jams, shove and push, bigger school buildings, dusty libraries, polluted air, chemically treated water and artificial parks — he felt mentally superior to what he thought was an underprivileged, short-on-brains cousin. He even gave his philosophy on how to treat animals in the forest. He said, "Just be friendly to them and they will be friendly to you."

It was hard for the country boy to keep from laughing as he thought of the first lesson coming up for Cousin Inexperience. The next day they went into the woods and ran across a skunk. Country Cous said, "Hold up, come back."

But City Cous kept going as he said, "Let me show you how to be friendly to him," not knowing it was a skunk. Well, it took just about two weeks (all his vacation) to get the odor off him.

In dealing with a skunk, four-legged or two-legged, experience will soon teach you to keep your distance.

The burnt child is afraid of fire.

The scalded dog fears even cold water.

He knows the current best who has swum the river.

Experience costs a lot, but I don't know how you get it without paying the price.

Where Is Happiness Found?

Blessed is every one that feareth the Lord; that walketh in his ways. For thou shalt eat the labor of thine hands: happy shalt thou be, and it shall be well with thee. Psalms 128:1,2

There are first-hand witnesses who testify to where happiness is not found:

• *Not in unbelief.* Voltaire, one of the most vocal infidels, said, "I wish I had never been born."

• *Not in education.* The well-learned Solomon wrote, "For in much wisdom is much grief: and he that increaseth knowledge increaseth sorrow."

• *Not in pleasure.* Lord Byron is an example of this. He sought it madly. Disappointed, he wrote, "The worm, the canker and the grief are mine."

• *Not in fame and possession.* Lord Beaconsfield (Disraeli) had both. Yet, he pitifully wrote, "Youth is a mistake, manhood a struggle, old age a regret."

• *Not in military glory.* Alexander the Great conquered the world of his day. Then he wept because, as he said, "There are no more worlds to conquer."

• *Not in money.* Jay Gould was so wealthy his name is still proverbially used in this sense. But when dying he said, "I suppose I am the most miserable man on earth."

• *God has placed happiness in simple things:* conscience void of offense, peace with self, love of others and being loved, giving oneself to a cause bigger than self, kind words and helping hands that make others rejoice, a memory that forgets the wrongs one suffers, and a realization that the gift of life is wonderful. It is not a destination reached but a journey.

Roast Preacher

And why beholdest thou the mote that is in thy brother's eye,
but considerest not the beam that is in thine own eye?
Matthew 7:3

As the family sat down for their Sunday dinner, they had more than roast beef. They had roast preacher. The father said, "The sermon this morning was very boring."

"What tore me up, he kept repeating himself," commented the mamma.

Then Aunt Jane: "He's hard to follow."

Next, Cousin Mary stated, "A mighty poor sermon topic."

But it was little Johnny who shook them up with his expressed perception: "I thought it was a pretty good show for a quarter."

After a few hard swallows the father said, "Why that preacher can't see his mistakes, I don't know." Then he put hypocrisy's thickest icing on the cake by saying, "I think I could see my mistakes, if I had any."

Really, if a person had no faults of his own, he wouldn't get so much joy from pointing out the faults of others. Critics are like peas in a pod; they all look alike and smell like spoiled leftovers. And the paradoxical thing is that while they think they know how to do everything perfectly, they are usually failures. In most cases they are faultier than the ones they fault.

The jury, passing on the prisoner's life,
May in the sworn twelve have a thief or two
Guiltier than him they try.

William Shakespeare

Baby

And when she saw that he was a goodly child, she hid him three months. Exodus 2:2

When Moses was born the Egyptians were killing all Hebrew baby boys. So the mother hid him for three months. Only for three months because baby wouldn't wait. Then she put him in a water-proof basket and placed it in the river, hoping the baby's life would be spared. It worked.

Baby is something that won't wait. A few tomorrows and your baby stands as tall as you. Whatever joy you derive from the child's babyhood and whatever early shaping of the mind you intend to do, you must hurry. "As the twig is bent, so grows the tree."

Baby is a mutual ownership, belonging half to mother and half to father. Furthermore, he or she is half of mother and half of father.

This precious little one is a helpless creature that lies, sits, crawls and wobbly walks. Which way are you leading and pointing your child? A little life with lots of future. May that future not be thwarted.

Baby has no appreciation of time, so he or she may get the days and nights mixed up. Rest assured, the parents will know.

Infant babe — so little — makes hands busier, nights longer, days shorter, clothes shabbier, eyes sleepier and purses lighter; BUT, love stronger, happiness greater, closeness tighter, hope brighter, play better and singing sweeter.

Baby is a little jewel you wouldn't take a billion dollars for; but when you have the number you wish, you wouldn't give ten cents for a hundred more.

If You Run With the Goats

Be not deceived: evil communications [associations] corrupt good manners [morals]. I Corinthians 15:33

When our son Paul was a little boy he had some special friends. One of them lived on a little acreage where happy children could play in the great outdoors. Another special attraction this friend had was some goats and a little wagon for the goats to pull.

There were times when the goats chose to be unruly and butted them down, but each time those boys got back up. What a lesson! Life has its blows, jolts and kicks that flatten us; but as long as we can get back up, we're still in the struggle and still in reach of victory.

One day Paul came home smelling like a goat — and that's not a savory odor. I jokingly said, "Son, if you run with the goats you'll smell like a goat." He was too young then to comprehend the full import of those words. Later he learned and heeded the message. Now, with two sons of his own, he understands even more fully the power of association and influence.

Jesus truly wants us to learn this lesson on influence. I know He does. For He told us what a little leaven could do to three measures of meal (Matthew 13:33).

Since we are all creatures of influence, there is protection and elevation in associating with righteous, honorable people.

> *Whatever others do or say*
> *Can lead you aright or astray.*

Furthermore, in most instances the very company in which you are apt to improve the most will be the least expensive.

Rid Your Burden by Forgiving

Forbearing one another, and forgiving one another, if any man have a quarrel against any: even as Christ forgave you, so also do ye. Colossians 3:13

At a morning service in an evangelistic meeting a lady came forward during the singing of the invitation song. She sat on the front pew directly in front of a lady on the second pew. Apprehension and nervousness ran through the audience. You could see it. You could feel it. The respondent came forward to confess her sins, ask for the prayers of the church, and to be restored to the fellowship of God and the church.

After the service was dismissed the woman on the second pew walked around and took the other woman's hand and said, "I'm so glad you came. I hold nothing against you. May God bless you."

Later I learned that the poor respondent woman's son had killed the other woman's husband and son. It was reported that the murderer was being investigated by the grandjury for bootlegging. He warned the other two to skip the country and not testify. An argument followed and the father and son were fatally shot.

There were trials for murder. Naturally the families (members of the same church) were pitted against each other. The trials ended with a death sentence and the prodigal son's having to die in the electric chair. After the murder, his broken hearted mother never returned to church until this day.

Later that afternoon the woman who had lost her husband and son and who had welcomed the other woman back in the spirit of love and forgiveness said, "I feel like a great burden has been lifted from my back. I feel better now than I have felt in years."

Politeness Opens Doors

What counsel give ye me to return answer to this people? And they spake unto him, saying, If thou be kind to this people, and please them, and speak good words to them, they will be thy servants for ever. II Chronicles 10:6,7

A gracious lady gave Jimmy an orange. His reaching for it and saying nothing prompted his mother to ask, "Now what do you say to the lady, Jimmy?"

"Peel it," said Jimmy.

Everyone should learn to say: "Thank you." "I appreciate." "I'm grateful." "It was nice of you." "Excuse me." "I beg your pardon." "I'm sorry."

Politeness is simply an expression of good will and kindness. It comes easily when it springs from good nature, love and excellent training.

Courtesy is a part of true religion and thus should be an urgent part of religious training. We must learn to be civil in dealing with each other. Man, being the offspring of God, is sacred and should be treated with respect.

Courtesy gives a person extra help in handling the exchanges, connections and relationships with others. Contraiwise, the smartest tongue is handicapped when it wags in rudeness. Impoliteness — the ugly spirit — can be expressed in many ways, one of which is to shoot from the lip.

If stress or strife of the times causes you to become weak-kneed, perhaps you should let them buckle that you may fall on your knees, and in this position do a little thinking and praying for poise; then get back up and face the issues with well-bred manners.

Give Full Measure

But thou shalt have a perfect and just weight, a perfect and just measure shalt thou have: that thy days may be lengthened in the land which the Lord thy God giveth thee. Deuteronomy 25:15

When I was a boy working in my father's store we weighed many items at the time of purchase: beans, sugar, etc. One day my father observed that I was trying to guess the exact amount before putting the bag on the scales. Later he suggested, "Son, don't do it that way. Seldom ever will you guess it exactly. Half the time you will have too little and half the time you will have too much. When you have too much and have to take out some, the customer will say to himself, 'You tightwad, why didn't you leave it in there?' Be sure you don't have enough and then take the scoop and keep pouring until you bring it to the mark. That way you create the impression the customer gets everything coming to him. We want that reputation."

The reputation for honesty is no empty echo in the community; it sounds and sounds and sounds, and the people listen. Though your reputation is not necessarily what you are, only what people think you are, still it is to be sought.

Business can't thrive where honesty is questioned. Integrity is the absolute essential of every worthwhile endeavor.

Indeed, honesty is more than the best policy, it is the manifestation of you — the real you. Hence, you will never obtain a full life from giving short measures, for it shrinks the *you*.

Feathering your own nest at the expense of dishonestly plucking the feathers of others turns soft feathers into prickly thorns that will pierce you.

Big Results From Little Beginnings

For it was little which thou hadst before I came, and it is now
increased unto a multitude. Genesis 30:30

The other morning I had breakfast with a friend who stated that some six or seven weeks ago he had turned a key that was very hard for him to do. He had turned for the last time the key on a lock that would close a jewelry store he opened forty-two years ago. He said, "I opened that business with one counter of jewelry. That was the beginning of the whole chain." The chain now consists of more than two hundred big department stores.

Big results, both good and bad, can come from little beginnings. The break in the dam and the flooding of the town downstream began with the oozing through of one drop of water. The execution of John the Baptist had its beginning in one rash promise — a promise to give a girl anything she wished. Also, the fate of Lot was determined by a small matter. He pitched his tent toward Sodom, but later landed in that wicked city and lost his family. This powerful nation of ours had its beginning with the landing of a few settlers.

There is power in little things and little beginnings. No matter how little you may think you are, God can lift you tall and make you powerful. He can kindle a fire within you.

Thus out of small beginnings greater things have been produced
by His hand that made all things of nothing, and gives being to
all things that are; and, as one small candle may light a thou-
sand, so the light here kindled hath shone unto many, yea in
some sort to our whole nation.

William Bradford

An Island of Butter

The Lord is my shepherd; I shall not want.   Psalms 23:1

And that's optimism.

We need optimism, the expectant and victorious view, for all the circumstances of life; and the more gloomy the situation is, the more we need the bright outlook.

Have you heard the story of the two frogs that fell into a churn of milk? One was a pessimist; thinking there was no hope, he made no effort to stay afloat. He went down. The other was an optimist; believing something good would happen, he kept kicking and in time there was an island of butter. He crawled on it and jumped out.

In making coffee in the morning, I heat water in the teakettle. I have observed that when it's up to its neck in hot water, it keeps on singing.

The right mental attitude is one of the prerequisites of success. No optimism, no victory. Expecting to win helps one to fulfill his own expectations. And if he doesn't, he has still won for trying.

When I was a boy growing up, we had a dog that was the most optimistic creature I ever saw. He was the very ultimate in optimism. He never sounded a discouraging bark, yet I assure you he did have just causes. He chased scores of rabbits and never caught a one in his life. Did he ever get discouraged? Never. He was always ready to try again, evidently thinking this time he would win.

In the intervening years, I too have chased a lot of rabbits, figuratively speaking, and if I don't catch one occasionally I get discouraged. Then I need to think about that optimistic and faithful dog.

If He Had Known

But if ye had known what this meaneth, I will have mercy, and not sacrifice, ye would not have condemned the guiltless.
Matthew 12:7

There is the enchanting story of two cowboys who were visiting in Colorado. While they were out walking, a bull spotted them and gave chase. After setting new track records one of them ran up a tree. The other one ran into a cave. But just as quickly he ran back out. The bull made a lunge and he sprang back into the cave. This darting in and shooting out continued several times.

Finally the man in the tree yelled, "You nitwit, why don't you stay in there? If you'll stay in there, after a while the bull will go away."

The in-and-out-of-the-cave man frantically shouted, "What you don't know is — there's a bear in this cave."

What we don't know often gets us in trouble.

Not until we have walked in the other fellow's shoes are we fully prepared to criticize his sensitive step — it just might be the shoes are too tight or there are holes in the soles.

We wouldn't have condemned the nodding man at church of a lack of interest, if we had only known he had been up most of two nights with a sick wife.

If the teacher had known the child's transient parents had moved him from school to school every few weeks, she would not have prejudged him as a slow learner.

As the Scripture says, "If ye had known . . . ye would not have condemned."

Like a Tree

And he shall be like a tree planted by the rivers of water, that bringeth forth his fruit in his season; his leaf also shall not wither; and whatsoever he doeth shall prosper. Psalms 1:3

In the above Scripture the upright man is likened to a tree, but in the next verse the evil person is compared to chaff. How impressive is the contrast. What an appropriate suggestion of a bad man — chaff. No roots, no substance, no life, no value, no future! But the good man is likened to a tree. Why a tree?

• *He is a fixed person.* "Planted by the rivers," his roots are deep. One of his laudable traits is stability. Steadfast and unmovable. Not wishy-washy. Not blown about by the fickle winds of popularity and temporary gain. You can deal with him.

• *He is a growing individual.* "Planted by the rivers of water," he has nutriment. It is intended that the spiritual part of man should continue to grow. While the outward part of man reaches the climax in growth and begins to weaken, the inward part is to be renewed and get stronger day by day.

• *He is a fruitful being.* "Bringeth forth his fruit." Successful. Productive. Fruitful of golden deeds. "In his season." Winter is sure to find out what summer has laid up. For a person's family and for the world to have fruit, one must produce.

• *He is a beautiful, living creature.* "His leaf also shall not wither." He retains his attractiveness, just like a tree holds its foliage. No ugly withering. Few objects in nature are as pleasing as a handsome tree. Its foliage beautifies the landscape. It crowns the hilltop. It touches up the mansion. But even more attractive is a righteous, fruit-bearing life. No mansion is pretty without it. How beautiful is a good life!

Trust Allays Fear

What time I am afraid, I will trust in thee.   Psalms 56:3

The lightning was flashing, thunder was roaring, black clouds looked angry, and the train was traveling fast. The tension and fear among the passengers was most evident.

One little boy, however, who sat by himself seemed completely unaware of any danger as the storm raged.

One of the passengers spoke to him: "Aren't you afraid to travel alone on such a stormy night?"

The lad looked up and answered with a smile: "No ma'am, I'm not afraid. My daddy's the engineer."

It was a wise resolve the Psalmist stated in the foregoing passage. We don't know the future, but we know the One who holds it. We *have seen* enough to teach us to trust God for what we *have not seen.*

> *I will not doubt though all my ships at sea*
> *Come drifting home with broken masts and sails,*
> *I will believe the Hand which never fails,*
> *From seeming evil worketh good for me;*
> *And though I weep because those sails are tattered,*
> *Still will I cry, while my best hopes lie shattered,*
> *"I trust in Thee."*

Learn From the Ant

Go to the ant . . . consider her ways, and be wise . . . provideth her meat in the summer, and gathereth her food in the harvest." Proverbs 6:6-8

One of the traits to attain is *drive* — the ant has it. And I have noticed that the get-aheaders have it, too, and almost indefatigable energy. It relentlessly impels them toward their objective. This is one of the reasons the "old boys with no chance" make it to the top. They come from the backwoods, the plains, the villages and the cities. It is not where they are from but what is in them that makes the difference.

The second lesson to learn from the ant is *togetherness* — the ant works with others. "Two are better than one" (Ecclesiastes 4:9). If you can't work with people, you are doomed to a lonely life of mediocrity.

And the third lesson is *thrift* — the ant stores meat in the summer for the winter. While the grasshopper is playing and living for the moment, the ant is toiling and filling her cupboard. This lesson was not given to make scabby skinflints. Rather it was given to teach us a basic principle of survival. We can't have by wasting. This self-preserving principle should not be scorned as a social crime. The lesson is divinely given and should not be humanly mocked.

By following the ant, Joseph preserved himself and his country through seven years of drought.

So our most painful sting is not from the ant but from our failure to follow her. That sting comes from ourselves.

Get Off the Merry-Go-Round

*Simon Peter saith unto them, I go a fishing. They say unto him,
We also go with thee. They went forth, and entered into a ship
immediately; and that night they caught nothing.* John 21:3

When I was a boy my father took the family into town to
a carnival filled with attractions to cause a country boy to look
with curious wonder.

He assisted me in getting on a wooden horse on the merry-
go-round, and round and round I went with that carnival
music blaring its allurement.

After it stopped, as we walked away, he said, "Son, there
was a lot of motion and sound, but you didn't go anywhere."
That was some more of my father's deep insight and down-
to-earth philosophy that has stuck with me and directed me.
It has been one of the rules by which I have measured my activities — am I getting anywhere? Frankly, I am not constituted
to be satisfied with defeat or stalemate.

Our God believes in progress. He did something productive
every day for six days and rested on the seventh (Genesis 1,2).

It is imperative that we constantly check our activities for
results. Unless we discipline ourselves to stay with the pay-offs,
we shall get diverted to the little merry-go-rounds of com-
paratively unimportant matters. On them we can actually slave
and make no gains.

I have observed much lost motion in church, in school and
in business. I have seen some ministers, educators and
businessmen work and toil, get compliments for their tireless
energy, and fail because their labors were not directed toward
the things that pay off. It's not enough to be busy — be
productive.

The Shepherd Hymn

The Lord is my shepherd, I shall not want. He maketh me to lie down in green pastures: He leadeth me beside the still waters. He restoreth my soul: He leadeth me in the paths of righteousness for his name's sake. Yea, though I walk through the valley of the shadow of death, I will fear no evil; for thou art with me: Thy rod and thy staff, they comfort me. Thou preparest a table before me in the presence of mine enemies: Thou anointest my head with oil: My cup runneth over. Surely goodness and mercy shall follow me all the days of my life: And I will dwell in the house of the Lord for ever. Psalms 23

It was David, the ancient shepherd boy, who pictorially expressed the hope of frail man in the eloquent and immortal Twenty-third Psalm.

For hundreds of years, on every shore and in every clime, it has dried the tears and healed the hearts of countless numbers who helplessly stood by and watched as husband or wife, son or daughter, father or mother, brother or sister slipped down through the valley of the shadow of death.

Its words have been upon the trembling lips of millions who slowly turned from the flower-decked mound where the earthly frame they loved so dearly was placed to sleep in hallowed ground.

And later, when time stood still in mournful shadows, as they tried to put back together a broken heart, they found peace in the way of life and death provided by the Good Shepherd.

Today man's needs are no different. And the shepherd's psalm is still a balm for hearts that ache and bleed and break.

He Does What He Must

I must work the works of him that sent me, while it is day: the night cometh, when no man can work. John 9:4

As seen in the above Scripture, Jesus had the dedication and courage to face and to do what He had to do. This attitude is ever relevant and ever descriptive of the ideal person. *He does what he must.*

He girds himself with determination and fights his daily battles out of true convictions, never failing love, and undying loyalty. He couldn't do otherwise and be himself. Our hats are off to him.

His business falls apart. Has to be closed. Old doors close behind him; now he must open some new ones. As a giant among men, he does.

His investments fail and his plans are shattered. Yet he keeps an unfaltering trust that God will see him through.

His wife is ill, bills are pressing, house payments are coming due. Two jobs are necessary to stay solvent. He takes them without a whimper.

Moral questions arise on the job. Right seems to be out of vogue. But he doesn't worry about the flow of popularity. For he knows it floods and dries up according to the whims and fancies of man. Moreover, it is more important to him to live with the approval of his conscience.

He is knocked down again and again; nevertheless he stays in the ring. In every round he is determined to score. The world can't beat a man that won't stay down. He arises and does what he must. "He alone is great, who by a life heroic conquers fate."

A Lion in the Street

*The slothful man saith, There is a lion without, I shall be slain
in the streets.* Proverbs 22:13

This poor fellow didn't want to work. He said there is a lion
in the streets. When an excuse is needed, a friendly kitten can
be pictured as a devouring lion.

Excuses! Excuses! Excuses! How freely you come! How
worthless you are!

Two men on Sunday morning were out on the lake fishing.
About 10:30 one of them looked at his watch and his mind
flashed back to where he should be. Feeling that slight touch
of conscience, he said, "Hubert, we really ought to be in
church."

Hubert answered, "Well, I couldn't have gone. My wife is
sick."

Offering an excuse when we fail is an effort to keep the ego
inflated. We just don't like to admit failure or wrong. All have
done it, I have, you have, and it seemed to give a little temporary relief from pain by thwarting the admission of any deficiency. However, this becomes more hurtful than any pain that
ensues from admitting a fault. It is most injurious to refuse to
see and face ourselves as we really are. It keeps us from cor-
recting our mistakes and from improving our character.

The world doesn't accept excuses. Neither does the Lord. We
are going to be judged now and later by our performance —
not by excuses. This is right, for it is as Shakespeare said:

> *The fault, dear Brutus, is not in our stars,*
> *But in ourselves.*

Shall We Live Again?

*For which cause we faint not; but though our outward man
perish, yet the inward man is renewed day by day.*
                                        II Corinthians 4:16

Victor Hugo, the renowned French poet, novelist and
dramatist, expressed in his declining years some eloquent and
encouraging thoughts on immortality. They continue to echo
in many hearts the world over. They are as relevant as man
himself who lives and dies.

"I feel in myself the future life. I am like a forest once cut
down; the new shoots are stronger and livelier than ever. I am
rising, I know, toward the sky.

"You say the soul is nothing but the resultant of the bodily
powers. Why, then, is my soul more luminous when my bodily
powers begin to fail? Winter is on my head, but eternal spring
is in my heart. I breathe at this hour the fragrance of the lilacs,
the violets and the roses, as at twenty years. The nearer I approach the end the plainer I hear around me the immortal sym-
phonies of the worlds which invite me. It is marvelous yet simple. It is a fairy tale, and it is history.

"For half a century I have been writing my thoughts in prose
and in verse: history, philosophy, drama, romance, tradition,
satire, ode and song; I have tried all. But I feel I have not said
the thousandth part of what is in me. When I go down to the
grave I can say like many others, 'I have finished my day's
work.' But I cannot say, 'I have finished my life.' My day's
work will begin again the next morning. The tomb is not a
blind alley; it is a thoroughfare. It closes on the twilight; it
opens on the dawn."

And That Is Dying

Blessed are the dead which die in the Lord from henceforth: Yea, saith the Spirit, that they may rest from their labors; and their works do follow them. Revelation 14:13

It adds joy and zest to life to have a hope that takes the sting out of the thought of dying. We do not want to go now, but we do want to know that all can be well when going time comes.

We like to think of it as the completion of our pilgrimage to the distant land; and that those who have preceded us are enjoying the love of there even much more than the love of here; and that they are waiting to welcome us. It is expressed well in the following:

I am standing upon the seashore. A ship at my side spreads her white sails to the morning breeze and starts for the blue ocean.

She is an object of beauty and strength and I stand and watch her until at length she is only a ribbon of white cloud just where the sea and sky come to mingle with each other. Then some one at my side says:

"There! She's gone!"

Gone — where? Gone from my sight — that is all. She is just as large in mast and hull and spar as she was when she left my side and just as able to bear her load of living freight — to the place of destination.

Her diminished size is in me, not in her and just at the moment when some one at my side says: "There! She's gone!" other voices are ready to take up the glad shout "Here, she comes!"

And that is dying in the Lord.

Nearer, My God, to Thee

And God appeared unto Jacob . . . And Jacob set up a pillar in the place where he talked with him, even a pillar of stone. Genesis 35:9-14

The inspiring hymn, "Nearer, My God, to Thee," was written by Sarah Fuller Adams, who was born in 1805. She wrote many lyrics, but her claim to fame is found in the authorship of this one hymn.

One night she had a graphic dream in which she saw herself standing by the mounds in Bethel where Jacob once pitched his tent. There she saw Jacob, an exile, to whom God had revealed Himself. She awoke feeling that God was with His people everywhere, no matter how desolate the place is. At once she wrote the words of the hymn.

This hymn has been emotionally associated with the Titanic disaster. As the ship was sinking, taking more than a thousand down to a watery grave, it has been stated that the band played the tune of the hymn and passengers and crew joined in the singing. The hymn that comforted them has comforted millions.

Nearer, my God, to Thee,
Nearer to Thee!
E'en though it be a cross
That raiseth me;
Still all my song shall be,
Nearer, my God, to Thee,
Nearer to Thee.

When the End Comes

For we know that, if our earthly house of this tabernacle were dissolved, we have a building of God, a house not made with hands, eternal in the heavens. II Corinthians 5:1

When the end comes, it's only a new beginning. For when this life has run its course we shall continue to live and to serve in a better realm. "And his servants shall serve him: And they shall see his face" (Revelation 22:3,4).

> *When Earth's last picture is painted,*
> *And the tubes are twisted and dried,*
> *When the oldest colors have faded,*
> *And the youngest critic has died,*
> *We shall rest — and, faith, we shall need it —*
> *Lie down for an aeon or two,*
> *Till the Master of All Good Workmen*
> *Shall set us to work anew!*
>
> *And those that were good shall be happy;*
> *They shall sit in a golden chair;*
> *They shall splash at a ten-league canvas*
> *With brushes of comet's hair;*
> *They shall find real saints to draw from —*
> *Magdalene, Peter and Paul;*
> *They shall work for an age at a sitting*
> *And never get tired at all!*
>
> *And only the Master shall praise us,*
> *And only the master shall blame;*
> *And no one shall work for money,*
> *And no one shall work for fame;*
> *But each for the joy of the working,*
> *And each in his separate star*
> *Shall draw the Thing as he sees It*
> *For the God of Things as They Are.*

The Master Is There

Yea, though I walk through the valley of the shadow of death,
I will fear no evil: for thou art with me.   Psalms 23:4

There is a comforting story of a Christian physician who was caring for one of his patients in the patient's home. This was years ago. As the physician was leaving, the sick man said: "Doctor, am I going to get well?" The doctor hesitated and said, "I don't always know, but I do know you're a pretty sick man."

Then the extremely ill man took the physician by the hand and continued, "I don't want to die; tell me what's on the other side."

The doctor replied, "I wish I could tell you but I don't know."

They talked for a moment about the mystery of life and death, and then the doctor prepared to leave. As he opened the door to go, a dog sprang into the room and delightfully leaped on him. Turning to the patient, the good physician resumed: "Did you observe that? This is my dog. Never before has he been in this house. He did not know what was inside here. He knew nothing except that his master was here, and so he leaped in without any fear. I cannot tell you what's on the other side, but I know the Master is there — and that's enough for anyone. When he opens the door, I expect to pass in without fear. There I shall dwell in His house forever."

RESIGNATION

There is no flock, however watched and tended,
But one dead lamb is there!
There is no fireside, howsoe'er defended,
But has one vacant chair!

Henry W. Longfellow

With You Always

And, lo, I am with you alway, even unto the end of the world.
Matthew 28:20

There is the promise of divine presence in all the days.

• *In days of loneliness*, which come to all. There can be the loneliness of the rich as well as the poor, the king as much as the peasant. At times all suffer a loneliness hard to share, except with the God who created us. We call this sharing, this closeness, the communion of our spirit with the Eternal Spirit.

• *In days of sadness*. There are days when the singer has no song and the musician has no music. Occasions arise that sadden the most buoyant and dampen the hope of the most hopeful. But the promise, "I am with you all the days," lifts the spirit of the sorrowful and encourages the downhearted.

• *In the days of monotony*. Many people find the daily routine slavishly monotonous. In days of danger, opposition, threat or persecution, they rise to valor; but in easier days they find the humdrum experiences of life very boresome and grinding. But the knowledge of the Lord's presence should give your ordinary living a new appeal. He can help you through the common days.

• *In days of struggle*. The sea of life is not always smooth; neither is the wind always favorable. It takes a lot of hard rowing. But when the sailing is the harshest and sternest, inspired by Him who promised to be with us, we say:

> *List not to the angry waters*
> *Of life's ever restless sea;*
> *Believers of the Lord, remember,*
> *"As thy days, thy strength shall be."*

House of Many Mansions

For we know that, if our earthly house of this tabernacle were dissolved, we have a building of God, a house not made with hands, eternal in the heavens. II Corinthians 5:1

A move from one house to another does not end the life of the tenant. When this old house — this body — shall have broken down, man shall be given a fairer dwelling made for eternity.

THE TENANT

This body is my house — it is not I;
Herein I sojourn till, in some far sky,
I lease a fairer dwelling, built to last
Till all the carpentry of time is past.
(In a new house away from) this lone star,
What shall I care where these poor timbers are?
What, though the crumbling walls turn dust and loam —
I shall have left them for a larger home.

Frederick Lawrence Knowles

Fashioned by a mighty hand that doeth all things well, our new bodies, made to last world without end, shall never know harassment and hurt, sickness and sorrow, despair and death; for the Great Giver shall design them to be like unto his own glorious body. For the Bible, in speaking of our Lord, says, "Who shall change our vile body, that it may be fashioned like unto his glorious body, according to the working whereby he is able even to subdue all things unto himself" (Philippians 3:21).

It is in this triumphant faith that we live in the soothing solace that only a part of us shall ever die.

The Most Popular Book

All Scripture is given by inspiration of God, and is profitable for doctrine, for reproof, for correction, for instruction in righteousness: That the man of God may be perfect, thoroughly furnished unto all good works. II Timothy 3:16,17

An unknown author once said of the Bible:

"This old book contains the mind of God, the state of man, the way of salvation, the doom of sinners, and the happiness of believers. Its doctrines are holy, its precepts are binding, its histories are true, and its decisions are immutable.

"Read it to be wise, believe it to be safe, and practice it to be holy.

"It contains light to direct you, food to support you, and comfort to cheer you. It is the traveler's map, the pilgrim's staff, the pilot's compass, the soldier's sword, and the believer's charter. Here paradise is restored, heaven opened and the gates of hell disclosed. Christ is its grand object, our good its design, and the glory of God its end.

"It should fill the memory, rule the heart, and guide the feet.

"It is a mine of wealth, a paradise of glory, and a river of joy. It is given you in life, will be opened at the judgment, and will be remembered forever. It involves the highest responsibilities, will reward the greatest labor, and will condemn all who trifle with its sacred contents."

Thus it is easy to see: Why there is a copy in almost every home in the land. Why it is the most read book in public gatherings. Why it is the most popular source book for writers. Why its comfort has been on the lips of countless numbers who confidently slipped away into the world beyond.

Exaggeration

*And they brought up an evil report of the land . . . saying
. . . and there we saw the giants, the sons of Anak, which come
of the giants: and we were in our own sight as grasshoppers, and
so we were in their sight.* Numbers 13:32,33

Highly exaggerated!

Evangelist Billy Sunday was always plain and unique. At the
close of one of his sermons a woman approached him and
asked contemplatively, "I wonder if you can help me? I have
an awful habit of exaggerating."

"Certainly, madam," replied Sunday, "just call it lying."

The rumor was out that Mark Twain had passed away. A
sympathizer went to the home to pay his condolences. He
knocked on the door and Twain answered. The startled man
finally got out these words, "I heard you were dead."

The famous humorist replied, "I would say the report was
greatly exaggerated."

Those accustomed to exaggeration find it hard to tell the
whole truth without twisting at least some portion of it into
a lie.

The love of exaggeration is a love to enhance, improve and
make a better story. There are people who really enjoy spill-
ing news, for it puts them in the spotlight by making them the
center of attention; and the bigger the story, the bigger they
feel.

However, it's incredible that a person would pursue attention and limelight at the risk of losing credibility. How much
more one is respected when he follows this straight principle
of unadornment, "I am what I am; and what I say is, *is.*"

How to Overcome Tensions

*When thou liest down, thou shalt not be afraid: yea, thou shalt
lie down, and thy sleep shall be sweet.* Proverbs 3:24

Anxieties and tensions are the normal reactions when our
safety and well-being are threatened. They are our defenses.
However, sometimes we become too anxious and too tense,
which is hurtful. This means that we should learn to deal with
our difficulties without overly reacting. Here are some
suggestions:

• *Talk it out.* Don't bottle up your bother. Talk opens the
high pressure valve and allows some tension to escape. Be
cautious, however, in picking one with whom you talk.

• *Leave it for awhile.* It is helpful to escape from the vexing problems long enough to recover your bearing and get your
balance. Later come back to the difficulty.

• *Be not self-willed.* Life is made up of give and take. Compromise truth? No! Opinions? Yes! Remember — you could be
wrong.

• *Work off your indignation.* Don't let the sun go down on
your wrath. Do something constructive — it calms the nerves.

• *Take life one day at a time.* The load will get too heavy
if you pile on your back all the burdens of the weeks and
months ahead.

• *Expect realistic accomplishments.* Some people expect too
much of themselves, which is frustrating. We don't have to be
supermen — just good people who use their talents.

• *Be able to take criticism.* The best people get criticized.
What people say about you does not change what you are.

God's Garden

She hath done what she could.   Mark 14:8

That's all that can be expected of any person — 100% performance.

A grand little lady in New England came up with a novel idea in serving the Lord and in reaching for fulfillment in life. Next door to her humble house she had a vacant lot that had been growing weeds and creating worries. She decided to turn the liability into an asset for the church and the world. She decided to use it for a vegetable garden and to raise all the kinds that grow in that area.

She called her project *God's Garden*. The name was appropriate. For all the vegetables she didn't use she either gave to needy people or sold them and gave the money to the church.

One night she attended church, exhibiting her abiding interest and cheerful smile. Doing for others always brings satisfaction and happiness. She was a living example of the correctness of Christ's principle that it is more blessed to give than to receive.

That night after church, she went home and went to bed. The next day neighbors found that she had done more than go to sleep: sometime during the night she had gone to sleep in Jesus. The moment came for her to move into another garden, one more beautiful and meaningful than earth has ever known, cultivated by Him who said, "I go to prepare a place for you."

The people in the Northeast still remember the little old lady who tilled *God's Garden*. The frosts of many winters have cut down the vegetables, but the memories she planted in human hearts continue to live.

The Most Important Values

While we look not at the things which are seen, but at the things which are not seen: for the things which are seen are temporal; but the things which are not seen are eternal. II Corinthians 4:18

The Cathedral of Milan greets the visitor with some deep and self-examining philosophy. There are three inscriptions on the arches over the triple doorway.

One is a beautifully carved wreath of roses, and beneath it is the notable pronouncement, *All that pleases is but for a moment.*

Another is a sculptured cross and these encouraging words are below, *All that troubles is but for a moment.*

But the main central entrance has beneath it this masterpiece in priorities, *That only is important which is eternal.*

Pleasures are fleeting, troubles are momentary, and man who knows both is soon ridden away on the pale horse. Everything in the earth shall bow to death and pass away. Nothing material can withstand the ravages of time. Even the earth itself "shall pass away with a great noise and the elements shall melt with fervent heat."

But God shall keep on living. He is from everlasting to everlasting. His word shall never pass away. It has been maliciously sentenced to death by foolish men, but it is indestructible. And the spirit of man lives on and on. Things eternal!

So, what are the major values? The answer is simple: Only the invisible things that defy time and answer not to death's call. They — and they only — can be considered the most important.

The Donkey in the Lion's Skin

For if a man think himself to be something, when he is nothing, he deceiveth himself. Galatians 6:3

There is helpfulness in an age-old fable about a donkey that found a lion's skin and put it on. Disguised as a lion, he went into the woods and pastures and threw the flocks and herds into a dreadful fear.

At last, he met his owner who saw his long ears sticking out and recognized him. The owner promptly took a stick and hit him over the head, which brought him back to his senses.

Notwithstanding he was dressed in a lion's skin, he was still just a donkey.

The lesson is: People should be what they seem to be.

The fable points up the vain pretense of putting on airs and assuming to be wiser, richer, more learned and of higher rank than one really is. Such persons are ever in danger of being found out; and when they are, they will in a greater degree suffer the ridicule and humiliation of the donkey in the lion's skin.

The really honest person — in all conditions of life — will show himself in his true garb and in his own character. He will not for temporary gain pretend to be something he is not. He will not pretend to be better than he is to impress people; furthermore, he will not condescend to do anything worse than he is. He will act in the spirit of the proverb: "Be the same thing you would be called." May each be able to say with Lewis Carroll:

> You may charge me with neglect or want of sense —
> We are all weak at times;
> But the slightest approach to a false pretense
> Was never among my crimes!

Too Slow

And Jonathan cried after the lad, Make speed, haste, stay not.
And Jonathan's lad gathered up the arrows, and came to his
master. I Samuel 20:38

After the woman's husband was laid to rest, she was the only mourner to get in the big funeral limousine. She had no children and no other relatives. On the way home from the cemetery the funeral director said, "Mary, I want to tell you something, and I don't want you to be offended. I mean it as a compliment. I've been secretly in love with you for all these years. That's why I have never married. Because of John I wouldn't say anything about it, but now he's gone. All of my life I've been too slow about everything, but this time I'm coming in early. So Mary, if you should ever think of marrying again, just remember I asked you first."

"Tom, I appreciate this very much," she replied, "but the doctor has already asked me."

Don't you feel sorry for him? Always a foot behind and a minute late.

Too slow — that's the best description of some people. They're always running behind. Late at work, late at church, late at appointments. They need to reset their timing and rewind themselves.

In the everyday affairs of life we have to run fast just to stand still. But we can hasten without being in a break-neck hurry. Hasten slowly. There's a vast difference between rashness and haste. A prudent haste is great protection against loss and waste. Certainty is better than haste, but when we are certain we should hasten.

The world is moving on, unless we hasten we will be left behind.

He Fainted at Church

For consider him that endured such contradiction of sinners against himself, lest ye be wearied and faint in your minds. Hebrews 12:3

While the man was sitting on a pew at church he keeled over in a dead faint. There was no purpose in preaching to him. He couldn't listen. No need to call him to sing. He couldn't sing. Neither could you call him to pray. He couldn't pray. Nor was there any point in passing him the contribution plate. He couldn't give.

The poor fellow was completely incognizant, unconscious, and had to be carried out. There he was unable to accomplish anything. For he was in a faint. In this comatose state, he only breathed. This is true of those who faint spiritually. While they may breathe in the church, their heart is in another world.

Here are some safeguards against fainting in business, home and church:

• *First, don't expect a life free of all hardships.* If you do, you will not be conditioned to face them when they come.

• *Second, renew your strength.* This is accomplished by waiting on the Lord. Then you can rise with the wings of an eagle; can run and not get weary; can walk and not faint.

• *Third, see the goodness of many blessings.* Think how many more things are good than bad.

• *Fourth,* by increasing your faith and trust in God, you *build up your courage* to stay in there and keep struggling.

• *Fifth, pray.* I have never known a praying person to spiritually faint. Prayer puts us in touch with a Higher Power.

The Ghost of Procrastination

And now why tarriest thou? Acts 22:16

Putting off an easy thing today makes it hard tomorrow — or even impossible. Procrastination is the world's biggest and cruelest thief. It steals what people cannot afford to lose: opportunity, accomplishment and success.

There were at first a little grass and weeds in the farmer's crop. A few tomorrows later they took over and the crop was lost. At first there was only a tiny leak in the roof. A few tomorrows saw the house flooded.

By doing our duty today, we have less trouble tomorrow. Today is cash in hand. Tomorrow is only a dim, promissory note.

TOMORROW

He was going to be all that a mortal should be
   Tomorrow.
No one should be kinder or braver than he
   Tomorrow.
A friend who was troubled and weary he knew,
Who'd be glad of a lift and who needed it, too;
On him he would call and see what he could do
   Tomorrow.

The greatest of workers this man would have been
   Tomorrow.
The world would have known him, had he ever seen
   Tomorrow.
But the fact is he died and he faded from view,
And all that he left here when living was through
Was a mountain of things he intended to do
   Tomorrow.

Edgar A. Guest

The most upright thing about him is his tombstone, which says something nice about him because he is down.

Run Rabbit Run

In all labor there is profit: but the talk of the lips tendeth only to penury. Proverbs 14:23

A group of men and women stood on a hillside watching a dog chase a rabbit. They shouted, "Run, rabbit, run! Run for your life! Run! Run! Run!

After circling in the chase two or three times and as the people cheered again, the poor rabbit yelled back, "Ladies and gentlemen, I appreciate your words of encouragement, but why doesn't someone chase off the dog?"

They didn't talk too much, they did too little. They were vain talkers. Clouds without water. Rivers that were dry. A disappointment.

Some talkers seem a help, but their limp arms never move.

Talking comes cheap, so cheap that some talk when they have nothing to say. And the only reason some others listen is because they know it will be their turn next.

Some think help is only a one way street in which all assistance is coming their way and none going back to the other fellow. That was the view of the self-centered woman who arose one morning and said, "I wonder what nice thing somebody can do for me today." It had never dawned on her that she, like everybody else, is here to help others; instead, she thought she was here for others to help.

It is the practical law of nature that we help one another. Not just talk. Help each other. The Apostle Paul commanded, "Bear ye one another's burdens" (Galatians 6:10).

God give us hands that move with the tongue.

Old Jiggs

*Where no wood is, there the fire goeth out: so where there is
no talebearer, the strife ceaseth. As coals are to burning coals,
and wood to fire; so is a contentious man to kindle strife.*
Proverbs 26:20,21

Old Jiggs — that was the name of our dog. I liked that dog
and I should have, because he liked me. Furthermore, he had
some jobs to do, just as I did, and he always did them faithfully and well.

My father's store had wooden floors. Nearly all floors were
made of wood back in that day. Customers would sometimes
drop a cigarette on the floor. This was a potential fire hazard
— a wooden floor, strewn bits of paper and cardboard, and
a dropped cigarette.

Now back to Jiggs — we trained him from the time he was
a pup to put out cigarettes and burning paper. He was our
fireman in that store, and one that could smell better than we
could. He wouldn't hurt anybody, but he was death on cigarettes and little fires. His whiskers stayed scorched all the time.

Years have passed and I've thought about old Jiggs many
times. There's a great lesson to learn from him. He didn't start
fires — he put them out.

Too bad some people in church, in business, in school, and
in every other circle don't act like Jiggs. They generate sparks
and build fires in our society.

Anyone can cause trouble, but it takes a righteous talent to
prevent it (if possible) and to maintain peace.

It's a thousand times better to be like Jiggs — when strife
begins to flame, put it out.

Handling Discouragement

Rejoicing in hope; patient in tribulation. Romans 12:12

The name of Thomas Edison is greatly cherished because his inventions have blessed the world: incandescent light, telephone, storage battery, microphone, talking movies and many more.

In a biography written by his son, we are informed of some of the battles bravely fought by this unique genius. An incident in 1914 reveals the grit, the unconquerable spirit, the adjustment and the optimism of this great man. In a freezing December night the alarm of "Fire! Fire!" was sounded. Edison's plant was on fire. Though fire equipment from eight surrounding towns came to fight the blaze, everything was destroyed.

But it was neither the building nor the records that worried the son. His father was missing. Had he been working (for he worked day and night) and died? If he survived, had it broken the spirit of the sixty-seven year old man? Then to his relief, his father came running to him and said, "Where's Mom? Go get her. Tell her to hurry up and bring her friends. They'll never see a fire like this again."

The next day with the fire barely under control, Edison summoned his employees and said, "We're rebuilding." He ordered one employee to rent all the machine shops in the area. Another was told to get a wrecking crane. Then, as if he had almost forgotten, he asked, "Oh, by the way, anybody know where we can get some money?"

He could handle disappointment. He tried again and again — many times — before his inventions worked. Now he was tried by fire. But hope never yields to disappointment. Hope makes way for another chance, another dream.

Present Tense Living

Today if ye will hear his voice, harden not your hearts. Hebrews 4:7

Many people are mixed up in their tenses. Some are living in the future; others are living in the past. But happy and victorious living is in the present tense.

Yet, there are blessings to be gained from our past. A past mistake can be a warning. We should not stumble on the same rock twice. Also, inspiration from a past success can give present strength.

And the hope of the future can enrich and stimulate us for the present. But, so far as living is concerned, life is strictly a matter of the present tense. Note:

- "Whosoever heareth these sayings of mine, and doeth them, I will liken him unto a wise man" (Matthew 7:24) — present tense.

- "Search me, O God, and know my heart: try me, and know my thoughts: And see if there be any wicked way in me, and lead me in the way everlasting" (Psalms 139:23,24) — present tense.

- "Who comforteth me in all our tribulation, that we may be able to comfort them which are in any trouble" (II Corinthians 1:4) — present tense.

Duty is in the present tense. Not yesterday! Not tomorrow! Do you think you will grasp your potentialities and ideals some uncertain tomorrow? No, you will not! Your tomorrow will be only the result of your today. The possibilities of life are in the present tense.

The People at the Top

*To every thing there is a season, and a time to every purpose
under the heaven: . . . a time to plant . . . a time to gather
. . . a time to get.* Ecclesiastes 3:1-6

Prosperous people definitely intended to pull ahead. A singleness of purpose kept them on the road that led to their goal. Success begins with a purpose.

In every success story there is a determined man or woman, bent on rising above the ordinary. This force of will to be or to achieve is actually the first sign of greatness and the starting point in a successful career.

*Singleness of purpose is one of the chief essentials for success in
life, no matter what may be one's purpose in life.*
John D. Rockefeller, Jr.

Also, they know that their getting to the top is their own responsibility. Not the other fellow's. Not the community's. Not the government's. They know that with God's help it is up to them. Knowing that their compensation must come from their own hands — "the recompense of a man's hands shall be rendered unto him," Proverbs 12:14 — they climb their ladder rung by rung.

Furthermore, have you noticed that the people at the top have a habit of doing the things which experience proves are most likely to work? And negatively, have you observed that they make it a point not to do the things that have a record of failure?

Oh yes, they find roadblocks as all people do, but they themselves are not roadblocks. They do not stand in their way.

Would You Sell the Parrot?

Thou shalt not go up and down as a talebearer among thy people. Leviticus 19:16

Five preachers met for a friendly gathering to exchange views and encourage one another. During the session one preacher said, "Our people come to us with open hearts, confess their sins, and express certain needs. Don't you think it would be good for us to do the same: We're frail, have weaknesses, make mistakes, and have needs like everybody else. We are all made from the same clay."

After some discussion, it was agreed that they should do the same; that confession is good for the soul.

The first one confessed that he enjoyed going to night clubs, and sometimes when away from home he would sneak in and visit but not participate. The second confessed to liking to play cards but that he would never play for more than a dime. The third confessed to enjoying cigars and to indulging occasionally. The fourth confessed that sometimes he drank a little in an effort to quiet his turbulent feelings. The fifth one didn't want to confess. But the others pressed him, "We confessed ours, now it's your turn. What is your secret weakness or sin?"

After much insistence he answered, "It's gossiping and I can hardly wait to get out of here and start talking."

All of us need to learn that Jesus said, "Go into all the world and preach the gospel"; that He didn't say, "Go into all the world and preach the gossip."

Will Rogers has given some timely advice: "So live that you wouldn't be ashamed to sell the family parrot to the town gossip."

The One Whose Presence Is Most Needed

For where two or three are gathered together in my name, there am I in the midst of them. Matthew 18:20

The story has been told that one day the telephone rang in the minister's office of the Washington church, which was attended by President Franklin Roosevelt. A desirous voice inquired, "Do you expect the President to be in church Sunday?"

"That," answered the preacher, "I cannot promise. But we expect the Lord to be present, and we fancy that should be incentive enough for a reasonably large crowd."

A government head errs, but not the Lord — "Who did no sin, neither was guile found in his mouth" (I Peter 2:22).

A government leader is sometimes a respecter of man, but not God — "Of a truth I perceive that God is no respecter of persons" (Acts 10:34)

A government official may be political in his decisions, but not the Great Judge — "As I hear, I judge: and my judgment is just" (John 5:30).

A President will die and leave us, but not God — "Hast thou not known? hast thou not heard, that the everlasting God, the Lord, the Creator of the ends of the earth, fainteth not, neither is weary?" (Isaiah 40:28).

Therefore it is wiser for us to place the honor and the glory where it belongs — on the Lord, not on man.

Something Special

What is man, that thou shouldest magnify him? and that thou shouldest set thine heart upon him? Job 7:17

The brilliant Daniel Webster said:

> *If we work upon marble,*
> *It will perish;*
> *It we work upon brass,*
> *Time will efface it;*
> *If we rear temples,*
> *They will crumble into dust;*
> *But, if we work upon immortal souls,*
> *If we imbue them with principles,*
> *With the just fear of God*
> *And the love of fellow man,*
> *We engrave on those tablets*
> *Something which will brighten all eternity.*

Man is a creature of great potential for this world and a sure thing for everlasting existence in the ceaseless ages to come. This marks him as something special. All of this we would expect, for he is the handiwork of God made in God's own image, a little lower than the angels. This makes him Heaven's masterpiece.

Despite the laudatory remarks, man is weak and subject to temptation. Oh, how contemptible he is unless raised above the degradation of sin.

While man is weak like a reed, he is a thinking reed to be cultivated. Man — the object of God's love — is clay to be molded into a masterpiece of distinction. Man — an intellectual being — is born without manners, and is a challenge to be shaped into a vessel of accomplishment, culture and refinement. Man — an eternal being — is spirit housed in a corpse, and spirit does not die. So in working with man, we work with the immortal.

Prepared for a Prepared Place

I go to prepare a place for you. John 14:2

There is an intriguing story about a preacher who decided to leave a church where he had preached two years. With moist eyes, he stood up in the Sunday morning service and bid good-bye to a sad congregation.

"Brothers and sisters," he said, clearing his throat and restrainnng his emotion, "I wish to say farewell. The Lord has called me to another place. I don't think the Lord loves you very much; for none of you ever dies. He doesn't seem to want you. And you don't seem to love each other; for I have never married any of you. And neither do you seem to love me; for you don't pay me enough to live substantially.

"And now, brothers and sisters, I am resigning. I have accepted a position to be the chaplain in the state penitentiary. In closing, I am reminded of the Scripture, 'I go to prepare a place for you . . . where I am, there ye may be also.' "

I would like to believe the preacher was kindly and humorously teasing them a little. If so, it is proof he liked them; for we don't tease the people we don't like.

The story does, however, emphasize the need of preparation to enter a prepared place. Even if it is a penitentiary, one has to qualify (which is on the low side) to enter it.

There is a prepared job out there for you, but you have to be prepared to do it. The school is a prepared place, but the student must be prepared to appropriate it. The church is a prepared body, but a person must be prepared for its fellowship.

Jesus said, "I go to prepare a place for you," but it is a prepared place for prepared people.

Is It Meddling?

Preach the word; be instant in season, out of season; reprove, rebuke, exhort with all long-suffering and doctrine.

II Timothy 4:2

A mechanic went to hear a visiting evangelist in a little town. The preacher preached that night on money, and presented the sermon under three points.

• *First point, "Make all you can."*

The mechanic nudged his wife and said, "That man is the best I've ever heard. He's no nitwit. He knows what it's all about. He is one smart man."

• *Second point, "Save all you can."*

This excited the mechanic and he whispered again, "This beats anything I've ever heard. He's smart enough to be President. This town has never had a preacher that could hold a candle to him." The preacher commended hard work and thrift, denouncing laziness and waste. The mechanic couldn't keep quiet. He whispered, "I've believed in this all my life. Salvation has finally come to us."

• *Third point, "Give all you can."*

"Oh my," exlaimed the mechanic, "now he's gone crazy. He has quit preaching and gone to meddling."

Isn't it strange that some people's conception of great preaching is a sermon that compliments them and rebukes others?

Remember — your preacher didn't write the Bible. He is not responsible for any word in it, but he is definitely responsible for preaching every word in it. And when it is preached, people judge themselves by their reaction to it.

Leaning Trees

*When I call to remembrance the unfeigned faith that is in thee,
which dwelt first in thy grandmother Lois, and thy mother
Eunice; and I am persuaded that in thee also.* II Timothy 1:5

The grandmother inspired and swayed her daughter, and the daughter influenced her son. His name was Timothy.

In my first visit along the California coast I observed that all the trees leaned from the ocean back to the East. This was caused by the wind that blew in from the Pacific. The wind's pressure was applied to the trees and now they lean accordingly.

A little cloud blew up and a gale from the opposite direction struck those trees with gusty force that bent and twisted them back the other way. But only temporarily. When the storm subsided, they yielded back to their original leanings. They had become old and would not depart from the way they grew up. Bend? Yes, but not permanently. Reminds me of Solomon's assertion on rearing children: "Train up a child in the way he should go: and when he is old, he will not depart from it" (Proverbs 22:6).

At church I noticed a little girl carrying a copybook her teacher had given her. An impressionable way to teach. Then I was struck with the idea, however, that the parent's life is the child's most effective copybook. The parent's impressions are more indelible and far-reaching than all others — more than the minister, the Sunday school teacher, the public school teacher or any other person.

A Page of Example

Ye are our epistle written in our hearts, known and read of all men. II Corinthians 3:2

There are four gospels, Matthew, Mark, Luke and John, and the fifth is You, which is the one most read by your associates.

The Gospels of Matthew, Mark, Luke and John,
Are read by more than a few,
But the one that is most read and commented on
Is the gospel according to You.

You are writing a gospel, a chapter each day,
By things that you do and words that you say,
Men read what you write, whether faithless or true.
Say, what is the gospel according to You?

Is it love? Is it forgiveness? Is it helpfulness? Is it fairness? Is it truthfulness? Is it ethics? Is it kindness?

Is it courtesy? Is it tolerance? Is it Bible study? Is it church attendance? Is it sacrifice? Is it clean speech? Is it unselfishness? Is it bigness?

These qualities will make you an effective living epistle, admired and loved by those who read you. And read you, they will!

A page of example is worth a book of preach.

Success Requires Activity

Then said Jesus unto him, Go, and do thou likewise. Luke 10:37

While a little girl was playing with some lettered blocks she made a startling discovery.

Her mother had requested her to spell the word "good," and explained how important it is for a little girl to be good and act good.

After a little while the girl ran into the kitchen and joyously exclaimed to her mother: "Come and see the two nice words I made out of the word 'good.' " It was the words, "go" and "do."

From a child's play we have a powerful lesson on successful pursuit — that it demands more than play.

We can't just play neighbor — we must go and do.

We can't just play business — we must go and do.

We can't just play government — we must go and do.

We can't just play education — we must go and do.

We can't just play church — we must go and do.

We can't just play good — we must be good.

They Don't Know My Son

But Joshua the son of Nun, which standeth before thee, he shall go in thither: encourage him: for he shall cause Israel to inherit it. Deuteronomy 1:38

School lasted only six or seven months a year in our little village. I grew up believing that the most important factor in education is not the length of the school term but the depth of the student's mind.

We had all the grades except the last year. When I reached that level I moved into town, lived with my grandmother, and went to school there. On registration day I was kindly but firmly told that no one from a small school with such short terms could possibly finish in one year; that it was much harder than a country school; that it always took two years for a student with my background to graduate.

I replied, "If you don't mind, please see that I have all required courses and enough credits so that I can finish, in the event I pass."

"All right, but we just don't want you to be disappointed."

I didn't believe it, but the thought of it cast gloom over me. Later, feeling the despondency, I told my mother what the school official had said. I shall never forget her sweet assuring words: "They don't know my son."

The nine months soon became history and graduation night came. Not only did I pass, but I received a college scholarship. The point is not the scholarship but the encouragement my mother gave. At times everybody needs it. Encouragement is oxygen to the heart. Giving it can save a person from fainting.

Cause and Effect

And David said, What have I now done? Is there not a cause?
I Samuel 17:29

Every effect must have a cause.

In a Sunday morning worship service one of the men was leading the congregation in prayer. This is no criticism — I wouldn't dare do that. Nearly all had heard his rhetoric so often they could go three words ahead of him at any point in the prayer. This particular wording was always included: "O Lord, since we last called upon Thee, the cobwebs have come between us and Thee. We pray that Thou will remove the cobwebs that we may look upon Thy face once again."

At this very point in his prayer, one worshiper spoke out a little louder than he intended: "O Lord, kill the spider."

That's right. It's good to get the cobwebs cleaned out, but it's better to kill the spider. Remove the cause and the results shall be ended.

Many wish to deal with effects instead of causes, which is the short view. But wisdom demands that we get to the bottom of things.

The Bible has a powerful statement on cause and effect: "Whatsoever a man soweth, that shall he also reap" (Galatians 6:7).

None is succeeding or failing, gaining or losing, well or ill, happy or miserable, by chance. All of life is regulated by the inflexible rule of cause and effect.

Honor this law and we shall be blessed. Violate it and we shall be hurt.

Eyes Can Play Tricks

Against an elder receive not an accusation, but before two or three witnesses. I Timothy 5:19

A man came into my office terribly distraught. His voice trembled with emotion. He thought he had nearly set himself up to violate one of the Ten Commandments: "Thou shalt not bear false witness."

He said, "I drove by a tavern and I thought I saw one of the elders of the church sitting there, drinking intoxicants. No question in my mind, I was certain. He wasn't taking a little for 'his stomach's sake.' However, I decided to drive by more slowly and take another look. I was wrong. It wasn't the elder. The boozer certainly looked like him, but wasn't.

"If I hadn't gone back and looked again, the chances are I would have said he was hitting the bottle. It scares me to think of the injury I might have done him."

Due to the imperfection of man, a single witness is no witness. People don't always see what they think they see. The varying testimonies of witnesses to wrecks prove this. Be doubly, doubly sure before accusing a person of wrong.

It's easy to understand why God commanded that an accusation be substantiated by at least two or three witnesses. Though one is honest, he still might be mistaken in what he thought he saw or heard.

Even if the innocent brother mentioned above had been accused, I'm sure he would have recovered from it. But what about the accuser? Perhaps his fate would have been somewhat like that of the dog, of which Oliver Goldsmith wrote:

The man recovered of the bite,
The dog it was that died.

Retreat to Fight Again

Now when Pharoah heard this thing, he sought to slay Moses.
But Moses fled from the face of Pharoah, and dwelt in the land
of Midian: and he sat down by a well. Exodus 2:15

Moses fled from Pharoah, but he returned to attack again. He made havoc of Pharoah's kingdom by delivering the children of God from their bondage.

There are times to advance and there are times to retreat. We can make an honorable retreat, and an honorable retreat is in itself a victory.

> *He that fights and runs away*
> *May live to fight another day.*
>
> Butler

In Texas' War of Independence the defenders of the Alamo died to the last man from the guns and bayonets of an overwhelming army, led by General Santa Anna, President of Mexico. Then General Santa Anna and his army went on to attack Sam Houston and his ragged volunteer army, hoping to soon smash the revolution. But Houston retreated and retreated and retreated until the timely moment came. When the Mexicans were enjoying their siesta and least expecting an attack, the Texans turned and in a brief time slaughtered and captured the whole army, including President Santa Anna.

Knowing when to retreat and when to attack gave birth to a new nation, the Republic of Texas, which ten years later voluntarily became a part of the United States.

Today that knowledge of when to retreat and when to attack still wins victories. It can build a business, effect sales, shape the thinking of social and political groups, and make converts to Christianity. When you have gone far enough for the time, pull back and wait for another day.

Putting Together a Successful Life

I have put my life in my hand. I Samuel 28:21

For a triumphant and happy life one must:

• *Think* — it is the source of human power. "For as he thinketh in his heart, so is he" (Proverbs 23:7).

• *Work* — it is the power of production. "Let him labor . . . that he may have" (Ephesians 4:28).

• *Be thrifty* — it is the means of preservation. "Gather up the fragments that remain, that nothing be lost" (John 6:12).

• *Play* — it is the secret of perennial youth. There are several references in the Bible to games and contests which show that they were an acceptable pastime (II Timothy 2:5).

• *Read* — it is the foundation of knowledge. "Till I come, give attendance to reading" (I Timothy 4:13).

• *Be sensitive* — it is the heart that beats with the joys and sorrows of others. "Rejoice with them that do rejoice, and weep with them that weep" (Romans 12:15).

• *Be friendly* — it is the road that leads to friends. "A man that hath friends must show himself friendly" (Proverbs 18:24).

• *Think of others* — it is the way to enlarge your own heart, view of life and fruitfulness. "Look not every man on his own things, but every man also on the things of others" (Philippians 2:4).

• *Honor God* — this is the conclusion of the whole effort. "Let us hear the conclusion of the whole matter: Fear God and keep his commandments: for this is the whole duty of man" (Ecclesiastes 12:13).

The Rainbow Speaks

I do set my bow in the cloud, and it shall be for a token of a covenant between me and the earth. Genesis 9:13

A little city boy went with his father on his first vacation. They went to the mountains where they camped, hiked and saw its wonders. On one of their hikings, standing on a peak, the daddy pointed out a beautiful and colorful rainbow.

The television-oriented youngster, who had seen many a commercial, commented, "It really is pretty. What's it advertising?"

I don't know the father's answer, but I do know what he could have said: "It's advertising the grace of God and His promise to never send another flood to destroy the earth. After Noah's flood, God made this promise, and set the rainbow in the sky as a sign of the promise."

Furthermore, all of nature is one big signboard after another declaring the glory of God and His handiwork. Many of nature's sights are so enchanting that we first gaze on them in breathless silence, and then when breath is restored we exclaim, "O Lord our Lord, how excellent is thy name in all the earth! who has set thy glory above the heavens" (Psalms 8:1).

> And now sold on the advertising,
>> On the mountains,
>> On the plains,
>> On the seas,
>> On bended knee,
> The little cares that worried me,
>> I lost them yesterday.

Religion Without Ice

Greet Priscilla and Aquilla, my helpers in Christ Jesus.
Romans 16:3

One of the truly renowned helpers in the Lord's work was a little lady who lived in a small town. When she moved there she found no congregation of the church of which she was a member. She immediately made an inquiry and located two other members, a man and his wife. Through her insistence they decided to establish a congregation of the three.

Then she got busy and located a hall they could rent for their assembly. It was a second floor, reached only by climbing a stairway. The same hall was used on Saturday night as a dance hall. She and the couple would get up early on Sunday morning and clean up the rubbish and disarray of the night before. This hall wasn't their choice, but it did put them in operation for the Lord.

Wanting an evangelistic meeting, she wrote a preacher she knew in Oklahoma, explained the circumstances, and invited him to do the preaching. She told him they had no money, could not pay anything, could only keep him and pay his bus fare. The self-sacrificing preacher came.

But he was not the only one to sacrifice: This widow did without ice the entire summer (had no electric refrigerators then) to save enough money to pay the bus fare.

The church prospered. Hard struggle, but it grew. Today it stands as a reminder of what one dedicated woman can do in the Master's vineyard. Strong people just naturally find a way to make an impact. Light shines wherever it is. Salt seasons whatever it touches.

And Touched Them

And Jesus came and touched them, and said, Arise and be not afraid. Matthew 17:7

Touch has a tongue that says what a lonely and burdened world wants to hear. It is the natural touch, energized by a friendly heart, that communicates a feeling that is hard to put into words. Sometimes when the tongue is listless and cannot utter the thoughts that arise within your heart, a warm touch on the shoulder will speak your message.

IN A FRIENDLY SORT O'WAY

When a man ain't got a cent,
*   and he's feeling kind o' blue,*
An' the clouds hang dark and heavy,
*   an' won't let the sunshine through,*
It's a Great Thing, O my brethren,
*   for a feller just to lay*
His hand upon your shoulder in
*   a friendly sort o' way!*

Oh, the world's a curious compound,
*   with its honey and its gall,*
With its cares and bitter crosses,
*   but a good world, after all.*
An' a good God must have made it —
*   leastways, that is what I say,*
When a hand is on my shoulder
*   in a friendly sort o' way.*

James Whitcomb Riley

O for the touch of a loving hand!

A Priceless Mother

Her price is far above rubies. Proverbs 31:10

Solomon the wise man has paid a lofty compliment to the worthy mother: "Her price is far above rubies." No quantity of precious stones can equal her worth. It is utterly impossible to appraise her true value.

She is good to both her husband and children. "She will do him good and not evil all the days of her life" (Proverbs 31:12). It is no problem for her to be good, because she is good. It comes as naturally as breathing. I have observed that good people are good to all; and evil people, when circumstances are trying, are evil to all.

Another one of her invaluable attributes is *she works willingly.* "She . . . worketh willingly with her hands" (Proverbs 31:13). She finds joy in unselfish service to her loved ones. Moreover, her attendance to the family's needs is rendered cheerfully; and we know why — her heart is in it. Willing work contributes to a pleasant and happy home life.

"*She riseth also while it is yet night,* and giveth meat to her household" (Proverbs 31:15). Her diligence enables the members of the family to enter their labors without delay, interruption and tension. This has a major influence in giving the cheerful and unconquerable spirit to the father and children as they face their day. The husband does better in his work and the children do better in school. Fortunate are they!

No wonder her husband praises her (Proverbs 31:28). She has the approbation of her husband and children, because she has earned it. And their appreciation gives her more satisfaction and joy than a golden palace filled with a thousand wardrobes.

My Mother

And Adam called his wife's name Eve; because she was the mother of all living.   Genesis 3:20

Believing that many will be glad to see the following poem reprinted and to have it at this season of the year, I make it a part of this book. It has been a classic for nearly two centuries and has touched the hearts of countless numbers.

MY MOTHER

Who fed me from her gentle breast
And hushed me in her arms to rest,
And on my cheek sweet kisses prest?
    My mother.
When sleep forsook my open eye,
Who was it sung sweet lullaby
And rocked me that I should not cry?
    My mother.
When pain and sickness made me cry,
Who gazed upon my heavy eye
And wept, for fear that I should die?
    My mother.
Who ran to help me when I fell
And would some pretty story tell,
Or kiss the part to make it well?
    My mother.
Who taught my infant lips to pray,
To love God's holy word and day,
And walk in wisdom's pleasant way?
    My mother.
When thou art feeble, old and gray,
My healthy arm shall be thy stay,
And I will soothe thy pains away,
    My mother.
And when I see thee hang thy head,
'Twill be my turn to watch thy bed,
And tears of sweet affection shed —
    My mother.

Jane Taylor

Mother — The Heroine

Now there stood by the cross of Jesus his mother. John 19:25

Every influential and forceful mother has courage as a basic element of character. Fearlessness is a quality of the heart — not a circumstance of surroundings. It depends on what we have in us — not what we have about us. It is a dynamic, internal power that controls behavior as the person faces difficulties, trials and dangers.

Physical courage is seen as a person risks life for another or a cause. The soldier who gives life for his country is honored among the nation's heroes; but we often forget the heroism of those who live and serve and die a little everyday in the home.

It takes the bravest kind of courage to face the everyday affairs of life. It is on this battlefield that mothers display a heroic nature that is unexcelled. It is here that they unflinchingly triumph amidst all the opposition and friction, strain and heartbreak of life.

Brave is the woman who knows how to handle the anxieties, cares, disappointments and sorrows of life. If she does not know what to do with a poor batch of bread, a bad-fitting garment, a soiled carpet, a torn pair of trousers, a broken dish, an unkind word spoken, a misrepresentation, a letdown, a society snub, and a cross look she will fret and worry herself and her family, or go into a pout, or fill her soul with hate and resentment and thereby destroy her loveliness and usefulness.

The universal need for all the services a mother renders compels her to become a creature of bravery. Too much is at stake for her to be otherwise. And every victory won fits her to win another.

Rock Me to Sleep

My son, keep thy father's commandment, and forsake not the law of thy mother: Bind them continually upon thine heart, and tie them about thy neck. When thou sleepest, it shall keep thee; and when thou awakest, it shall talk with thee.

Proverbs 6:20-22

The most wonderful world is the child's world, for it is the realest world — no shams, no baseness. It is to our good that a child's world is always around. One of our blessings is the ability to walk into this world occasionally for a renewal of spirit by reverting to it in memory.

Backward, turn backward, O Time, in your flight,
Make me a child again just for tonight!
Mother, come back from the echoless shore,
Take me again to your heart as of yore;
Kiss from my forehead the furrows of care,
Smooth the few silver threads out of my hair;
Over my slumbers your loving watch keep;
Rock me to sleep, Mother — rock me to sleep!

Tired of the hollow, the base, the untrue,
Mother, O Mother, my heart calls for you!
Many a summer the grass has grown green,
Blossomed and faded, our faces between:
Yet, with strong yearning and passionate pain,
Long I tonight for your presence again.
Come from the silence so long and so deep;
Rock me to sleep, Mother — rock me to sleep.

Elizabeth Akers Allen

Your Second Chance

Suffer little children, and forbid them not, to come unto me; for of such is the kingdom of heaven. Matthew 19:14

A childless neighbor said, "Children are such a comfort in your old age."

"Yes, and they help you to reach it faster," replied the fatigued, nerve-tattered mother.

But a child is your second chance. Moreover, a child teaches the parent — including how much patience you have. Also he teaches you that he's an individual and that you can abandon all cut and dried theories on rearing children. John Wilmont (1647-1680) said, "I had six theories about bringing up children; now I have six children and no theories."

Jesus put a child in the midst. What He did is an apt example for parents — keep them in your midst as much as you can. Give them plenty of love. And the chances are the only bad luck you will ever have with them is *they will grow up.*

SEND THEM TO BED WITH A KISS

O mothers, so fatigued, discouraged,
  Worn out with the cares of the day,
You often grow tired and impatient,
  Weary of the noise and the play;
For the day brings so many vexations,
  So many things going amiss,
But mothers, whatever may vex you,
  Send the children to bed with a kiss.

For some day their noise will not vex you,
  The silence will hurt you far more,
You will long for their sweet childish voices,
  For a sweet childish face at the door;
And to press a child's face to your bosom,
  You'd give all the world for just this,
For the comfort 'twill bring you in sorrow,
  Send the children to bed with a kiss.

All the Way to the Moon

But his mother kept all these sayings in her heart. Luke 2:51

Mama has just made a new observation. A startling one. Her precious ten-year-old boy has started coming to the table with washed face and hands. No prompting on her part. It brought tears to her eyes.

The little boy, sparked with wonder and excitement and with a frog in his pocket, will soon outgrow his careless and sometimes vexing childhood. Time passes fast. He will soon need many pockets, brief cases and filing cabinets to carry the weighty responsibilities of manhood. Ere long he will be running fast — not to catch butterflies, but to endless appointments.

Perchance there will be pressures to serve on committees. None will be like his present committee to dig the worms for the fishing trips, but he will have to dig into human events. Now he has a dog to protect him; later he must learn to protect himself from the wolves (two-legged ones).

Another tear is shed when mama recalls the times when she deemed it necessary to spank him for some infraction and he would say, "Mama, I love you all the way to the moon." That put her into orbit and into a new world.

Already the little boy imagination is beginning to give way to a new absorption: how to spell Cape Canaveral, and a new imagination: how to reach the stars.

It is understandable why mama wipes a tear. She is watching a boy grow into a man. One day he may reach the stars, but more importantly, she prays that he may never lose sight of the God who created them.

A Prayer for Mothers

Give ear, O Lord, unto my prayer; and attend to the voice of my supplications. Psalms 86:6

Our Father in Heaven, the one in whom we live and move and have our being, we thank Thee for mothers, the makers of humanity, the torch-bearers of life and the foundation of civilization. We are grateful for our own dear mothers who bore us in travail and loved us all the more for the pain we brought; who suffered for us in body, mind and soul; who gave us a confident security by their tireless sacrifices and undying devotion; for the agony with which they watched over us in sickness and nursed us back to health; for the sorrow that pierced their hearts when we were foolish; for the smiles of appreciation and joy that played across their faces when we achieved some little accomplishment; for the thousand little tasks they performed daily to make life better for us.

O, God of our being, we implore Thee to grant support, patience and courage to deserving mothers that they may not break under their heavy burdens in life's most strenuous tasks. As each new day dawns, may faith undimmed and optimism unclouded shine anew in their deserving hearts.

And for us we pray, our Father, that the hallowed memories of such illustrious mothers may inspire us to nobler living and lift us to higher ground. May we live the praises due them. In Christ's name. Amen.

Standard of Ethics

And if I have taken anything from any man by false accusation,
I restore him fourfold. Luke 19:8

This is exceedingly ethical.

A man explained to his son, "Ethics is vital to a workable and confident society. For instance, a friend paid me back today a loan with a new hundred-dollar bill. Later I discovered there were two hundred-dollar bills stuck together. This immediately presented a question of ethics: Should I tell your mother?"

But ethics can't be confined to family relationship and interest, with everybody else free to be ripped off.

Here is a five way test of ethics:

1) *Is it free from deception?*

2) *Is it honest?*

3) *Is it the truth?*

4) *Is it fair?*

5) *Is it in keeping with the Golden Rule?*

Ethics is concerned with what is right, not with mere legalism that considers only what is within the law.

Room at the Top

The desire accomplished is sweet to the soul. Proverbs 13:19

Also, trying to reach the goal sweetens the quest.

Every year thousands of people go through certain portions of the White House that are open to the public. It is a popular tour for students. Teachers hope that it will do more than satisfy their curiosity, that it will light within the heart the fires of ambition and patriotism. After one teacher had taken her high school students on this tour, she later asked them to write their impressions of the visit. Many interesting replies were given, but the one that most affected the teacher stated: "I was glad to get to visit my future home."

The lightning won't strike for every child to become President, but every person can soar high when ambition gives him eagle's wings.

One of the most expressive prayers of ambition was penned by the famous Henry David Thoreau:

> Great God, I ask Thee for no meaner pelf
> Than that I may not disappoint myself,
> That in my action I may soar as high
> As I now can discern with this clear eye.

There are two reasons why there is room at the top: First, so few get there. Second, of those who do, some of them go to sleep and fall off.

If you would rise, get on ambition's ladder and round by round climb, climb. Don't look down, you might get dizzy. And when you have once attained the utmost round, turn not your back to the ladder and look in the clouds and scorn the lowly base from which you did ascend.

This Might Happen to You

Wherefore let him that thinketh he standeth take heed lest he fall. I Corinthians 10:12

The residents of a little village were distressed, because motorists raced through their village at murderous speeds, paying no attention to the large warning sign, "Drive Slowly," erected at a visible place at the entrance. In their desperation, they finally dragged a badly wrecked car to the spot and placed over it the sign, "This Might Happen To You." The effect was overwhelming.

Perhaps we should put up signs concerning all the end results we don't want, and add this warning signal: "This Might Happen to You." Then take heed that it doesn't.

This shall happen to you:

• *Poverty* — if you deal with a slack hand (Proverbs 10:4).

• *Want* — if you waste your substance (Luke 15:13).

• *Strife* — if you are contentious (Proverbs 26:21).

• *Cynicism* — if you see only the faults of others (Matthew 7:3).

• *Misery* — if you think only of self (Philippians 2:4).

• *Poor health* — if you live without the medicine of merriment (Proverbs 17:22).

• *Family disruption* — if you do not work for peace (Romans 14:19).

Remember — the worse wreck is a human wreck. Watch your driving and where you're headed.

My Faith Looks Up to Thee

Let us draw near with a true heart in full assurance of faith. Hebrews 10:22

This immortal hymn was written by Ray Palmer, an American minister, when he was only twenty-two years old.

One day in 1830, sitting in his little room, he was engrossed in thinking of his personal problems. Discouraged and almost overwhelmed, he then and there took paper and pen and wrote this hymn and put it away without showing it to anybody.

Years later, he met Dr. Lowell Mason on the street in Boston. Dr. Mason asked him to write a hymn for a new hymn book he planned to publish. Palmer suddenly thought of the one he had written years before. A copy was made and he gave it to Mason.

A little time passed and the two met again on the street. Hardly taking time to greet him, Dr. Mason said, "Mr. Palmer, you may do many things; you may live many years and accomplish much, but you will be known to posterity as the man who wrote, "My Faith Looks Up to Thee."

> *My faith looks up to Thee,*
> *Thou Lamb of Calvary,*
> *Savior Divine!*
> *Now hear me while I pray;*
> *Take all my guilt away;*
> *O let me from this day*
> *Be wholly Thine.*
>
> *When ends life's transient dream,*
> *When death's cold, sullen stream*
> *Shall o'er me roll,*
> *Blest Savior, then, in love,*
> *Fear and distrust remove;*
> *O bear me safe above,*
> *A ransomed soul!*

Distractions on Every Hand

I am doing a great work, so that I cannot come down: why should the work cease, whilst I leave it, and come down to you? Nehemiah 6:3

Years ago I had a very insistent man to visit me. He explained that they were buying a camp for boys and girls. In these threatening times for young people, it would provide uplifting associations, clean recreation, and even Bible study, supervised by honorable personnel. Different groups could go there for periods of two weeks. Then he asked me, " What do you think of it?"

"I think it's excellent," was my reply.

"Then you'll get out there and call on the church members and raise money to help pay for it?"

"No, I can't do that."

He continued, "If you think it's excellent, then why can't you do it?"

"Yes," I responded, "I believe it can be a good and fruitful endeavor. But just look up and down these streets. I have more work now than I can do. I can announce it, and I can pray for it, and I can personally give a little, but I can't do your job. I must stick with mine."

Such requests to take me away from my own job — one for which I was employed — to engage in another has occurred many times. Though I regretted to say *No*, the demands of my own work were too pressing to say *Yes*. Since you can't do everything, you must decide which has priority and do it. If I had permitted these extra requests to come ahead of my work, I never would have accomplished the things God has brought to pass in my life.

And This Is Success

This book of the law shall not depart out of thy mouth; but thou shalt meditate therein day and night, that thou mayest observe to do according to all that is written therein: for then thou shalt make thy way prosperous, and then thou shalt have good success. Joshua 1:8

The word "success" appears only once in the Bible, in the above verse. In a further consideration, we offer some specifics.

And this is success —

A good name is rather to be chosen than great riches, and loving favor rather than silver and gold. Proverbs 22:1

And this is success —

A wise son maketh a glad father. Proverbs 10:1

And this is success —

Her children arise up, and call her blessed; her husband also, and he praiseth her. Proverbs 31:28

And this is success —

Because I delivered the poor that cried, and the fatherless, and him that had none to help him. Job 29:12

And this is success —

Nay, in all these things we are more than conquerors through him that loved us. Romans 8:37

And this is success —

I have fought a good fight, I have finished my course, I have kept the faith: Henceforth there is laid up for me a crown of righteousness. II Timothy 4:7,8

Lost and Found Column

He that findeth his life shall lose it: and he that loseth his life for my sake shall find it. Matthew 10:39

Jesus, the author of the above words, ran His own lost and found column; and there is more to it than watches and diamonds, dogs and cats — man's happiness is there. He that finds his life within himself loses it; but he that loses his life outside of himself finds it.

The world's greatest book on psychology is the Bible. The highest cause in which you can lose yourself is God's religion, for it includes all the principles that can take you out of your selfish self and extend you to God and to others.

Those who live in the shell of self habitually focus their attention inwardly until outside interests have little appeal. The result is discontent and boredom, and even worse — one becomes the prison for his soul.

Oh, doom beyond the saddest guess,
As the long years of God unroll,
To make thy dreary selfishness
The prison of a soul.

John Greenleaf Whittier

On the other hand, one can find a new life of delight in simply losing self in another interest. Getting out of the hull of self will take the emptiness out of life and fill it with rapture. As the little flower seed never becomes beautiful and fragrant until it breaks out of itself and grows up and blossoms, so it is with man.

If you would find the good life, break out of that shell of self-centeredness, grow up and lend a helping hand. The world needs it; even more, you need to give it.

Reaching for the Better Life

Therefore leaving the principles of the doctrine of Christ, let us go on unto perfection. Hebrews 6:1

Here are some noble principles that assure a meaningful and illustrious life:

• *Walk with God.* The direction is right. The journey is joyful. And it gives no room to go astray.

• *Be a friend to man.* Help those in need. It is bread cast on the waters. It always returns.

• *Behave yourself like an adult.* Don't whimper like a baby. Don't fuss like a child. Don't quit like an adolescent.

• *Be a watchman on duty.* Guard your speech, guard your faith, guard your honor.

• *Treat everybody with respect and courtesy,* for each is the image of God.

• *Honor every commitment to God and man.* It is better not to vow than to vow and break it.

• *Be an example.* People follow better than they take orders.

• *Keep a cool head.* Hot heads don't solve problems. Operating with a short fuse makes for a quick explosion.

• *Keep a warm heart.* Be tender, sympathetic, kind. A heart that feels with others is always welcome.

• *"Let all that you do be done in love"* (I Corinthians 16:13). When motivated by love, any mistake you may make will be only one of judgment.

Dealing With Disappointment

Simon Peter saith unto them, I go a fishing. They say unto him,
We also go with thee. They went forth, and entered into a ship
immediately; and that night they caught nothing. John 21:3

Disappointment! Disappointment! Comes in many ways and in many forms. But the letdown is always the same, the lower you sink is determined by the value involved and the higher you had hoped.

ON THE TAKE

She took my hand without a blush,
She took my candy with a rush,
She took the costly wrap of fur,
She took the diamonds I bought her,
She took my flowers and did ware,
She took my time I could spare,
She took my ring with loving smile,
She took my rides mile after mile,
She took my kisses, happy girl,
She took my plans for our new world,
She took everything I could buy,
And then — she took the other guy.

In all of this and in all disappointment there is pain, for disillusionment always hurts.

Life has its disappointments: Courtship without marriage. Clouds without rain. Trees without fruit. Crops without harvest. Business without profit. Education without practicality. Work without promotion. Home without love. Manuscript without publisher.

But it is better to hope, plan, pursue and be disappointed than to expect nothing. That kind of living is not living — only a disappointing existence.

The War That Each Must Fight

Dearly beloved, I beseech you as strangers and pilgrims, abstain from fleshly lusts, which war against the soul. I Peter 2:11

Concerning the war that rages, we further read: "For the flesh lusteth against the Spirit, and the Spirit against the flesh; so that ye cannot do the things that ye would" (Galatians 5:17).

There is a conflict of two powers and man is caught in the middle. If he wills to do good, he is opposed by the flesh; if he wills to do evil, he is countered by the Spirit. The Christian life is one long conflict between the opposing forces of the flesh and the Spirit. The inclinations and desires of the flesh are contrary to those formed in us by the renewing of the Spirit. They can never be harmonized. One set of principles must win over the other.

It is a war for the soul on the battlefield of life. How may the better nature win?

First, resolve to triumph. There is power in resolution.

Second, fortify yourself with prayer. "Watch and pray that ye enter not into temptation."

Third, strengthen yourself with the Word of God. The Psalmist did this: "Thy word have I hid in mine heart, that I might not sin against thee."

Fourth, fight off evil by staying busy doing good. Idleness makes one vulnerable to attack.

Fifth, trust God as if all depended on Him; and strive with all your might as if everything depended on you. This double power will suffice.

Every victory won strengthens us to win another.

Lights for a Dark World

That ye may be blameless and harmless, the sons of God, without rebuke, in the midst of a crooked and perverse nation, among whom ye shine as lights in the world. Philippians 2:12

The Constitution and the Bill of Rights assure all citizens some very precious rights. But there are two exceedingly important rights they do not guarantee: The Right to Know and The Right to Glow. Actually upon them rest all other rights.

Centuries ago Christ launched His movement to enlighten a benighted world. He selected twelve apostles to whom He handed the torch. You know the inspiring story of their heroic devotion to the history-making cause. After His crucifixion those disciples in just a few years had faithfully and tirelessly spread Christianity throughout the world.

Today the faint-hearted say, "I am only one among billions. What can little me do?"

Alone we are all weak, but shining together we are powerful.

It has been reported that an unusual request was made in a religious service in which 90,000 had assembled. The lights were turned out and jet darkness settled over the crowd which sat there in curious silence. Then there came a voice over the loud speaker, cutting through the blackness: "Look this way. I'm going to light a match." Immediately there was the small gleam of the tiny flame. Again the speaker spoke: "Now I want each of you to light a match, please." Here and there flames appeared, more and more, until the stadium was aglow with brightness.

It all started with one match. If each will shine, it will light our nation and our world.

A Psalm of Life

Blessed are the dead which die in the Lord from henceforth: Yea, saith the Spirit that they may rest from their labors; and their works do follow them. Revelation 14:13

There are two sublime thoughts that are exceedingly encouraging. One, while man's body dies, his spirit continues to live. The second, man's works continue to live and follow after him.

Life is real! Life is earnest!
  And the grave is not its goal;
"Dust thou art, to dust returnest,"
  Was not spoken of the soul.

In the world's broad field of battle,
  In the bivouac of life,
Be not dumb driven cattle!
  Be a hero in the strife.

Lives of great men all remind us
  We can make our lives sublime,
And, departing, leave behind us
  Footprints on the sands of time.

Footprints, that perhaps another,
  Sailing o'er life's solemn main,
A forlorn and shipwrecked brother,
  Seeing, shall take heart again.

Let us, then, be up and doing,
  With a heart for any fate;
Still achieving, still pursuing,
  Learn to labor and to wait.

Henry W. Longfellow

What Makes Me

For as he thinketh in his heart, so is he. Proverbs 23:7

Said in few words:

A person consists of what he thinks.

The tranquil life comes from thinking; so does the troubled one.

The most necessary task for man is to think wisely.

Thinking is the hardest work in the world; it is easier to stay in the rut.

Thoughts are mightier than the hand.

A moment's thinking is worth an hour's work.

When one thinks, he does more than "hitch his wagon to a star" — he becomes a star. And shine he does.

If people would think for themselves, they would avoid much exploitation.

Thinking without acting takes you no where.

The person who says just what he thinks should stop and think.

If you think, there is a good chance you will go aright; it is the thoughtless that go astray.

Think With Wings

But they that wait upon the Lord shall renew their strength; they shall mount up with wings as eagles; they shall run, and not be weary; and they shall walk, and not faint. Isaiah 40:31

Are you weary? Do you feel defeated? Are you about to faint? Then put wings on your thoughts. Think positively. Think constructively. The measure of a person is in his thoughts. "For as he thinketh in his heart, so is he" (Proverbs 23:7). This was Solomon's total of a person: his strength or weakness, his courage or cowardice, his peace or confusion, and his happiness or gloom. Indeed, we are what we think.

Each of us needs to recognize that he can change his life by changing his attitude.

Most assuredly, there is power in believing. What you believe, in keeping with reality, has a way of happening. Believe that life is a wonderful, glorious, thrilling experience, and your belief will go far in creating the fact. Anybody who starts thinking he is strong, will find strength; if he thinks he can bear what is placed upon him, he will hold up; if he thinks he can overcome, he will triumph. He is giving his thoughts wings.

But the opposite is just as true. Think negatively and your life will be shrouded with gloom and despair. One negatively sick man said, "I always expect the worst and I have never been disappointed yet."

Positive, optimistic and unshaken thinking is the power to open new worlds to us. If you are dissatisfied with the little world your thoughts have created and pulled in around you, then change your thinking and a new world will open up.

The Hardest Thing to Keep

Whoso keepeth his mouth and his tongue, keepeth his soul from troubles. Proverbs 21:23

The hardest thing for any person to keep is his tongue. He can keep his house, his car, his job, his health, his payments, his credit up, and his weight down, easier than he can keep his tongue.

THE TONGUE

"The boneless tongue so small and weak
Can crush and kill," declared the Greek;
"The tongue destroys a greater horde,"
The Turk asserts, "than does the sword."

The Persian proverb wisely saith,
"A lengthy tongue — an early death,"
Or sometimes takes this form instead,
"Don't let your tongue cut off your head."

"The tongue can speak a word, whose speed,"
Says the Chinese, "outstrips the steed,"
While Arab sages this impart:
"The tongue's great storehouse is the heart."

From Hebrew with the maxim sprung:
"Though feet may slip, ne'er let the tongue";
The sacred writer crowns the whole:
"Who keeps his tongue, doth keep his soul."

Knowing it is difficult for us to keep the tongue, God has given us this admonition in the sacred writings: "Let every man be swift to hear, slow to speak" (James 1:19).

It is fitting, therefore, that we pray: "Let the words of my mouth, and the meditation of my heart, be acceptable in thy sight, O Lord, my strength, and my redeemer" (Psalms 19:14).

Our Heritage

One generation passeth away, and another generation cometh: but the earth abideth for ever. Ecclesiastes 1:4

Hugh Black has said: "All things we cherish, our order of life, our institutions, all that we call our civilization, have come to us as a heritage from the past.

"They are the labors of countless generations of men and women who have lived and died. Craven must we be, if we lay down the load and put an end to the dream.

"It is a long way we have come, a long and toilsome climb, and there are blood marks on every flinty track. The checkered human career has in it deeds of high emprise, acts of sacrifice, tales of heroism that glorify the race. Lives have been lived with patience and courage and selfless love that create in us reverence for man.

"They make it easy for us to believe great things of the race to which they and we belong. We are unworthy of our past heritage and our present privilege if we forget the great society of the noble living and the noble dead."

When we take all this into consideration we see there is hope for the human race. In every infant born — regardless of parentage and circumstances — the hope of mankind is born anew. That child is born with a spark of divinity that lends itself to knowledge, refinement, virtue, brotherhood, and the power to make this old earth turn a little easier. It makes us very glad that Noah and his family didn't miss the boat.

Hard on Religion

Watch and pray, that ye enter not into temptation: the spirit indeed is willing, but the flesh is weak. Matthew 26:41

One of my jobs when I was a boy was to milk at least one or two cows twice daily. An old contrary cow can really try your nerves — and your religion. I know. I've had my vexing episodes with them. I have been in the milk shed bright and early, when the temperature hovered just a little above zero. The cow's tail was loaded with cockleburs she had picked up in the pasture. Without provocation I've had her to suddenly kick, knock over the milk pail, come down with her foot on my frozen foot, and simultaneously whisk and rake that cocklebur tail across my cold face. Now that was hard on religion.

I wondered how any living thing could get that mean. I never hurt her, but I must admit I did threaten her. I would tell her, "You do that just one more time and we're going to have steak for dinner instead of milk."

Now looking back to yesteryears I'm grateful for the experiences. Wouldn't take for them. I learned a little more about self-control and a lot more about the value of a glass of milk. We have to live to be prepared for living. Every problem overcome gives us a little more grit and power for the next one.

Life has its provocations. I've had many since the encounters with the cows. When some seemed unbearable, memory would flash back to boyhood days and I would tell myself: "When you were just a boy and the cow stepped on you and raked you with her tail, you handled it; and you can handle this." Each time it gave me strength.

Bobby and the Concrete

Verily, verily . . . John 3:3

And that's concrete.

On Sunday morning the preacher spoke tenderly and eloquently on *The Compassionate Jesus.* One of his points was that Jesus loved little children, gathered them to Him and blessed them. It was a moving sermon of great substance.

The following week he was in a different role; he was the director of the church's Vacation Bible School. The children were fresh out of school, possessed with the vacation spirit, and ready to turn loose their pent up feelings.

After a few days the preacher's nerves became edgy. An added pressure was the contractor's pouring of concrete on the parking lot. Then the breaking point came. The minister spotted Bobby stepping in the concrete. He thundered, "Bobby! Bobby! Bobby!" (getting louder each time). "Get out of there! Don't you know better than that?"

Bobby (mother's little never rebuked darling) went home crying. Immediately the irate mother called the nerve-tattered preacher and reminded him of last Sunday's sermon. "It was excellent rhetoric," she said, "but what about the practice? If you love Bobby, why did you speak so harshly to him?"

"Listen, lady," replied the minister, "I love Bobby, but I must admit, I'm being tempted to love him in the abstract — not in the concrete."

Really, Christianity is a concrete religion. It pertains to the practical and particular as opposed to the general. It centers our thoughts on that which is real and involves us in the living of actual events.

Grow Until You Outgrow Your Shell

*The righteous shall flourish like the palm tree: he shall grow like
a cedar in Lebanon.*   Psalms 92:12

A man once said, "If you think I'm awful now, be glad you
didn't know me when I was worse. I am making improvement." Ounce by ounce improvement shall in time make a ton
of difference.

It is incumbent upon us to grow. The status quo is not good
enough. The challenge is for improvement. It is difficult to remain stationary; one either progresses or retrogresses. There are
two major lessons to learn in growing: learn to be in control
of self, and learn to be under the control of God.

It takes time for good substantial growth. "Tall oaks from
little acorns grow," but not in a day.

> *Little by little each can grow strong,*
> *Fighting the battle of Right and Wrong;*
> *Little by little the Wrong gives way —*
> *Little by little the Right has sway;*
> *Little by little each longing soul*
> *Struggles up nearer the shining goal.*

It is wonderful and exhilarating that we can grow into a
larger and more beautiful person. Growth is a lifetime activity. Grow, grow, grow until you outgrow your shell and move
into a more stately mansion. Oliver Wendell Holmes put it this
way:

> *Build thee more stately mansions, oh, my soul,*
> *As the swift seasons roll!*
> *Leave thy low-vaulted past!*
> *Let each new temple, nobler than the last,*
> *Shut thee from heaven with a dome more vast,*
> *Till thou at length are free,*
> *Leaving thine outgrown shell by life's unresting sea!*

The Good Man's Triumph

They that seek the Lord shall not want any good thing.
Psalms 34:10

This Psalm has been called "The Good Man's Triumph." There are many present and eternal advantages in seeking and serving the Lord. Here are some of His assurances:

• *Shall not want for salvation* — "For thou, Lord, art good, and ready to forgive" (Psalms 86:5).

• *Shall not want for rest* — "Come unto me, all ye that labor and are heavy laden, and I will give you rest" (Matthew 11:28).

• *Shall not want for direction* — ". . . leaving us an example, that ye should follow his steps" (I Peter 2:21).

• *Shall not want for companionship* — "Lo, I am with you alway, even unto the end of the world" (Matthew 28:20).

• *Shall not want for light* — "He that followeth me shall not walk in darkness" (John 8:12).

• *Shall not want for peace* — "When a man's ways please the Lord, he maketh even his enemies to be at peace with him" (Proverbs 16:7).

• *Shall not want for help in time of trouble* — "In the day of my trouble I will call upon thee: for thou wilt answer me" (Psalm 86:7).

• *Shall not want for confidence in death* — "Yea, though I walk through the valley of the shadow of death, I will fear no evil" (Psalms 23:4).

According to Your Faith

According to your faith be it unto you. Matthew 9:29

The man took a little Bible from his pocket and said, "I owe all my success to this book. I wouldn't have made the grade without it. I was a good clerk in a store and had ambitions to have my own store, but I was shackled with inferiority. Ambition pulled me one way and misgivings pulled me another. The result was tattered nerves. In my desperation, I went through the Bible and underscored the verses I thought would help me the most in overcoming my problem of doubt and defeatism. Then I memorized certain ones. I said them everyday. At first they seemed like empty words, but later they gradually took on meaning and became an integral part of me. They changed my whole outlook on life and brought optimism and happiness to my troubled spirit."

In addition to the above Scripture, two others he marked are:

He staggered not at the promise of God through unbelief.
Romans 4:20

For we walk by faith, not by sight. II Corinthians 5:7

God gave each person a mind which is his "thought factory"; there his thoughts are turned out. As to whether the thoughts are positive or negative depends on what he believes or disbelieves. This is how simple it is: Have doubt — fail and be unhappy; or believe — succeed and be happy.

Believe in God, yourself and others, and it will put you in gear to make things start happening. Your belief becomes your thermostat which allows you to warm up, to be optimistic and cheerful in meeting the daily challenges of life. Faith gives life energy and zest.

A Tight Place

He went away sorrowful: for he had great possessions.
Matthew 19:22

A rich but miserly old man in the Northeast was asked several years ago to make a contribution to a statue of George Washington, to be erected in New York.

"Washington! Washington! How useless!" the rich man exclaimed. "Why, Washington does not need a statue. I keep him enshrined in my heart!"

The solicitor gave point after point as to why it should be done, but to no avail. Naturally he became a little perturbed and indignant at the millionaire's closeness.

"Well," he quietly remarked as he rose to leave, "all I can say is if the Father of our Country is in your heart, he is in a very tight place."

Even the most greedy, however, will give in death that which he cannot carry with him.

There is a fable about a pig which lamented his lack of popularity. In speaking to a cow he admitted that cows give milk and cream, but insisted that pigs give more. He said, "We pigs give bacon, ham, and pork chops, and people even pickle our feet. I don't see why you cows are esteemed so much."

The cow thought for a moment and replied, "Maybe it's because we give while we're still living."

Living and giving go together for an enrichment and happiness that cannot be obtained in death's gift.

One of the major thrusts of the Bible is to develop within man the big heart that relates to worthy causes and human needs.

The Greatest Gift

*And this they did, not as we hoped, but first gave their own
selves to the Lord, and unto us by the will of God.*
II Corinthians 8:5

The charming story has come to me concerning some Christian natives in a foreign land. The missionary who converted them later taught them sacrifice, which is the basis of Christianity. God sacrificed His Son. The Son sacrificed His life. And the early Christians sacrificed their lives; if not in one final act, they did in daily activities.

To simplify and facilitate the lesson on giving, the missionary drew a large circle on the ground, and had them to place their gifts within it. Different gifts were offered: corn, watermelons, shells, beads, a puppy, whatever one had. One poor native walked into the ring and said, "I give myself."

That's the greatest of all gifts — self. Self is a rarer gift than gold. All gifts fade into nothingness when the giver holds back himself. One thing that can impede the growth of Christianity today is the gift without the giver — gifts from the hand but not the heart.

The same imbalance — gift without the giver — can be injurious to the rearing of children, the sustaining of the husband-wife relationship, and the continuance of employee-employer connection. If the heart isn't there, it's only routine service. When self is no part of rich gifts, how paltry they are!

> *Not what we give,*
> *But what we share —*
> *For the gift without*
> *The giver is bare.*
>
> James Russell Lowell

A Friend to Man

To him that is afflicted, pity should be showed from his friend. Job 6:14

There is no higher calling than to be a friend to man. Neither is there a better way to help self. For in doing for others we actually do for ourselves. Every act of kindness shown to fellow pilgrims makes us a little stronger and happier.

About 700 B.C. Homer said of an ideal man, "He was a friend to man, and he lived in a house by the side of the road." Centuries later Sam Walter Foss gave us a very meaningful poem titled by the same wording:

THE HOUSE BY THE SIDE OF THE ROAD

Let me live in a house by the side of the road,
  Where the race of men go by —
The men who are good and the men who are bad,
  As good and as bad as I.
I would not sit in the scorner's seat,
  Or hurl the cynic's ban —
Let me live in a house by the side of the road
  And be a friend to man.

I see from my house by the side of the road,
  By the side of the highway of life,
The men who press with the ardor of hope,
  The men who are faint with the strife.
But I turn not away from their smiles nor their tears,
  Both parts of an infinite plan —
Let me live in a house by the side of the road
  And be a friend to man.

When We Are Wrong

*Zaccheus . . .said . . . if I have taken any thing from any man
by false accusation, I restore him fourfold.*   Luke 19:8

A man sold my father a cow soon after she had been bitten by a mad dog. My father, unaware of this, put the cow on the range. In a few days she had developed hydrophobia, and this crazed, charging animal almost killed my father. Later the seller apologized: "I was wrong. I'm sorry."

Nobody is perfect. Everybody commits wrong. "For all have sinned." As great as the Apostle Peter was, he was not above wrong. The Apostle Paul says, "But when Peter was come to Antioch, I withstood him to the face, because he was to be blamed" (Galatians 2:11). And concerning himself, Paul said, "I count not myself to have apprehended" (Philippians 3:13). He was still imperfect.

But one area in which we can be perfect is the correction of wrongs. We can change, apologize, restore, make amends, make restitution. We can right our wrongs. Repentance, which is demanded of all of us, requires restitution.

If wrong has been done, refusing to admit it will not blot it out. This only adds wrong to wrong. When wrong, we can't make it right by committing another wrong to try to cover it up; or by persecuting the person we have wronged.

Neither will the approval of others change wrong into right. Abraham Lincoln said, "If the end brings me out wrong, ten angels swearing I was right would make no difference."

The only right and honorable way — when we're wrong, say so; when we can correct it, do so. To err is human; to correct is to be a better human.

An Appeal to Logic

For every house is builded by some man; but he that built all things is God. Hebrews 3:4

This Scripture is an appeal to logic. The house didn't just happen. It had to have a builder. Neither did the world. It had to have a Creator.

There is so much illogical thinking today. Some is about as ridiculous as a man's trying to drink the ocean dry, or rid the ocean of sharks with a minnow seine.

Logic is the mother of all arts and the safeguard of society's sanity. Disregard it and you will pay the price. Unsound thinking has an extremely high price tag.

Many of the wise sayings are nothing but worded logic. And the art of being wise is the art of perceiving the logical. It's plain common sense.

Note these maxims of common sense:

> *Don't expect a full barn unless you fill it.*
> *Don't run with the hare and hold with the hound.*
> *An ounce of prevention is worth a pound of cure.*
> *As the twig is bent so grows the tree.*
> *If you want eggs, be willing to put up with the hen's cackle.*

The Bible is filled with logic. Here are some examples:

> *Doth a fountain send forth at the same place sweet water and bitter* (James 3:11)?
> *Neither do men light a candle, and put it under a bushel* (Matthew 5:15).
> *For whatsoever a man soweth, that shall he also reap* (Galatians 6:7).

Shape your life by logic. The best place to get it is the Bible. Read it to be wise.

Make Me Somebody

Make me to go in the path of thy commandments; for therein do I delight. Psalms 119:35

The highest and most ideal life is one consecrated to God and dedicated to helping and serving man, expressed by the Psalmist in the prayer which says, "O Lord . . . make me." It is elevating for a person to have the noble ambition to be somebody and for his life to be useful and helpful. It is uplifting that we, too, have such consummate aims, as follows:

• *Make me a channel* of blessing that flows into the lives of others.

• *Make me a vessel* of salvation to those who stand in need of pardon.

• *Make me a light* that shines in a world darkened by wrong, exploitation and sin.

• *Make me a soldier* that defends the true and the right.

• *Make me an ambassador* of peace in a world torn by strife and war.

• *Make me a tree* planted by the rivers of water that produces good fruit for a morally and spiritually famished society.

• *Make me a healing balm* for the hearts that mourn and break.

• *Make me an example* for those who might not change, if they did not have a pattern to follow.

God is ready to help. Are we ready to ask?

The Clouds Pass

Weeping may endure for a night, but joy cometh in the morning. Psalms 30:5

Every life must have some clouds, some more and worse than others. But the clouds pass.

I am very fond of the encouraging words of William Cowper, one of the world's great poets:

> God moves in a mysterious way
> His wonders to perform,
> And plants His footsteps in the sea
> And rides upon the storm.
>
> Ye fearful saints, fresh courage take,
> The clouds ye so much dread
> Are big with mercy and shall break
> With blessings on your head.

Pain passes. All of us have some pain, ranging from mild to severe. But our bodies have been made to adjust to circumstances. Time is needed for pain to pass. If it doesn't, God can give us the strength to bear it. He did for Paul who had a thorn in his flesh, whatever that was. The thorn remained but so did God who strengthened him.

Sorrow and grief pass. That black cloud hangs awfully low at times. Not being able to see through it, we just walk through it by faith. At first it seems the hurt will never lessen, but it gradually eases as we adjust to the loss and revise our living.

It is comforting to know that the clouds can break with blessings on our head. "Our light affliction, which is but for a moment, worketh for us a far more exceeding and eternal weight of glory" (II Corinthians 4:17).

I'm Still Standing Up Inside

My son, despise not thou the chastening of the Lord, nor faint when thou art rebuked of him: For whom the Lord loveth he chasteneth, and scourgeth every son whom he receiveth.
Hebrews 12:5,6

A teacher said to a child who had been misbehaving, "Richard, this is the fifth time this week I have had to punish you. What do you have to say?"

Richard replied, "I'm glad it's Friday."

The ending of the school week would not end the problem. It was deeper than that.

An even smaller child has illustrated this fact. Oh, how we learn from children! Three-year old Jimmy kept standing up in his highchair, although his mother kept reseating him and admonishing him to stay seated. After the fourth time Jimmy stayed down, but he testingly said, "Mommy, I'm still standing up inside."

The mother disciplined Jimmy because she loved him. God also chastens us for the same reason — He loves us. I don't know the form or manner in which the chastening always comes. But I know the God who administers it. This means it is for my good. And whatever is for my good — though unpleasant at the time — should be endured patiently, looking forward to the end result of a better person and happier days.

I Shall Not Pass Again This Way

When a few years are come, then I shall go the way whence I shall not return. Job 16:22

> *The bread that bringeth strength I want to give,*
> *The water pure that bids the thirsty live;*
> *I want to help the fainting day by day;*
> *I'm sure I shall not pass again this way.*
>
> *I want to give goodness and joy for tears,*
> *The faith to conquer crowding doubts and fears;*
> *Beauty for ashes may I give always;*
> *I'm sure I shall not pass again this way.*
>
> *I want to give to others hope and faith,*
> *I want to do all that the Master saith;*
> *I want to live aright from day to day;*
> *I'm sure I shall not pass again this way.*

The certainty of the proposition, "I shall not pass again this way" dictates to us that whatever we intend to do we need to get busy and do it now. Too much time has already been lost; therefore, it is incumbent upon us to fully use the fleeting moments that are left.

Our little day passes so quickly. The shadow we cast lengthens so fast until it gradually fades into night. "I go whence I shall not return, even to the land of darkness and the shadow of death" (Job 10:21). The day is passing — so grab the light and race with the sun to accomplish your purpose.

> *Fill up each hour with what will last;*
> *Buy up the moments as they go;*
> *The life above, when this is past,*
> *Is the ripe fruit of life below.*

The Power of Little Things

Behold, how great a matter a little fire kindleth. James 3:5

In the same vein and logic we can say:

How great a strife a little word ignites.
How great a liar a little fib commences.
How great a murderer a little hate kindles.
How great a wrath a little temper foments.
How great a fool a little riches can manifest.
How great a drunkard a little wine produces.
How great an apostasy a little error starts.
How great a destruction a little neglect effects.

But also:

How great a church a little beginning starts.
How great a movement a little vision awakens.
How great a person a little child becomes.
How great a lump a little leaven changes.
How great a friendship a little effort produces.
How great a joy a little smile gives.
How great an encouragement a little word provides.
How great an appreciation a little gift stirs.
How great a satisfaction a little good yields.
How great a beam a little candle throws.
How great a business a little planning begets.
How great an oak a little acorn becomes.

Greatness is inherent in people, qualities, things and circumstances, just as it is in an oak.

I am little and I know it, but with God's help I can be a powerful force.

Honor Father

Honor thy father and mother. Ephesians 6:2

One of the ancient duties enjoined upon mankind is to honor parents. It is old in origin but just as new in its essentiality and practicality as ever. It is an urgent need of each new generation. A person can no more outgrow this need than one can outgrow the need of basic character.

A flagrant disregard of this divine law to honor father has in it the seeds of frustration, violence and degradation. A violation of it will produce in the children a mischievous self-assertion and a bitter resentment of all authority and superiority. So one of the preventions of juvenile delinquency is to honor father and accept his headship in the family

Disrespect, ingratitude and neglect toward father is a deadly force that destroys individual character, which in turn pulls down our whole social structure; for the family is the cornerstone of society. Affection, devotion and respect to father are cardinal virtues, and a society divested of them cannot long survive.

Now for a little confession — father is much more deserving of honor than we could appreciate when we were young. Youth has to grow up. Time is an effectual teacher. The years are wrought with strong opposition and staggering blows from a world youth thinks is easy to conquer. Sons and daughters may not learn this until father is either old or dead, but there is one thing sure — they will learn.

And all the while nature is planning a sure reversal of the order. By and by, those children will grow up and have children of their own, and the drama of parents and children will be re-enacted all over again.

Father — An Ideal

We have a father, an old man. Genesis 44:20

The demands upon a father are great. Our world demanded courageous minds, watchful eyes, ready hands, true faith — actually many hearts in one — and God answered the call by giving the world fathers. The qualities of his heart seem to be a thousand hearts, and each heart an absolute necessity to fatherhood. This makes him an ideal, which is aptly stated in the poem:

AN IDEAL

I wish I were as big a man,
 As big a man,
 As bright a man,
I wish I were as right a man in all this earthly show,
As broad and high and long a man,
 As strong a man,
 As fine a man,
 As pretty near divine a man as one I used to know.

I wish I were as grave a man,
 As brave a man,
As keen a man,
As learned and serene a man, as fair to friend and foe;
I wish I owned sagaciousness
 And graciousness,
 As should a man
Who hopes to be as good a man as one I used to know.

I'd be a creature glorious,
 Victorious,
 A wonder-man,
Not just-as-now-a blunder man whose ways
And thoughts are slow,
 If I could only be the man,
 One-half of one degree the man,
I used to think my father was, when I was ten or so.

       Benton Braley

The Heroic Father

*O my son Absalom! my son, my son Absalom! would God I had
died for thee, O Absalom, my son, my son!* II Samuel 18:33

We esteem father because of his heroism. His sweat and tears
and blood, shed for us, testify to his heroic nature. He who
struggles for others when the easy way is to run is a hero, call
him what you will. You know the brave story of his sacrifices
— rigorous toil, long hours, maybe two jobs, unremitting
thrift, the slow accumulation of savings, at times bitter
discouragement, but also the outpouring of happiness as he
realized his hopes for his children.

Too often we forget the price that father paid. We enjoy the
fruits of his labors but fail to see the labors themselves. The
world sees the glitter of the gold and not the sweat of the
sacrifices of him who wielded the pick in yonder mountainside.

Perhaps we have been woefully negligent in honoring the
heroic father who takes the wounds of the everyday struggles
of life. We are protected because he courageously dared. The
highest and noblest spirit is "that a man lay down his life for
another." Father did this not in one supreme gift but in the giving of himself little by little, day by day. The daily conflicts
of earning a living and heading a household brought out the
slumbering qualities of the hero.

> Not at the battle front merit of in story,
> Not in the blazing wreck, steering to glory;
> Not while in martyr-pangs soul and flesh sever,
> Lives he — this hero now; hero forever.
>
> James Braidwood

We say to father — living or dead — your deeds, your
unselfish deeds, your glorious deeds, shall never die. They shall
ever be hallowed in the cherished memory of grateful children.

Father Refuses to Weaken

For my father fought for you and adventured his life.
Judges 9:17

Father knows he cannot weaken because his children believe in him; he cannot falter because they trust him.

Years ago a father and a son were traveling over a dangerous mountain trail. They came to a place where a huge rock jutted out over the precipice, leaving only a hanging portion as the pathway. With much difficulty and danger, the father traversed the perilous spot. Then holding to the rock with one big hand, he reached the other out over the cliff and told the boy to step on his hand and thus pass around the rock to safety: "Do not fear to step on my hand. It is strong. It will not give way." The boy did and the hand held.

Examples which are less dramatic could be cited by the thousands. It is a common practice in the everyday struggles of life. Father extends his hand over countless precipices and chasms and says, "Step on it. It will not give way." There is too much faith in him for his big manly hand to weaken, and by more trust in it and more usage it becomes as iron.

This is father's prayer:

> However humble the place I may hold
>   On the lowly trails I have trod,
> There's a child who bases his faith in me;
>   There's a dog who thinks I'm a god.
>
> Lord, keep me worthy — Lord, keep me clean
>   And fearless and undefiled,
> Lest I lose caste in the sight of a dog,
>   And the wide clear eyes of a child!

C. T. Davis

A Father's Tribute to His Son

A wise son maketh a glad father. Proverbs 10:1

One of the grandest tributes a father ever gave to a deceased son was given by Charles G. Dawes. The son, Rufus Fearing Dawes, had drowned. The father had been Comptroller of the Currency under President Cleveland and had held other high positions. The father's tribute was read by the minister at the young man's funeral. Among other things, the father said:

"I have taken him with me among the greatest in the nation, and looked in vain for any evidence in him of awe or even curiosity. He has taken me, asking me to help them, among the poor and lowly of earth. . . . He did not smoke, nor swear, nor drink. He was absolutely clean. I never saw him angry. In twenty-one years he never gave me just cause for serious reproach. He was extremely ambitious. He was extremely proud. Upon one occasion, years ago, when I mistakenly reproached him, he patiently explained my error, and then peremptorily demanded and received an apology from me . . . My boy lived long enough to 'win out.' Whatever the years would have added would be only material. In a man's character is his real career."

This tribute came from memories. The son was taken, but the father was left a world of precious memories which meant more than the world itself. Our memories are companions and he who has them is not alone. Beautiful memories are helpful friends which inspire man to reach upward to the higher and nobler life.

To our dead who have fallen asleep in the Lord, we say: *Though you have moved on, a lot of you remains here. To live in hearts that love you is not to die.*

Make Me a Child

Little children . . . for of such is the kingdom of heaven.
Matthew 19:14

> Last night my little boy confessed to me
> Some childish wrong;
> And kneeling at my knee
> He prayed with tears—
> "Dear God, make me a man
> Like Daddy—wise and strong.
> I know you can."
>
> Then while he slept
> I knelt beside his bed,
> Confessed my sins,
> And prayed with low-bowed head,
> "O God, make me a child
> Like my child here—
>   Pure, guileless,
> Trusting thee with faith sincere."

Nothing is as thirsty as a child who has just gone to bed. The parent who desires the purity of a child is also thirsty— for the living water of which the Lord spoke.

The child is very believing — believes everything he or she is told. So do the godly parents, *if* that word has come from the Lord. Faith and faithfulness are linked together. The Bible says, "Be not faithless, but believing" (John 20:27).

No human is as forgiving as a little child. Adults must be forgiving to be childlike and to find forgiveness for themselves.

So that's my prayer: Make me a child.

Only Six but He Could Read

Till I come, give attendance to reading, to exhortation, to doctrine. I Timothy 4:13

My little grandson had just finished the first grade. He could read unusually well, and I was very proud of him. Feeling the need of his comradeship, one day I took him with me to the hospital where he waited in the reception room. There we met friends who were reading a newspaper. This presented an opportunity for the six-year-old to read the newspaper for them. They marveled at his reading skill.

This is an accomplishment God intends for all of us to attain and use often. I know He does, because our God is the God of literature. He wrote the Ten Commandments on tables of stone. The Lord commanded Jeremiah, "Write thee all the words that I have spoken unto thee in a book" (Jeremiah 30:2). And Jesus said, "But these are written, that ye might believe" (John 20:31). But why did He write, if He did not intend for us to read?

The person who does not read has no advantage over the person who can't read.

Reading gets you out of the rut of your own thinking and allows you to look into the mind of another. It will increase your knowledge, boost your spirit, augment your thinking, enhance your self-confidence, and enlarge your usefulness on the job.

Always have a good book at hand, in the living room, in the bedroom, in the bathroom — a book of condensed thought, sound maxims, wise directions, and inspirational uplifts. Resolve to engage in a little reading everyday. Though it is only a little, it will make a big difference in a year.

Keeping on Keeping on

Behold, we count them happy which endure. James 5:11

The teacher thought she was making an impression in her lecture on perseverance. In describing the gritty, never-turn-back person, she said, "He drove straight down the road to his goal. He never looked to the left or right, but pushed forward, moved by the drive to get there. His purpose was definite and inflexible. Neither friend nor stranger could have turned him from his course. All who crossed his path should have known that he was coming head-on. What would you call such a man?"

One student spoke up: "A truck driver."

Perseverance! Endurance! Stickability! No amount of talent, education, finesse or looks will serve as a substitute for the old bulldog spirit of hanging in there. Without it, a person is doomed to failure or mediocrity.

"Faint heart never won fair lady" — nor outran one either.

It won't do you any good to be on the right track, if you stop.

And you won't need to make a "comeback" if you keep going. So if you're chugging along on the right road, never quit.

DON'T QUIT

When things go wrong, as they sometimes will,
When the road you're trudging seems all uphill,
When the funds are low and the debts are high,
And you want to smile, but you have to sigh,
When care is pressing you down a bit,
Rest, if you must — but don't you quit.

I Have the Edge

For to him that is joined to all the living there is hope: for a living dog is better than a dead lion. Ecclesiastes 9:4

I have the edge, for I have life. Here is an outline of Life: Tender Teens, Teachable Twenties, Tireless Thirties, Fiery Forties, Forceful Fifties, Serious Sixties, Sacred Seventies, Aching Eighties, Nappy Nineties . . . shortening breath, Death.

As long as I stay above the latter, there is still hope for me. For where there's life there's hope. For this reason, a living dog is better than a dead lion.

Life is an opportunity to improve — every today is another chance.

Life lets me think — may my thoughts be constructive, elevating and uplifting.

Life lets me talk — may my speech be true, pure and helpful.

Life lets me do — may my efforts center on the things that count the most and last the longest.

For a greater edge and more fruitful living, let each look to God who is the giver of life. For He holds the key.

Indeed, life is a story in volumes three:

The Past
The Present
The Yet-to-be
The first is finished and laid away,
The second we're reading day by day,
The third and last of volume three
Is locked from sight;
God holds the key.

Tact the Best Tactics

I think myself happy, King Agrippa, because I shall answer for myself this day . . . Especially because I know thee to be expert in all customs and questions which are among the Jews: wherefore I beseech thee to hear me patiently. Acts 26:2,3

The above passage, which is the introduction of the Apostle Paul's speech in the defense of himself, is a classic in diplomacy. Inasmuch as the apostle saw the need of tact, then surely all of us should.

Abraham Lincoln was asked to define diplomacy. After musing a moment, he said: "I guess you might say that it's the knack of letting the other fellow have your way." In another definition of tact, Lincoln said, "It is the ability to describe others as they see themselves."

It is the flair to make a point without sticking the person. Diplomacy is the art of telling a person where to get off when he thinks he's getting on. Tact is a virtue that adapts to circumstances. It is remembering a woman's birthday without remembering her age.

Tact is response to mind reading. Diplomacy is the genius to deal with a man as though he has an open mind when he has a hole in his head. It is the art of saying "nice doggie" at the sound of growls.

Lest we be misled, tact based on double talk is not tact but hypocrisy, and should be shunned.

Furthermore, no matter how good diplomacy may be, in some instances it won't work. I had a wolf pup when I was a boy; and, as he grew up, I learned that pitching steaks to him wouldn't make him a vegetarian. Nevertheless, tact is the best tactic. Use it freely.

I Carried You

In all their affliction he was afflicted, and the Angel of his presence saved them: in his love and in his pity he redeemed them; and he bare them, and carried them all the days of old. Isaiah 63:9

Perhaps we have all read and loved the anonymous but beautiful *Footprints:*

"One night a man had a dream. It was plain to him that he was walking along the beach with the Lord. Across the sky flashed scenes from his life. For each scene, he noticed two sets of footprints in the sand; one belonging to him, and the other to the Lord.

"When the last scene of his life flashed before him, he looked back at the footprints in the sand. He noticed that many times along the path of his life there was only one set of footprints. He also noticed that it happened at the very lowest and saddest times in his life.

"This really bothered him and he questioned the Lord about it. 'Lord, you said that once I decided to follow, you'd walk with me all the way. But I have noticed that during the most troublesome times in my life, there is only one set of footprints. I don't understand why when I needed you most you would leave me.'

"The Lord replied, 'My precious, precious child, I love you and I would never leave you. During your times of trial and suffering, when you see only one set of footprints, it was then that *I carried you.'* "

Thy mercy, O Lord, held me up.
Psalms 94:18

Surely he hath carried our griefs and borne our sorrows.
Isaiah 53:4

The Basis of All Improvement

Examine yourselves. II Corinthians 13:5

Not the other poor soul!

Did you ever notice that when you point a finger at some-one else three of your fingers are pointing at you? This is significant. For there are at least three times as many reasons to look at self as the other fellow.

• *First, I can live only one life* — mine, not the other person's.

• *Second, I am responsible for what I do* — not for what someone else does.

• *Third, I am the master of my fate* — no one else is.

Indeed, much is gained by an earnest self-examination. It is the foundation of all progress; self-knowledge is a prerequisite to self-improvement. The most successful people are those who know themselves. See yourself as you are and go from there. Never be satisfied with your faults and weaknesses. The desire to improve shows of what stuff you are made.

So it is highly incumbent upon each of us to pull back the drapery of his life and ask himself a few questions. And there is no greater accomplishment than a consciousness of sincerity as the examination proceeds.

SOMEBODY

Somebody did a golden deed;
Somebody proved a friend in need;
Somebody fought a valiant fight;
Somebody lived to shield the right;
Was that "somebody" you?

Some More Chalk

Blessed is he whose transgression is forgiven, whose sin is covered. Psalms 32:1

At a preachers' luncheon a preacher stated in his speech that he dreamed he had gone to heaven and looked and Grandpa was not there.

They laughed.

Then it was Grandpa's time to reply, and he said, "You know, that's funny, Jim, I had a dream last night, too. I dreamed I went to heaven and the Lord gave me a piece of chalk and said, 'Go over there and write down all your sins.' And just at that time I met you leaving. I said, 'Jim, what are you doing? Why are you going that way?' And you said, 'I'm going to get some more chalk.' "

And they roared.

One thing sure, sin is not what it's cracked up to be — "The way of transgressors is hard" (Proverbs 13:15).

Another thing sure —"All have sinned and come short of the glory of God" (Romans 3:23).

Moreover, another thing sure, unless sin is checked it feeds on itself and multiplies — "For our transgressions are multiplied before thee, and our sins testify against us" (Isaiah 59:12).

And another thing sure, God loves us though we are sinners — "But God commendeth his love toward us, in that, while we were yet sinners, Christ died for us" (Romans 5:8).

And still another thing sure, God is anxious to forgive — "Though your sins be as scarlet, they shall be as white as snow; though they be red like crimson, they shall be as wool" (Isaiah 1:18).

Don't Be Too Hasty

For ye shall not go out with haste, nor go by flight: and the God of Israel will be your reward. Isaiah 52:12

We are told that the idea for the steam engine was born in the daydreaming of James Watt as he watched a teapot bubble. Such original ideas spring from wonder and imagination.

Ideas refuse to be rushed. They come in their own way and in their own time.

However, the motto today is: "Don't just stand there. Do something. Anything!" This is because we tend to confuse mere bustle with actual achievement. But years of observation and personal experiences have taught us that these maxims are not vain rhetoric:

> *Do in haste and repent in leisure.*
>
> *Good and haste seldom meet.*
>
> *He that is hasty fishes in an empty pond.*
>
> *Hasty people have never hastened the sun.*
>
> *Make haste slowly.*
>
> *Haste is ever the parent of failure.*
>
> *Haste makes waste — and frustration and ulcers.*

Wouldn't all of us in this fast, restless, nervous world get more out of our years — and have more years — if we spent more time in doing some helpful thinking? This would free the mind to think out the answers to some of our problems, to make things better, and to develop into the kind of people we would like to be.

You Will Be Missed

Then Jonathan said to David, Tomorrow is the new moon: and thou shalt be missed, because thy seat will be empty.
I Samuel 20:18

It should be the ambition of all of us to live so that when we are gone, whether it be death or a move into another community, we are sure to be missed. I can't think of anything more tragic than for a departed person not to be missed.

It is possible for you to be missed for many reasons:

• *You will be missed because your seat will be empty.* Empty chair in family circle. Empty chair in office. Empty chair in civic club. Empty seat at church. Occupying a pew at church is more important than many people think. First, it helps us. Moreover, it shows whose side we are on in a struggle for a better world. What if no one attended? What if the congregation should die?

• *You will be missed because your tongue will be silenced.* We have been blessed many times by a wise, considerate, helpful tongue. It gave direction. It gave encouragement. "A word fitly spoken is like apples of gold in pictures of silver" (Proverbs 25:11).

• *You will be missed because your ears will be deaf.* We shall miss those ears into which we have poured our troubles. All of us need someone in whom we can confide. It means much just to have someone to listen to us.

• *You will be missed because your hands will be stilled.* Those hands have worked that others could have. When Dorcas was gone, those left behind wept and looked at the garments she had made. Her hands had contributed to her good works and almsdeeds.

Puff of Wind

Make no friendship with an angry man; and with a furious man thou shalt not go; Lest thou learn his ways, and get a snare to thy soul. Proverbs 22:24,25

I recall very vividly the first time I ever drove across the Great Divide in Colorado. I was struck with the awesome thought of influence and responsibility. I was at the very dividing line in which a raindrop may go on its way to either the Atlantic Ocean or the Pacific Ocean. Then I thought on the momentous power of a little puff of wind in determining the destiny of a raindrop, how that it can send it on its way to one ocean or the other.

Then I made the serious and searching application. I thought deeply on the force and consequence of human influence. I realized more fully that a little human sway at a critical point in another's life can mark the fate of that person.

Blow winds of influence, blow! If you're going the way I want to go, fine; if not, I will grab a limb and hold on to where I am.

Our friends and associates write their names in our guest books, but they do more — they make imprints on our heart.

Many a tearful parent has said to me, "Oh, if my son (or daughter) had not gotten with the wrong crowd!"

For your present and future good, select your associates carefully, because:

- *A person is known by the company he or she keeps.*

- *Good company is a good coach.*

- *Bad company teams you with a losing coach.*

Judge Not

Judge not, that ye be not judged. For with what judgment ye judge, ye shall be judged: and with what measure ye mete, it shall be measured to you again. Matthew 7:1,2

Our limited knowledge of the facts, our unacquaintance of the hidden chain of circumstances, and our incognizance of all the provocative causes keep us from being infallible judges.

Upbringing, bias, likes and dislikes, beliefs and disbeliefs, loves and hates influence a person's judgment of others. This disqualifies every human as a perfect judge. This is clearly exemplified in that a woman's love for a man makes her a very poor judge of character.

Furthermore, we are inclined to judge people by what they have instead of what they are. This prevents a flawless judgment.

Another thing — our judging the inefficiences and mistakes of another may be an indirect way of trying to call attention to our superiority and to lift ourselves by stepping on someone else. It can be an effort to compliment self by pointing out another's fault. It can be a sneaky way of saying, "Look how bad that fellow is, but look how good I am."

In light of the above facts, isn't it better to leave judging to the Perfect One?

> Judge not! though clouds of seeming guilt
>   may dim thy brother's fame;
> For fate may throw suspicion's shade upon
>   the brightest name;
> Thou canst tell what hidden chain of
>   circumstances may
> Have wrought the sad result that takes
>   an honest name away.
>   Judge not!

Passing the Buck

And I said unto the king, If it please the king, and if thy servant have found favor in thy sight, that thou wouldest send me unto Judah, unto the city of my fathers' sepulchres, that I may build it. Nehemiah 2:5

The reason Jerusalem was in decay and disarray was because the buck had been passed too long. Now Nehemiah was willing to accept the buck and rebuild the city.

Will Rogers, one of America's favorite humorists, stated that there have been three periods in American history: Passing of the Indian, Passing of the Buffalo, and Passing of the Buck.

Why the Passing of the Buck?

1) I won't have to assume the responsibility.
2) I won't have to be a target for criticism.
3) If it fails, I won't be blamed.
4) Instead, I can blame the other fellow.
5) If it fails, I can be a post-mortem expert.

Let's give the buck-passer his due; he is especially talented and quick in the utterance of two sets of four words: "Let George do it"; and if it fails, "It is George's fault."

When the buck is passed to George, of course he sometimes fails. But George gets the recognition, the honor, the role of leadership, the thrill that comes from challenge, the victory over boredom, and the joy of the struggle.

The greatest reason for any persons's tackling the job that falls his lot to perform is that he is a man, which demands responsibility and performance. He cannot live like a cow or horse that is content to whisk away the flies and eat the grass around the hoofs.

Doing Good

Who went about doing good. Acts 10:38

This passage has reference to Christ. Every footprint He left on the sands of time points toward doing good. If we would walk in those prints, we *must* do good. Christianity demands more than confession. It requires that good be done.

Trying to get to heaven in a vessel of selfishness — help me only — is about like trying to sail the Atlantic Ocean in a paper sack.

It was easy for Jesus to do good because He was good, and that's the secret of doing good. Flowing wells don't have to be pumped.

Unless good comes out of us to help others, there is not much good in us. Understandably, the better we are, the more good we do.

Doing good is one argument the atheist can't knock. So the words of John Wesley are very pertinent:

> *Do all the good you can,*
> *By all the means you can,*
> *In all the ways you can,*
> *In all the places you can,*
> *At all the times you can,*
> *To all the people you can,*
> *As long as ever you can.*

By doing good you give this old earth a little semblance of heaven. The good we do never dies. It lives on and on after we are gone. "They may rest from their labors; and their works do follow them" (Revelation 14:13).

Salute an Illustrious Day

Render therefore unto Caesar the things which are Caesar's; and unto God the things that are God's. Matthew 22:21

Old Glory will be displayed more prominently, even on our front porches, and will head parades that march up and down our streets. Old Glory will be saluted on every hand.

Many will go to the park. Many will play ball. To fight the heat, many will go swimming. There will be much eating. Perhaps too much. Hands will shake. Faces will smile. Children will have fun. The spirit of freedom with its joys will be in the air.

There will be many speeches. Many too long. But the people will tolerate them because Old Glory will be there and referred to in honor.

When the sun slips over the western horizon, night settles down, and the stars come out to play twinkle, the culminating thrill will be a display of fireworks. Every sound will be a sound of freedom. Every light that blazes the sky will remind us of a light provided by freedom.

It is the Fourth of July — America's Independence Day.

It all started when some brave colonists, outraged at the tyrannical demands of a king, said, "We've had enough," and then put it in the form of a declaration and backed it up. Declaration of Independence.

What was won more than two hundred years ago must not be lost now by indifference and selfishness. Let us be aware that freedoms can be lost one by one as well as all at once. If we don't like what our government has become, it is our fault. For we the people are the government and determine its course.

Nutshell Messages

Hear instruction, and be wise, and refuse it not. Proverbs 8:33

Little statements of facts have big messages. Here are enough to completely reshape any person's life:

No one's vision is ever so keen as when he sees an opportunity to do good.

No one ever stands so tall as when he stoops to lift another who has fallen.

No one can walk both sides of the street at the same time.

No one can climb the mountain with one step.

No one can be great without serving.

No one can shine and not be seen.

No one can build a lasting house on the sand.

No one can find ease in walking the transgressor's way.

No one is stronger than he thinks he is.

No one can be braver than his conscience.

No one is better than his word.

No one is right just because he thinks he is right.

No one can find the truth who will not consider and weigh the opposite of what he believes.

No one can go forward while back-stepping, or walk straight while going in circles.

No one can serve God in Satan's kingdom.

Butter in a Lordly Dish

*He asked water, and she gave him milk; she brought forth
butter in a lordly dish.* Judges 5:25

Why the lordly dish? It was used only when the most distinguished and notable people were entertained in the most grandiose style. It was a gesture of the best for the best. Jael made the guest Sisera feel very important, greatly honored, and highly extolled, which allayed any suspicions that he was in any danger. However, he was in grave peril — just didn't know it. He was caught in the trap of flattery. His suceptibility to honeyed treatment cost him his head. He was beheaded.

Flattery has caused many a person to lose his head; if not physically, at least spiritually. People get caught up in the intoxication of flattery and fall for tricks and schemes that otherwise could not entrap them. They like to eat out of that lordly dish.

There is an expressive and spicy chapter in Solomon's Proverbs that gives an account of a man's capture by a flattering woman who wished to entice him. This is not fanciful. It is real. Solomon said, "With her much fair speech she caused him to yield, with the flattering of her lips she forced him. He goeth after her straightway, as an ox goeth to the slaughter, or as a fool to the correction of the stocks; till a dart strike through his liver; as a bird hasteth to the snare, and knoweth not that it is for his life" (Proverbs 7:21-23).

Then why are we duped by flattery when we know it's not true? First, we like to hear it, though we know it's false. Second, even though we see through the blarney, it shows that the flatterer sees in us something worth courting. This necessitates that we be cautious of the lordly dish and see the poison within it. So let's just look at it — not swallow it.

The Fighter

But call to remembrance the former days, in which, after ye were illuminated, ye endured a great fight of afflictions. Hebrews 10:32

My father used to say, "It's not the size of the dog in the fight but the size of the fight in the dog that counts."

Fighting for a noble cause ennobles the fighter, but to refuse labels one as either complacent or cowardly. And all defeat has to do to prevail is for good people to refuse to fight.

I must forever be on guard
  Against the doubts that skulk along;
I get ahead by fighting hard,
  But fighting keeps my spirit strong.

My victories are small and few,
  It matters not how hard I strive;
Each day the fight begins anew,
  But fighting keeps my hopes alive.

My progress has been slow and hard,
  I've had to climb and crawl and swim,
Fighting for every stubborn yard,
  But I have kept in fighting trim.

My dearest plans keep going wrong,
  Events combine to thwart my will,
But fighting keeps my spirit strong,
  And I am undefeated still.

Samuel E. Kiser

So, with a renewal of bulldog tenacity, I say:

I'm wounded sore but not yet slain,
I'll just lie down and bleed awhile,
And then I'll rise and fight again.

A Little Rest and Re-creation

And they found fat pasture and good and the land was wide, and quiet, and peaceable; for they of Ham had dwelt there of old. I Chronicles 4:40

If we can't live in such a place, free, untouchable and un-bothered all the time, at least we should find such a refuge part of the time.

A local couple sent a playpen to their friends in Northern California who had been blessed with the arrival of their fourth child.

Two weeks later the mother responded with this note: "Thanks, many thanks, and thanks again for the pen. It comes in so handy — I sit in it every afternoon and read and think. In it the children can't get near me."

This whimsical note emphasizes the need of some quiet place for everybody. The crowded mind and the tired body cry out for relaxation, preferably for a place where we can lie down in green pastures and walk beside still waters. And there nature communicates with our spirit and whispers, "Tempest be still."

To re-create body, we should play and rest. To re-create mind, remove the worries and stress and then repose. To re-create cheerfulness, put trust in God and think on how many more things work than fail.

Recreation is not waste. It is re-creating that which is waning. Life is too sacred and time is too short not to follow a course that prolongs us.

All of us must find a way to make our own little land wide and quiet and peaceable.

A Little Lower Than Angels

What is man, that thou art mindful of him? And the son of man, that thou visitest him? For thou hast made him a little lower than the angels, and hast crowned him with glory and honor. Thou madest him to have dominion over the works of thy hands; thou hast put all things under his feet: All sheep and oxen, yea, and the beasts of the field; the fowl of the air, and the fish of the sea, and whatsoever passeth through the paths of the seas.

Psalms 8:4-8

Now this is man — "a little lower than the angels." He is adorned with the crown of reason, is internally endowed with a conscience, and in apprehension and action is closer to the angels.

"Thou madest him to have dominion over the works of thy hands." God has given him the glory and honor of being in charge of His creation — not the animals, not the fowls, not the fishes. This distinction belongs to man.

The earth and the universe are for man. The sun in the heavens is his lamp. Night is the shade for his window. His furnace is the energies stored up in the earth, and if they should be depleted he still has the sun. The vegetation and the flocks and the herds are for his sustenance and his clothing. The seas can float him around the world. Space permits him to travel faster. The breath-taking spectacle of sky, and sea and earth are for his good and happiness. God has given such to man, saying, "All this is for you. Have dominion over it. Be faithful to your stewardship."

Then, awed with His goodness and grateful for His favors, we exclaim in the sacred language of the Psalmist, "O Lord our Lord, how excellent is thy name in all the earth" (Psalms 8:9).

Little Boys and Girls

Children's children are the crown of old men; and the glory of children are their fathers. Proverbs 17:6

Reflecting on childhood gives zest to life. It renews the spark of life for older ones who are now running the last laps of their race.

I like the way Alan Beck has put it:

> BOYS come in assorted sizes, weights and colors. They are found everywhere — on top of, underneath, inside of, climbing on, swinging from, running around or jumping to. A boy is Truth with dirt on its face, Wisdom with bubble gum in its hair, and the Hope of the future with a frog in its pocket. A boy is a magical creature — you can lock him out of your workshop, but you can't lock him out of your heart.

> LITTLE GIRLS . . . the nicest things that happen to people. They are born with a little bit of angel-shine about them and though it wears thin sometimes, there is always enough left to lasso your heart — even when they are sitting in the mud, or crying tempermental tears, or parading up the street in Mother's best clothes. A girl is Innocence playing in the mud, beauty standing on its head, and Motherhood dragging a doll by its foot. A little girl . . . can muss up your home, your hair, and your dignity — spend your money, your time, and your temper — then just when your patience is ready to crack, her sunshine peeks through and you've lost again.

Truly, children are a gift from God.

The Egg

Watch therefore; for ye know not what hour your Lord doth come. Matthew 24:42

The egg — yes, *the egg*, because this one was different.

Years ago I was holding a gospel meeting in a little Alabama town, and a strange thing happened. In the late afternoon when the children gathered the eggs they found one that had this message indented in the shell: "Beware 12 o'clock tonight." The news soon spread through the town and pandemonium broke loose. As the night wore on, anxiety increased. Some who had not been to church in years attended that night. Little groups sat up in prayerful vigilance, waiting for the fateful hour to come. But when the clock struck twelve nothing unusual occurred — just a sigh of relief.

You say, "What's the explanation?" One of the young men had been to college and had gotten very bright. He learned that the shell of an egg can be softened by putting it in a certain solution and that words can be inscribed on it, and that by putting it in another solution it will harden, leaving the indentions. This he did and slipped it over in the neighbor's hen house.

What I had not been able to do with the help of the Bible that old hen easily did with the help of a prankster. She made them think on several important matters: their ways, the brevity of life, the uncertainty of time, and the end of the world.

Wisdom cries out that we live mindful of both life and death: as if today is the last, and as if we had a thousand more years. For life which has its opportunities also has its death which knocks on every man's door. And when belongs only to God.

The Art of Imagination

Eyes have they, but they see not: they have ears but they hear not. Psalms 115:5,6

The Psalmist was describing an idol made of silver or gold. But it also describes a person devoid of imagination. He has eyes that see not and ears that hear not.

Grandmother saw Billy running around the house slapping himself, and curiously asked him why.

"Well," said Billy, "I just got so tired of doing nothing that I thought I'd ride my horse for a while."

Little Billy's imagination came to his aid. If he keeps it going, his possibilities shall become unlimited.

Einstein said, "Imagination is more powerful than knowledge." Without it, thought comes to a halt.

Imagination gives fresh eyes to look at everything, as though you had just emerged from the darkness of night into the light of day. It lifts eyes to the unknown lands and charts new paths to higher goals.

Imagination breaks the barriers of old boundaries and projects your thoughts beyond them in search of creative answers to old problems.

This great human power — imagination — in the words of Shakespeare, "gives to airy nothing a local habitation and a name." Man, woman, boy or girl reaches into the heavens to grasp an idea and then brings it down to earth, clothes it in practicality, and makes it work.

Wander among the clouds. Then come down to earth. This is the art of imagination!

What Can I Do?

I can do all things through Christ which strengtheneth me.
Philippians 4:13

One thing to watch is the "can'ts" and "cans." I must learn that I can't get off dead center if I think I can't, that I can't aim low and rise high, that I can't succeed if I don't try. I need to learn that I can do much more than I have ever thought. It is a known fact that nearly everybody lives below his or her capacity.

It is stimulating, therefore, to think on what Horace Traubel has said:

> *What can I do? I can speak out when others are silent. I can say man when others say money. I can stay up when others are asleep. I can keep on working when others have stopped to play.*
>
> *I can give life big meanings when others give life little meanings. I can say love when others say hate. I can say every man when others say one man. I can try events by a hard test when others try them by an easy test.*
>
> *What can I do? I can give myself to life when others may refuse themselves to life.*

Every age is the age of the individual: individual mind, individual will, individual virtue, individual goals and individual responsibility.

What can I do? I can be a tiny light in a world of darkness. A soldier in the army of God. A sower that scatters good seed. A little leaven that affects the whole lump. True — life has its bitterness but is sweet to those who pour in the sugar.

Pass on the Praise

If there be any virtue, and if there be any praise, think on these things. Philippians 4:8

One of the moving principles of human nature is the desire to be appreciated. The hunger for recognition and praise makes for the highest excellence, for it spurs people to do their best.

Praise, however, should be limited to those who are worthy; for praise makes good people better but bad people worse. To acclaim those who don't deserve it is only satire in disguise.

• *Husband, praise your wife,* even though it may shock her. It will put a song on her lips as she works.

• *Wife, praise your husband,* even if it does cause him to think you want something. He will get over it. Compliment him. This will encourage him to do even better.

• *Parents, if your child is good, judiciously tell him about it.* Of course, there are times to censure; but don't forget the deeds and occasions deserving applause.

• *Teacher, if a student deserves honor, grant it to him.* This will inspire him to be a greater achiever. For the art of praising is the art of pleasing, and the art of pleasing can be the art of shaping.

• *Employer, if your worker does a good job tell him so.* He will appreciate this nearly as much as a raise. For a conscientious, dedicated worker does not work for salary alone.

• *Neighbor, if your neighbors are an asset* to the neighborhood and give you a secure feeling, tell them how fortunate you are to have them.

The Anchor Holds

Which hope we have as an anchor of the soul, both sure and steadfast. Hebrews 6:19

In carrying out the symbol given in this Scripture we can say that life is a voyage. Even the very best people find the voyage of life a little tumultuous at times. The anchor is very essential to a safe journey. There are at least two threatening sources of peril:

1) *The danger of drifting.* It is much easier to float with the wind and the tide than to go against it. This is the peril that carries many people into the worst conditions of life. They permit themselves to drift.

2) *The storms that strike.* There are the pressures of temptation. Secular anxieties. Physical infirmities. Family afflictions. Spiritual conflicts. All beat down upon us with a mighty wrath, and can wreck us unless we have an anchor that holds.

The only anchor that will not snap or budge in the tempest is hope. It is sure and steadfast. It steadies the soul. Those who are anchored to God can confidently face the tides and storms of this world. Let us remember that having an anchor does not preclude storms, but rather protects us in storms.

Every strain fixes the anchor deeper. It holds even in the hour of death. This was exemplified by a dying sailor. He was near the end. A friend said, "Well, mate, how is it with you now?"

The dying man with poise and assurance replied, "The anchor holds."

May all of us be able to say in both life and death, "The anchor holds."

Some Things I Have Learned
Since Leaving College

For I have learned by experience. Genesis 30:27

• *It pays to do much preventive work.* Then one doesn't have to do so much corrective work. The best way to cure trouble is not to let it happen.

• *The bad that is reported in most cases is not as bad as it is pictured.* The evil or threat or despair that gets reported is often highly exaggerated.

• *The good that is aired in most instances is not as good as it is portrayed.* It is easy for people and things to get pictured better than they really are.

• *The people's appraisal of a man is determined by whether or not he agrees with them.* If he does, he is applauded for his brilliancy; if he doesn't, he is scorned for being inferior.

• *Some people are against everything.* This keeps them from having to assume the responsibility of launching out. Their negative views have clobbered them.

• *There are others who are against any improvement unless they get the honor of thinking of it first.* Their pride demands that they be first — or not at all.

• *Some have too much pride to ever change when once they are wrong.* When they say that two plus two equals five, to them it will always be five.

• *It is a mistake to let people tell you too much about their sins.* Later they may be embarrassed in your presence and hate you, not because of what you have done but because of what you know about them.

Things Work Out

I have been young, and now I am old; yet have I not seen the righteous forsaken, nor his seed begging bread. Psalms 37:25

The Psalmist is a witness to the comforting thought that things work out. He had never seen the righteous forsaken.

We know that setbacks occur, but they are not failures unless we make them such. Let us recall that the roads we have taken had their bridges; and occasionally if one was out, the detour was not long.

Because it rains when we wish it wouldn't,
Because men do what they often shouldn't,
Because crops fail and plans go wrong,
Some of us grumble the whole day long.
But somehow in spite of the care and doubt,
It seems at last that things work out.

Because we lose what we hoped to gain,
Because we suffer a little pain,
Because we must work when we'd like to play,
Some of us whimper along life's way.
But, somehow, as day will follow night,
Most of our troubles work out all right.

So bend to your trouble and meet your care,
For the clouds must break, and the sky grow fair.
Let the rain come down, as it must and will,
But keep on working and hoping still,
For in spite of the grumblers who stand about,
Somehow, it seems, all things work out.

Rearing Children

And, ye fathers, provoke not your children to wrath: but bring them up in the nurture and admonition of the Lord.
Ephesians 6:4

A minister asked a six-year-old girl how many children there were in her family.

"Seven," she replied.

The preacher remarked that so many children must cost a lot.

"Oh, no, we don't buy 'em, we raise 'em," replied the child.

We don't buy them. It's the upkeep — upbringing — that's costly. And I'm not talking about money. I'm talking about bringing them up in the way they should go. It costs time, guidance, example, patience, work, play, study and thought.

Training is everything. Candied yams are nothing but country sweet potatoes that went to a cooking school.

Oh for a thousand pens and tongues to declare the urgency of rearing children properly! The future of the world depends on it. May today's children be the bulwarks of morality, the keepers of orthodoxy and the guardians of democracy.

Ably rearing children requires us:

- To love them and not to spoil them.
- To discipline them and not to domineer them.
- To lead them and not to master them.
- To protect them and not to smother them.
- To help them and not to hinder them.
- To hold them and not to possess them.
- To treasure them and not to hoard them.

Is Your Mainspring Broken?

Faith which worketh by love. Galatians 5:6

Years ago my watch quit running, which prompted me to take it to the jeweler. After examining it, he said, "The mainspring is broken." This was the source of energy that kept it ticking.

With the mainspring broken, time had gone off and left that watch. It couldn't stay up with a moving world.

Now from a spiritual viewpoint, we need to ask ourselves: What about my mainspring, my faith? For faith is the energetic power to move man. It moved Noah, of whom we read, "By faith Noah . . . moved" (Hebrews 11:7). Paul recognized this mainspring of life, by saying, "Faith which worketh." It works. It moves. It ticks.

Some people's mainspring is wound up tighter than others — that is, have more faith than others. Some have very little faith: "O ye of little faith." Others have more and are described as having "great faith."

There are many things to test your faith, but never let it break; and it shall sustain and comfort you amid the encircling gloom and when the night is dark. With your faith strong — your mainspring wound up — you can sing one step at a time:

> Lead, Kindly Light, amid the encircling gloom,
>   Lead thou me on!
> The night is dark, and I am far from home —
>   Lead thou me on!
> Keep thou my feet. I do not ask to see
> The distant scene — one step enough for me.
>
> John Henry Newman

Be a Winner

Know ye not that they which run in a race run all, but one receiveth the prize? So run, that ye may obtain.
I Corinthians 9:24

No matter what the contest is, be a winner.

Winston Churchill — that grand old statesman of World War II — had the spirit to win. Drive, determination, courage and eloquence were his trademarks. I can still hear his bolstering words spoken in deep, resonant tones. His forceful speeches which sounded the note of victory kept the British people from despair when the threat of defeat was upon them. In one of his speeches he said, "Victory at all costs, victory in spite of all terror, victory however long and hard the road may be."

Before Churchill's day it was Napoleon who said, "Victory belongs to the most persevering."

Very definitely — a winner doesn't quit. He may have been knocked down, and he may have been in the process of being counted out; but, he still doesn't quit.

It is not enough to try, to work, to run, to fight. It is the spirit that we bring to the effort that decides the outcome. It is morale that wins the victory.

We can lose a few battles and still win the war.

So we fight on and on. And then when the time comes to lay aside the armor and to be kissed by death, we can say in the heroic language of the Apostle Paul, "I have fought a good fight, I have finished my course" (II Timothy 4:7).

And that makes us winners.

Tanning Hides

Reprove, rebuke, exhort with all longsuffering and doctrine.
II Timothy 4:2

A few years ago a preacher called on one of the members who lived in the backwoods a few miles from town. The backwoodsman was out at the barn tanning hides of animals he had trapped. He was so engrossed in his work that he was unaware of the minister's presence until he tapped him on the shoulder. In startled confusion, the hunter apologized, "I'm ashamed that you found me in this condition. I'm so poorly groomed for company."

The preacher replied, "Oh, that's all right. There is not much difference between us. Our works are very similar. You tan dead hides, and I tan live ones."

Human beings are so constituted that there are times when they need to be complimented and other times when they need to be censured. All of one and none of the other makes for imbalance.

One of the specific guidelines for a preacher calls for rebuke — a little tanning: "Rebuke them sharply, that they may be sound in the faith" (Titus 1:13). You don't straighten out people by silently watching them get more twisted. There is no true course but to speak out.

And those who listen will judge themselves to be wise or foolish by their own reactions to what is said:

> *Reprove not a scorner, lest he hate thee: rebuke a wise man, and he shall love thee.* Proverbs 9:8

> *Give instruction to a wise man, and he will be yet wiser.*
> Proverbs 9:9

Tested by Disappointment

After they were come to Mysia, they assayed to go into Bithynia:
but the Spirit suffered them not.   Acts 16:7

Paul and his company wanted to go to Bithynia, but God had bigger plans for them. Disappointed! But appointed — to bigger works.

One of the hardest blows for any person to bear is disappointment. It comes in every form: broken love, broken home, job stalemate, friend's betrayal, surgery that fails to cure, loss of fortune, defeat in athletics, defeat in politics, church plans that fizzle, cancelled trip, and children who come back from college with unusual philosophies and different morals.

When I was a boy I watched my mother sift flour through a sieve. The fine flour went through easily, but the larger bits of grain were not affected by the shaking and remained on top. Life is like that. We go through testing periods, but if we are big enough — have big enough faith, hope, love and courage — we can endure the shaking and remain on top.

Sometimes we have to suffer disappointment and bafflement in order to reach higher levels. If Hawthorne had been permitted to keep working at the custom house, he never would have become famous as a writer. If Harry Truman had not failed at selling men's furnishings, he never would have become President. It was A. B. Alcott who said, "We mount to heaven mostly on the ruins of our cherished schemes, finding our failures were successes." And William Penn said, "No pain, no palm; no thorns, no throne; no gall, no glory; no cross, no crown."

You Tell on Yourself

For every tree is known by its own fruit. Luke 6:44

You can't fool very many people very long. For you tell on yourself. Living on false pretense is a vain and pitiful gesture. Avoid it. Sooner or later your true self will come through and be recognized.

A person — both the wise and the foolish — tells on himself by his words. "The tongue of the wise useth knowledge aright: but the mouth of fools poureth out foolishness" (Proverbs 15:2).

Also, a person makes himself known by his deeds. "Even a child is known by his doings, whether his work be pure, and whether it be right" (Proverbs 20:11).

> You tell on yourself by the friends you seek,
>   By the very manner in which you speak,
> By the way you employ your leisure time,
>   By the use you make of dollar and dime.
>
> You tell what you are by the things you wear,
>   By the spirit in which your burdens you bear.
> By the kind of things at which you laugh,
>   By the records you play on the phonograph.
>
> You tell what you are by the way you walk,
>   By the things of which you delight to talk,
> By the manner in which you bear defeat,
>   By so simple a thing as how you eat.
>
> By the books you choose from the well-filled shelf;
>   By these ways and more, you tell on yourself;
> So there's really no particle of sense
>   In an effort to keep up false pretense.

And all because a tree is known by its fruit. So just be what you really are. If that's not good enough, get busy and improve yourself.

Example Worked When Precept Failed

Likewise, ye wives, be in subjection to your own husbands; that, if any obey not the word, they also may without the word be won by the conversation [conduct] of the wives. I Peter 3:1

When words fail, example may win.

Years ago a farmer became very ill. Worse than any physical ailment, he was highly biased against Christianity. His getting sick was poorly timed; of course, there is never a good time. It was in the spring and his crops desperately needed working. The weeds and grass were about to get ahead of the corn and cotton.

A neighbor, an outstanding Christian, took his boys and hired help and went over to the helpless man's farm and worked out his crops, free of charge.

One day when this "Good Samaritan" and his crew were working in the fields, beneath the burning sun, the sick man's hardness began to soften. Looking through a window at the workers' sweaty toil, he said to his wife, "When they have their gospel meeting this summer, we're going to have to go."

The man recovered. The meeting was held. He and his wife did attend; furthermore, they were converted. He grew fast and was soon leading prayers and making talks. He had natural leadership ability that came to the front in a hurry.

A few years passed and the couple moved away. There was no congregation near, but this was no deterrent. It was only a challenge. He got busy, started one, and did the preaching. The church grew and became a great candlestick.

When people won't hear your sermon, try living one.

An Amazing and Ageless Production

Holy men of God spake as they were moved by the Holy Ghost. II Peter 1:21

The Bible — what a sublime product!

How amazing and marvelous is its authorship! It was written over a period of about 1600 years by about forty different writers with a cross section of abilities, accomplishments and occupations.

For instance, Moses was educated in the wisdom of the Egyptians and was a shepherd and a leader. Joshua, a soldier and a spy; Ezra, a famous scribe and a pious priest; Nehemiah, cupbearer to the king; David, shepherd, musician, war hero and king; Solomon, the wisest man on earth and a powerful king; Isaiah, a prophet; Ezekiel, a Jewish exile; Daniel, a statesman; Amos, a shepherd and peasant; Matthew, a tax collector; Peter and John, fishermen, "unlearned and ignorant men"; Luke, a physician; and Paul, a tentmaker and a scholar brought up at the feet of Gamaliel.

How could men so different in abilities, customs and occupations have written a book that is the lamp that outshines all other lights, the book of all splendors, the gesture of heaven to kiss the earth with its glories? There is no human explanation. The only conclusion is: "The Spirit gave them utterance" (Acts 2:4) — or expression. Men furnished the tongue or the hand. The Holy Spirit furnished the power behind it. Thus, "all Scripture is given by the inspiration of God" (II Timothy 3:16).

> *Whence but from heaven could men, unskilled in arts,*
> *In several ages born, in several parts,*
> *Weave such agreeing truths; or how or why*
> *Should all conspire to cheat us with a lie?*
> *Unmasked their pains, ungrateful their advice,*
> *Starvation their gains, and martyrdom their price.*

Love Is the Strongest Support

And Jacob served seven years for Rachel; and they seemed unto him but a few days, for the love he had to her.
Genesis 29:20

Perhaps no man who occupied the White House has ever received so much praise and so much malediction as Andrew Jackson. When he retired to the Hermitage on the outskirts of Nashville he had the supporting memories of his notable victory over Wellington's troops at New Orleans and his two terms as President.

Yet, those were not the things on which his thoughts lingered as life's sun was sinking lower everyday. They paled in insignificance in comparison with other things more precious. It has been said that visitors saw the old man sitting before the fire, and near by were his Bible and a miniature of his beloved wife — Rachel.

On her tomb in the Hermitage grounds is the inscription, the beautiful tribute Jackson composed to his companion of thirty-five years: "Here lie the remains of Mrs. Rachel Jackson, wife of President Jackson, who died the twenty-second of December, 1828. Age 61 years. Her face was fair, her person pleasing, her temper amiable, her heart kind. A being so gentle and so virtuous, slander might wound but could not dishonor. Even death, when he bore her from the arms of her husband, could but transport her to the bosom of her God."

What gave the greatest satisfaction and sweetest comfort to the old warrior were not the plaudits for his grand victory at New Orleans or his eight years as head of state, but rather the cherished memories of the affections and devotions of his loving Rachel.

I'll Make a Man Out of Myself Yet

*And that ye put on the new man, which after God is created
in righteousness and true holiness.* Ephesians 4:24

It has been reported that a student in a state university was expelled for participating in a shameful prank in which another student lost his life. Before leaving the campus, the dismissed student went to one of the professors and thanked him for what he had tried to do for him. One thing he said was, "I'll make a man out of myself yet."

Let the past lie in the realm of what cannot be changed. Let us be more concerned with the future, for it is there that we shall spend the rest of our lives. And the best way to meet it is to start with the present.

> *Life is a story in volumes three,*
> *The Past,*
> *The Present,*
> *The Yet-to-be —*
> *That's up to me.*

The only good in thinking on the past is to use it as an anvil on which a better person may be hammered out. This was the usage the Apostle Paul made of it. In speaking of his past he said, "Many of the saints did I shut up in prison . . . and when they were put to death, I gave my voice against them" (Acts 26:10). We know the change he made.

Starting anew is the constant challenge of life. When we speak of a faulty past, a cleansed present, and a helpful future, this is what life is really all about. It is saying, "I'll make a man or a woman out of myself yet."

Doing Good

Who went about doing good. Acts 10:38

That is what all of us are to do. We should aim and strive to do good. The world needs it and we need to do it.

What are some of the main elements that go to make up such a fruitful life?

• *Sympathy is the starter.* First, we must have a heart that goes out to others. If this feeling is lacking, all is lacking. It can be cultivated. Let us cultivate it.

• *The cheerful, hopeful life is essential.* People who are unhappy and despondent repel rather than help. This broadens the distance between them and others and leaves them too far away to be of any service. They are not close enough to help. We need the live, optimistic, enchanting view of life. Let us look up and then we shall live up; live up, and then we shall lift up.

• *A pure life is required.* No thirsty traveler can be blessed by drinking from an impure river. We are made better by just being in the company of good people. A pure life exerts an influence. It is powerfully contagious, goes out to affect others.

• *Open eyes that see needs are necessary.* The needs are there in one form or other. But we can't see them unless we get our eyes off ourselves. "Lift up your eyes and look." Then lift a hand. We are commanded to work in the vineyard—do good. Not just sit there and eat grapes.

No matter what our calling in life may be, remember that our greatest calling is to do good. This makes a better world!

Selfishness Profanes the Dignity of Man

Charity [love] . . . seeketh not her own. I Corinthians 13:5

A ten-year-old was enjoying an all day sucker. His playmate who had none looked with craving eyes. Finally the playmate said, "When you're through let me have the stick for a lick."

"When I'm through licking there won't be a stick left," was the reply.

There are adults who, figuratively speaking, will lick a stick to nothing before they will let anyone else have any.

We profane the dignity of man when we're concerned only with self. The higher traits of personality — thoughtfulness, consideration, helpfulness, benevolence and peacefulness — manifest themselves toward others. The selfish, however, live on the basis that everything should come only to self, as the water of a river flows to the sea.

A person perverts the life God has given him and hurts himself when he is interested in only three persons: Me, Myself and I.

A TEA PARTY

I had a little tea party
This afternoon at three.
'Twas very small —
Three guests in all —
Just I, Myself and Me.

Myself ate all the sandwiches,
While I drank up the tea;
'Twas also I who ate the pie
And passed the cake to me.

We hear it said, "Every man for himself." How much better it would be to say, "Every man for God, for others, and for self."

No End to What Spite Will Do

Thou hast seen it; for thou beholdest mischief and spite.
Psalms 10:14

A few years ago I visited in Natchez, Mississippi, and took the Natchez Pilgrimage Tour. It was fascinating to go through the elegant houses of yesteryears. One thing I found especially interesting was a picture hanging in Governor Holmes' House, which was built in 1794. It wasn't the picture itself I found so engaging but rather the story behind it.

Keene Richard was married to a very young lady. They lived together for awhile and she died. Nine years later Mr. Richard married again. The story is that the family of his first and deceased wife had a large picture (perhaps 5-x-5) painted of the deceased woman. She had a very sad, forlorn look and a white rose penned to the bosom of her dress, sitting on a coffin. They gave this painting to his new bride as a wedding gift.

What was in the heart of the givers, we don't know for sure; but it surely bears the interpretation of spite. For it definitely would be a tool of annoyance and irritation.

Spite comes in every ugly form from embittered and hateful hearts. It is the spirit of getting even, though the offense may be only imaginary. It seeks to get even, although the cost is high. But there are some who are so hardened and determined that they are willing to pay any price to strike at the one they despise. They are willing to give up one of their eyes if it will knock out both eyes of the one they wish to hurt.

Oh, how much sweeter life is when one is motivated by the spirit of love that is kind, thinks no evil, and bears all things!

Life Gets Better Day by Day

For which cause we faint not; but though our outward man perish, yet the inward man is renewed day by day.

I Corinthians 4:16

In reply to congratulations on his 86th birthday, Sir William Mulock stated:

I am still at work, with my hand to the plow, and my face to the future. The shadows of evening lengthen about me, but morning is in my heart . . . I have had varied fields of labor and full contact with men and things, and have warmed both hands before the fire of life.

The best of life is always farther on. Its real lure is hidden from our eyes somewhere beyond the Hills of Time.

The Bible pays a beautiful tribute to age: "The beauty of old men is the gray head" (Proverbs 20:29). "Days should speak, and multitude of years should teach wisdom" (Job 32:7). This is due to the lessons learned from rest and labor, health and illness, achievement and disappointment, ease and struggle, peace and war, sowing and reaping. They have experienced life in every form; they have seen the best of days and the worst of days.

The most adorable and lovely people in the world are those who have been mellowed and softened by the passing of many years. They radiate kindness and consideration, calmness and tranquility, knowledge and wisdom. Their lives have had double portions of laughter and tears, joy and triumph, heartbreak and ecstasy, and each has done its part in the enrichment process of forming a strong and noble character. And now, seasoned and matured by years of experience, they are living in their Golden Years. Look the world over for beauty, and you will find none greater than this.

The Goat Ate His Speech

I was dumb with silence, I held my peace, even from good; and my sorrow was stirred. Psalms 39:2

At a Vacation Bible School a special program was planned for the last day. All classes would meet in the auditorium. Parents were invited to this special event. Children who had shown outstanding talent were invited to recite. However, the morning of the program the minister received this note from a distraught mother: "Dear Preacher: I'm sorry Henry will not be able to be on the program. The goat ate his speech. Since the speech was very religious, my only consolation is we may have a better goat."

The goat got his speech. What is it that gets the speech of many adults and silences their tongue? Not the goat.

• *Could it be a lack of faith?* The Apostle Paul gave faith as the motivation, the compelling power, in his speaking: "We having the same spirit of faith, according as it is written, I believed, and therefore have I spoken; we also believe, and therefore speak" (II Corinthians 4:13). Deep convictions are anxious to speak out. When the fire of faith burns, then one speaks.

• *Could a lack of knowledge tie the tongue of some?* Feeling they are unknowledgeable, they decide not to say anything or only very little. They fear they might get in over their head. But any person with average ability can overcome this deficiency. Study will do it.

• *Could discouragement keep your tongue silent?* Be not dismayed. God's Word shall not return unto Him void, but shall accomplish what He pleases, and shall prosper in the thing whereto He sends it. If your words are His words, they will accomplish good, someway, somehow, somewhere, sometime. So take heart!

No Fear of Night

Thou shalt not be afraid for the terror by night.   Psalms 91:5

Night is feared because of crime. Under the protection of darkness more crimes are committed. However, it is not the night that brings danger but the ones who use it for cover.

Others fear the coming of night because of pain. A night of pain can be an eternity. But when the tired body calls for sleep the night is never long enough.

And others dread the night because of restlessness. They spend it in the misery of tumbling, tossing and growing gray.

For some people night has its haunts because of conscience. In the stillness of the night a biting conscience bites deeply.

Many find the night frightening because, if awake, sight is so short; and, if asleep, they know they have no awareness of approaching danger. There is so much fear in night that Edward Young said, "By night an atheist half believes a God."

But night was meant to bless us. It even kisses the grass with a fresh sparkling dew — think how much more it does for man. It is a time to rest, relax, sleep, and regain strength for the challenges of another day. Even the cattle lie down for a night's repose. It is a time to gather home. Thomas Gray said:

> *The curfew tolls the knell of parting day,*
> *The lowing herd winds slowly o'er the lea,*
> *The plowman homeward plods his weary way,*
> *And leaves the world to darkness and to me.*

As the shades of darkness are drawn about us, there can be an immunity from the fear of night.

The Child Within Us Lives Again

When I was a child, I spake as a child, I understood as a child, I thought as a child: but when I became a man, I put away childish things. I Corinthians 13:11

A slender, wrinkled, gray-haired woman in her fifties looked worn down. On that rain-chilled morning she was on the bus going to her job at the laundry. She looked terribly tired and in need of a little encouragement. No doubt, life had been hard for her.

Then suddenly out of the clouds and dampness of the day a thing happened. A station wagon had stopped in the halted lane next to the woman's window. A little girl, probably three, very cute and beautifully dressed, looked up out of that station wagon into that lonely woman's face. The little girl smiled and waved. The woman smiled and with a hand of honest toil waved back. The child was delighted and so was the woman. The face of each radiated with gladness. The smiling and waving continued until the traffic started up again.

Later when the woman got off the bus there had been a renewal of spirit and rekindling of energy within her. Her burden had been made lighter and her eyes twinkled with a new gladness.

This sort of thing happens all the time between children and adults. There are those unspoken acts of sharing a little of each other, which enriches both. Even the usually glum and bored people quickly come alive when there is communication with a child. In such a moment we find renewal of spirit, because the child within us lives again.

Children want to play, the parents want to play; and both will be better off if the parent spends on the child half as much money and twice as much time.

Some Things That Help Us to Live Better

The righteous shall flourish like the palm tree: he shall grow like a cedar in Lebanon. Psalms 92:12

• *Reading the Bible has a cleansing effect.* "Now ye are clean through the word which I have spoken unto you" (John 15:3). It is the mirror of the soul and lets us see ourselves as we are, which is the first condition of any improvement.

• *Prayer is a bulwark against evil.* "Watch and pray, that ye enter not into temptation" (Matthew 26:41). More things have been wrought by prayer than the world knows.

• *The ability to see one's faults is helpful.* "And why beholdest thou the mote that is in thy brother's eye, but considerest not the beam that is in thine own eye?" (Matthew 7:3). No wonder some people have difficulty making improvement — they can't see their faults, only the faults of others.

• *Helping others lifts us higher.* The doer is actually blessed more than the recipient. "It is more blessed to give than to receive" (Acts 20:35). Lending a helping hand gives a feeling of usefulness and importance. It will enhance your self-image which will encourage you to be a better person. Some people are too down on themselves ever to lift themselves up.

• *Wholesome associates bring out our better side.* "Know ye not that a little leaven leaventh the whole lump?" (I Corinthians 5:6). May that leaven be beneficial. In the presence of some people it is easy to be good. It gives you a sweet smelling savor.

• *Reflecting on the brevity of life is sobering.* "Whereas ye know not what shall be on the morrow" (James 4:14). Whatever stature you wish to attain, start working on it now. For hours and flowers soon fade away.

What Money Will and Will Not Buy

*For wisdom is a defence, and money is a defence: but the ex-
cellency of knowledge is, that wisdom giveth life to them that
have it.* Ecclesiastes 7:12

Will buy an education, but not wisdom.

Will buy tuition, but not knowledge.

Will buy books, but not brains.

Will buy a house, but not a home.

Will buy a bed, but not sleep.

Will buy food, but not appetite.

Will buy clothes, but not a man to put in them.

Will buy medicine, but not health.

Will buy finery, but not beauty.

Will buy amusement, but not happiness.

Will buy gifts, but not love.

Will buy employees, but not loyalty.

Will buy electricity, but not spark for your personality.

Will buy attention, but not respect.

Will buy communication, but not character.

Will buy a fine funeral, but not eternal life.

Will buy some men, but not God.

Will buy a lot of earth, but none of heaven.

While money has its values (also the possibility of liabilities),
it will not buy the most valuable needs of man. Such benefits
must be obtained otherwise and through other means.

Like a Parachute

And he said, How can I except some man should guide me? And
he desired Philip that he would come up and sit with him.
Acts 9:31

The above Scripture concerns the Ethiopian Treasurer. It is very evident he had an open mind.

The Justice of the Peace in a little town made preparations to go on vacation. His final act was to hang a sign on his office door: "Closed. But My Mind Is Still Open."

It's unique thinking like this that gets a man re-elected. Not only should the judge have an open mind, it should be true of all of us. We are the jurors. In the everyday affairs of life we hand down the decisions on ourselves. How tragic if the mind is closed and denies us the fulfillment of the possibilities within us.

Many boast of an open mind when it's only a vacant space. Others think they have an open mind when it's only an elastic conscience. The easiest way to build an undeserved reputation for having an open mind is never to think, just nod approval to everything the other fellow suggests. Obviously, this is not an open mind — just no mind. In such a case another sign should be hung out: "Closed for Repairs." The open mind examines and weighs a matter, free of prejudice and bias, and then decides what is true and right.

Many years ago our government wanted to develop the West, so it offered free lands for development. The greatest undeveloped territory in the world, however, is not the West, East, North or South; it's under our own hats, but can't be developed unless it is open.

Keep youd mind open — a piece of knowledge might enter. The mind is like a parachute. It operates only when it is open.

Can God Furnish a Table?

Yea, they spake against God; they said, Can God furnish a table in the wilderness? Psalms 78:19

Pessimism! The gloomy view!

A visiting minister was looking at the farmer's hogs. The preacher remarked, "Those are the finest hogs I've ever seen. You have enough meat standing there to feed your family two or three years."

"Yes, I know," replied the pessimistic farmer, "but only the Lord knows what's going to happen to us after that."

> 'Twixt optimist and pessimist
> The difference is droll,
> The optimist sees the doughnut,
> While the pessimist sees the hole.

The optimist's attitude is a stimulant; the pessimist's attitude is a tranquilizer. The optimist sees a tiny flickering flame of light; but the pessimist, when he hears of it, runs and throws water on it. An optimist thinks there will be a parking space in the next block; a pessimist thinks he will have a wreck before he gets there. An optimist makes the best of it when he gets the worst of it, but the pessimist makes the worst of it when he gets the best of it. The optimist enjoys his journey on the sea of life, but the pessimist stays seasick the entire trip.

Obviously, the wages of optimism are joy and success; and just as manifestly, the wages of pessimism are despair and failure.

I like what W. L. Phelps said, "I am an optimist because I believe in God. Those who have no faith are quite naturally pessimistic and I do not blame them."

Underneath the Stone

There is that maketh himself rich, yet hath nothing: there is that maketh himself poor, yet hath great riches. Proverbs 13:7

There is an age-old story involving a very rich man — materially and spiritually — who lived in a big house on a hill overlooking a village. He had become rich because he had been diligent in labor and thrift. Many others who had the same opportunities were poor. He and they illustrated Solomon's guideline on prosperity: "He becometh poor that dealeth with a slack hand: but the hand of the diligent maketh rich" (Proverbs 10:14).

Nevertheless, he tried to help them: planted trees, set up a park, did much for the children at Christmas, gave handouts, lent money, and worked to provide jobs.

One day the rich man got up early in the morning and placed a large stone in the middle of the road near his house. Then he hid behind the hedge to see what would happen. Later a poor man leading a horse came along. He raged, walked around the stone, and went on his way. Then a farmer came next. He ranted, drove around it, and went on his business. The day passed. Many had come, but did nothing to help.

At last, at nightfall, an old man came. He said to himself: "Somebody may fall over this stone in the night and get hurt. I will move it out of the way." Being thin and weak, he had to tug and tug, push and pull to get it moved. To his surprise, there lay a bag of gold underneath with this note: "This gold belongs to the one who moves this stone."

While gold is valuable, our greatest enrichment is what we do for others: rolling stones out of their way, lifting them up, pointing them to a better life.

The Bible Lives

Heaven and earth shall pass away, but my words shall not pass away. Matthew 24:35

The Bible lives. Century follows century — yet it lives. Empires rise and fall and are forgotten — yet it lives. Kings, dictators, presidents come and go — yet it lives. Hated, despised, cursed — yet it lives. Scoffed at by scorners — yet it lives. Despised and torn to pieces — yet it lives. Misunderstood and misrepresented — yet it lives. Abandoned by unbelief — yet it lives. Atheists rail against it — yet it lives. The Bible is the anvil that has withstood the constant blows of unbelievers.

THE ANVIL

Last eve I passed the blacksmith's door,
    And heard the anvil ring the vesper chime;
Then looking on, I saw upon the floor
    Old hammers worn with use in former time.
"How many anvils have you had?" said I,
    "To wear and batter all those hammers so?"
"Just one," said he; then said, with twinkling eyes,
    "The anvil wears the hammers out, you know."
And so, I thought, the anvil of God's Word
    For ages skeptic blows have beat upon;
Yet though the noise of falling blows was heard,
    The anvil is unharmed, the hammers gone.

Short but Potent

They think that they shall be heard for their much speaking.
Matthew 6:7

The richest treasures come in small amounts. Now let us see if we can get some powerful lessons out of some short statements.

- A smile has face value in every land.
- The way to get rid of a past is to get a future out of it.
- Blessed is he whose calendar has a Lord's Day in it.
- Every ending can be a new beginning.
- Money can feed you but not make you.
- The church is not a convention — don't send a delegate.
- Every day brings a clean page.
- A hungry soul may abide in a well-fed body.
- There is a difference between a home and a filling station.
- Some so-called open minds are open to everything.
- Don't argue — discuss.
- Redeeming the past enriches the future.
- One of the most useless things on earth is an excuse.
- A purchased friend never lasts.
- A diamond is a chunk of coal that stuck to its job.
- Grumblers, like Satan, take no vacation.
- Sapwood character makes poor building material.
- Tarry before you marry.
- Opportunity to do good is an opportunity to be good.
- Before passing judgment on the sermon try it out in practice.
- The war that will end war will not be fought with guns.
- The world at its best is man at his best.
- Almighty God cannot be exhausted.

Be Courteous

Finally, be ye all of one mind, having compassion one of another; love as brethren, be pitiful, be courteous. I Peter 3:8

My father taught me many valuable lessons as I grew up, working in a general merchandise store. One was: "Son, if others are rude, you don't have to stoop to their level. Be courteous. In the first place, it's right; in the second place, it keeps us in business."

> *IDENTIFY ME*
>
> *I come only from the well-bred.*
> *I am found in hovel and palace.*
> *I make faces smile and hearts warm.*
> *I unlock doors that rudeness has closed.*
> *I ease tensions and smooth relationships.*
> *I disarm enemies and make friends.*
> *I overcome prejudice.*
> *I am praised by many and condemned by none.*
> *I am little but produce big results.*
> *I cost nothing.*
> *I am COURTESY.*

So even common sense says, "Be not savage, cruel and rude." The impolite make life hard for themselves. They go out and butt heads when courtesy would often spare them the head-knocking ordeal. After all, we're not goats.

Rudeness is no hinge on which doors open. Neither is it a bridge that spans the difference between people. It is acid from which people pull back.

However, courtesy is the universal language appreciated on every shore and in every clime. Speak it! Speak it! And you'll be heard.

Corn on the Cob

And God said, Behold, I have given you every herb bearing seed, which is upon the face of all the earth, and every tree, in the which is the fruit of a tree yielding seed; to you it shall be for meat. Genesis 1:29

We were enjoying a very delicious meal, my wife and I and our five year old son, Paul. One of the dishes was corn on the cob, tender, sweet and juicy.

After Paul's corn disappeared like a train going through a tunnel, he passed his plate and said, "Will you put some more corn on my cob, please?"

This kind of talk is natural for a child. But what about us adults? Have we really forgotten who put the corn on the cob? And a thousand other things God has done for us?

In this age of expanding development, it's easy — if we are not thoughtful — to forget how much the Creator has done for us and how wholly dependent we are on Him.

Man plants but God gives the increase.

We can do much in appropriating and changing the created, but there our work ends. We can't start with nothing. We can't create. We are still human, and God is still God. As long as we can make this distinction there is hope for us.

We have come a long way. But from where? Name it and it will be a place God has given. And where are we going? Wherever it is, God is there. "Whither shall I go from thy Spirit? or whither shall I flee from thy presence?" (Psalms 139:7). His handiwork is stamped on everything we behold. He's still giving us corn on the cob.

Let Us Be Glad

The Lord hath done great things for us; whereof we are glad. Psalms 126:3

A friend suggested that we go to a gospel meeting in a neighboring city, and *I was glad.* "I was glad when they said unto me, Let us go into the house of the Lord" (Psalms 122:1).

• *Belief in the God of Forgiveness fills the heart with joy.* To Him we say, "Forgive us our debts." We need the slate wiped out. We need to start again. It makes for gladness.

• *Thanksgiving produces gladness.* You can find delight in counting your blessings. Most people in the world would be very happy to have what you have.

• *Commitment to a great and meaningful cause gives rise to gladness.* "I will very gladly spend and be spent," stated the Apostle Paul. Some people have nothing that really holds their interest and challenges them. Get involved.

• *Seeing a friend makes the heart glad.* "And when he seeth thee, he will be glad in his heart" (Exodus 4:14). The fellowship of kindred spirits is a delightful experience.

• *Additionally, gladness comes from confident living.* You can't be unhappy while you believe everything will turn out all right. Trust the Power greater than you. Learn to say, "I know whom I have believed."

• *Furthermore, hope will make your heart glad.* It has for all peoples through all the years, including the Psalmist who said, "I have set the Lord always before me . . . therefore my heart is glad . . . my flesh also shall rest in hope (Psalms 16:8,9). In His hand is the whole earth and for this reason we are glad, though there must be some sorrow.

Rock of Ages

From the end of the earth will I cry unto thee, when my heart is overwhelmed: lead me to the rock that is higher than I. For thou hast been a shelter for me. Psalms 61:2,3

This hymn, written by A. M. Toplady, was first published in 1775. One day when Toplady was walking in rocky terrain, he was hit by a severe thunderstorm. Seeking refuge, he could find nothing but a big split in the granite rock. He climbed into the narrow cleft and was sheltered from the storm. As lightning flashed and the thunder roared, he composed in his mind the words of this hymn. On arriving home he wrote down the verses. He died at the early age of thirty-eight, but the hymn he wrote will live forever.

Rock of Ages, cleft for me,
Let me hide myself in Thee;
Let the water and the blood,
From Thy riven side which flowed,
Be of sin the double cure,
Cleanse me from its guilt and power.

Not the labors of my hands
Can fulfil Thy law's demands;
Could my zeal no respite know,
Could my tears forever flow,
All for sin could not atone,
Thou must save, and Thou alone.

While I draw this fleeting breath,
When mine eyelids close in death,
When I rise to worlds unknown,
See Thee on Thy judgment throne,
Rock of Ages, cleft for me,
Let me hide myself in Thee.

Self-Love Is Essential

Thou shalt love thy neighbor as thyself.
Matthew 22:39

For a person to love others properly he or she must first love self rightly. Of course, the correct balance must be kept. In teaching against an imbalance, it is unfortunate that love for self has been attacked when it is actually a virtue essential to self-preservation. It is only a perversion of loving self that is wrong.

As seen in the above Scripture, the Second Commandment of the Law is based on self-love. This is proof that self-love when linked with a love for others is not evil.

A principal reason some people are so bitter toward humanity is they don't like themselves. It stands to reason that no one can love another when he does not even like himself.

Hence, it is fitting that we point out some of the fundamentals in learning to love self, which are as follows:

- See ourselves as the object of God's love, a creature worth loving.
- Expect of ourselves only that which is reasonable.
- Refuse to compare ourselves with other people.
- Accept ourselves as we are.
- Keep a clear conscience.
- Have the gratification of doing the best we can.
- Be the kind of persons we can be proud of.

All of this encourages self-respect and self-love, and then the person is ready to love humanity.

Joining Hands

We then, as workers together with him. II Corinthians 6:1

There is an intriguing story that emphasizes the absolute necessity of working together. A big can of paint, already mixed and waiting in the garage, said, "I'm going to paint the house."

The paintbrush bristled with displeasure and stormed, "No you won't, I'm going to paint it."

"Oh, you think you are?" snorted the ladder, which stood against the wall. "How far would either of you get without me?"

Just then the painter who overheard these self-centered remarks put in a word. "Perhaps I'd better go on vacation. I wonder if the house would be painted by the time I get back."

Let us remember that even the most efficient of us is only a tool in the hands of the Infinite Worker.

God does many things in which people have no part: Lifts the clouds, reddens the sunsets, keeps the stars in their orbits, sends the showers and the sunshine, sprouts the seeds, gives the seasons, paints the roses and lilies and perfumes them with their fragrance.

But there are other things just as beautiful and great in which He permits us to be His co-workers. By working with Him we have a part in putting the attractive tints and sweet savor on human souls. What a distinct honor to be a co-worker with God in transforming lives; in dispelling darkness and despair; in bringing light, purpose and happiness to human souls; in making known a cure for misery and sin! It is not our accumulation of wealth or attainment in society, but our service to others that is the real test of greatness.

Helpers or Honkers?

*If ye be come peaceably unto me to help me, mine heart shall
be knit unto you.* I Corinthians 12:17

A woman driver had the misfortune of having her car to
stall in heavy traffic. Furthermore, she could not get it started.
A man in the car behnd her expressed his impatience by blow-
ing his horn every few seconds. Finally, the perturbed and
shaken lady got out of the car, walked to the honker's car and
said, "I'm having difficulty starting my car. I'll make you this
proposition: if you'll try to start my car for me, I'll honk your
horn for you."

There are a lot more honkers than helpers. The reason —
it is easier to honk than to help, to talk than to work, to
criticize than to assist.

If you really want to help your fellow-man, lift a hand —
and that includes off the horn.

When we are stalled out there on life's highway, we are indeed thankful that God does not blow a horn at us. Instead,
He helps us. In recognition of His help, the Psalmist said, "My
help cometh from the Lord, which made heaven and earth. He
will not suffer thy foot to be moved: he that helpeth thee will
not slumber" (Psalms 121:2,3).

With deep appreciation we sing:

> *When other helpers fail, and comforts flee,*
> *Help of the helpless, O abide with me.*

We Receive in Kind

Judge not, and ye shall not be judged: condemn not, and ye shall not be condemned: forgive, and ye shall be forgiven: give, and it shall be given unto you." Luke 6:37,38

An attorney, a C.P.A. and I appeared before the Securities and Exchange Commission in Washington in behalf of a company in which I was interested. We met with three government attorneys who represented the Commission. At first they were the coldest, most unresponsive trio I had ever seen. Icicles formed from their breath. Nevertheless, we kept talking, suggesting, reasoning and probing, and all the time we kept completely cool, considerate, kind and courteous. After about three hours of our warmth and their coldness, they opened up and were the kindest and most helpful group you could ever want.

The next day when our business was completed (and we got everything we asked), as we were getting ready to leave, I said, "If you don't mind, out of curiosity, I would like to ask you a question."

"Go ahead."

"The first three hours you were so cold, and then you became so warm and helpful. What made the difference?"

"I'll tell you," one replied, "we were in a meeting in Houston last week, and some of those big Texans lost their temper, cursed us all out and told us to get back to Washington. We didn't know what to expect of you."

That's the way life is — kindness begets kindness; and kindness has won more triumphs than logic. This being true, you can be good to yourself by being good to others.

Bring on the Refreshments

The Lord give mercy unto the house of Onesiphorus; for he oft refreshed me, and was not ashamed of my chain.

II Timothy 1:16

After Paul became a prisoner in Rome, there was a special friend who sought him and refreshed him. His name was Onesiphorus. One thing that was especially refreshing was that this friend was not ashamed of Paul now that he was in jail. Paul, being only human, must have wearied in soul. What is so refreshing as the presence of a kind and sympathetic friend? We can imagine the words of sympathy, cheer, and hopefulness spoken by the free man to the prisoner.

How refreshing to one in trouble is a sympathetic friend. It lets the troubled person know that someone cares. Just the presence of some people is very rejuvenating. They don't have to say or do much. What they are and the affinity we have with them is refreshing like the morning air. Their unwavering faith and abiding love lift our drooping spirits.

Hundreds of years ago the Moors occupied Granada in Spain. Their empire has fallen. Their palaces have crumbled into dust. But there are the irrigating rivulets which they created. Today there is a murmuring music of those beautiful streams. The men who dug them are gone; but those refreshing streams continue telling their own story and doing their own work.

So let us cut channels through that refreshments may flow into the world's prisons—prisons of iron bars, and also the prisons of loneliness, disappointment, illness, bereavement, failure, sin and guilt. After we are gone they will keep on flowing. For good never dies. And those who drink will be refreshed.

Together in Marriage

Therefore shall a man leave his father and his mother, and shall cleave unto his wife: and they shall be one flesh. Genesis 2:24

This refers to our early parents Adam and Eve. Centuries have passed but it still constitutes the sweetest and most helpful, human relationship in all the world. The togetherness of it makes each stronger. Solomon has aptly stated: "Two are better than one" (Ecclesiastes 4:9). Let today bring what it will, a couple standing together, hand in hand, can handle it.

Fifty years since we launched our craft
To sail life's sea with each other;
We have kept the faith, we have held to the vow
As sweethearts— as father and mother.

There have been bonnie breezes most of the way,
We have had more sunshine than sorrows;
And if sometimes dark clouds have covered the sky,
They were followed by sunlit tomorrows.

Then more happy years to us, husband and wife,
Companions so tender and true;
Through fair and foul weather may we both sail together
To the Heavenly Harbor whose waters are blue.

Marriage is the end of a quest. Not the beginning of a conquest. Nor an inquest.

"Marriage is honorable in all" (Hebrews 13:4). Hence, marriage was designed to be an honorable estate, and even more — an entrance into a holy of holies.

The Candle Is Burning

Do this now, my son. Proverbs 6:3

A young man in training for the ministry was asked: "What are you now doing to make the world better?"

He replied, "Oh, I'm a student."

"Well," continued the questioner, "when you light a candle, do you light it to make the candle more comfortable, or that it may give light?"

"To give light" was the answer.

The inquirer then asked, "Do you expect it to give light after it is half burned, or when you first light it?"

He replied, "As soon as I light it."

"Very well" was the reply. "Go and do likewise. Begin at once."

Your life is a burning candle. Don't let it burn up in vain. Start shining now. Start living now. Start enjoying life now. Start reaching for your goals now.

Procrastination is the art of letting today vainly become yesterday. It is not one of the finer arts. By and by never becomes well done.

We can spend a lifetime just waiting for a better day. Every day is the best day of the year. More people fail for doing nothing than for doing wrong.

Go ahead and delay if you wish, but time will not tarry. At this very moment the candle is burning. Tomorrow there will be a little less.

Guidelines to Cope With Problems

My soul is weary of my life. Job 10:1

Guidelines from the immortal Twenty-third Psalm:

• *Approach your problem with the positive attitude* that you, with the help of the Good Shepherd, have the power and efficiency to handle it. Never underrate yourself. Never give way to the defeating negatives of "I can't." Rather, learn to say, "I shall not want" (Psalms 23:1).

• *Believe your waning strength can be restored.* Everyone gets tired and weary; and in this state it is easy to feel that you are no match for the problem. But take courage — your vigor can be restored; give yourself a little time and your force can build up again. "He restoreth my soul" (Psalms 23:3).

• *Be fearless in facing your difficulty.* "Cowards die many times before their death." Really, there's nothing to fear but fear itself. Jesus said to the disciples, "Arise, and be not afraid." Times and circumstances have changed, but He has not. "I will fear no evil" (Psalms 23:4).

• *Find fortitude in that you do not have to walk alone.* There are friends, members of the family and even the Lord to walk with you. "Thou art with me" (Psalms 23:4).

• *Affirm that your enemies, oppositions — things or people — cannot keep you from prospering.* "Thou preparest a table before me in the presence of mine enemies" (Psalms 23:5).

• *Believe that goodness shall accompany you.* There is much more goodness than badness for you; moreover, benefits can evolve from what you think at the time is dreadful. Rely on this assurance, "Surely goodness and mercy shall follow me all the days of my life" (Psalms 23:6).

She Insisted We Go to Church

Not forsaking the assembling of ourselves together, as the manner of some is; but exhorting one another: and so much the more, as ye see the day approaching. Hebrews 10:25

When I was away at college I returned to be with my mother who was to have serious surgery in a town thirty miles from home. As you perhaps know, any surgery back then was considered much more dangerous than now. Even today the prevailing view seems to be: "Any surgery I have is serious; any you have is minor."

The doctors set the time for her operation at 10:30 Sunday morning. That was church time in that town. My father, sister and brother-in-law were also there.

Would we go to church or skip it? We didn't have to answer the question. My mother answered it. She insisted that we leave her there alone and go on to church. She said, "I'll be all right; if not, there's nothing you could do anyway. Furthermore, if you honor God by worshiping Him, your prayers in my behalf might have a better chance of getting through."

We honored her — and God — by going to church. When we got back to the hospital the surgery was still in progress and everything was going well. After a few days she was able to go home. No other trouble has ever resulted from that operation.

I'm not saying there are never times when we should miss church. But I am saying that the command to assemble and worship is often broken too lightly. Over all, my mother's view would have to be held in great esteem and high respect. Her view has never emptied a church building and let it die a slow death. That which strengthens individuals and builds the church is not to be faulted.

Take No Chances

The devil, as a roaring lion, walketh about, seeking whom he may devour. I Peter 5:8

"Don't be afraid," said a mother to her little boy at a museum, "the lion is stuffed."

"Maybe so," responded the lad, "but he still might find enough room for a little boy like me."

He was taking no chances.

The boy's caution is actually good theology — and good sense. For the Bible says, "Resist the devil, and he will flee from you. Draw night to God, and he will draw nigh to you."

A man who decided to whip his alcohol problem quit parking his car in front of the liquor store. Instead, he began parking it down the street. He was taking no chances.

A wealthy man years ago wanted to hire a driver for his carriage. He tested some for the job. They were asked to drive over a narrow road which had been cut into the side of a mountain, leaving a dangerous cliff on the side. One driver drove as close to the edge as he could to show his skill. The next one hugged the bank, staying as far away from the edge as possible. Which one got the job? The one who took no chances.

Practicing safety is a matter of good sense. It is not wise to see how close you can get to evil without partaking. It is safer to heed this Biblical command:

Abstain from all appearance of evil. I Thessalonians 5:22

Safety lies in being cautious. There is no safety in skating on thin ice.

Singing in the Rain

Behold the fowls of the air. Matthew 6:26

A sweet and smart woman who had suffered several long months in painful illness said to her minister, "I have a lovely robin that sings outside my window. As I lie here in the early morning, he serenades me." As her face brightened, she continued, "I love him because he sings in the rain."

This is attractive and winning behavior on the part of the robin. And distinctive. When the storm silences nearly all other song birds, the robin sings on — sings on in the rain.

Here is a lesson for us humans to learn. Anybody can sing in the sunshine. But we need to learn to sing in the midnight hour or when the clouds are pouring out their rains.

Because a company was folding, an employee of several years lost his job. His comment was, "Best thing that ever happened to me. This will force me to get out and get a better job." He was singing in the rain.

A tornado destroyed a farmer's house. He reacted with this expression of gratitude and assurance: "Thank God no one was hurt. Now we will build a bigger and better home." He was singing in the rain.

A superintendent for an oil company in Texas suffered the loss of a hand from an accidental gunshot. He commented, "I can do more with one hand than most men can do with two." He was singing in the rain.

As a mother's baby lay cold in death, she said, "I can't see why it happened. But God can see down the stream of time where I can't see. I will keep on walking by faith." She was singing in the rain.

Human and Divine Rules

Let us walk by the same rule, let us mind the same thing.
Philippians 3:16

There are many rules in life — some human, some divine. We have no qualms in altering human rules if it is for the betterment. For example, some of the old rules of English grammar are giving way to change.

In mockery of the sometimes clumsy rule of not ending a sentence with a preposition, Berton Braley has written:

> *The grammar has a rule absurd*
> *Which I call an outworn myth:*
> *"A preposition is a word*
> *You mustn't end a sentence with!"*

And in the same spirit of scorn, Winston Churchill said, "This is the sort of English up with which I will not put."

But the divine rules remain as fresh, as relevant, and as needful as ever. They are as up to date as tomorrow. For they were given for the good of man, and his needs have not changed. For instances, look at these rules:

- *Golden* — "Therefore all things whatsoever ye would that men do to you, do ye even so to them" (Matthew 6:12).

- *Bible Study* — "Ye shall not add unto the word which I command you, neither shall ye diminsh ought from it" (Deuteronomy 4:2).

- *Sovereignty* — "Thou shalt worship the Lord thy God, and him only shalt thou serve" (Matthew 4:10)

- *Priorities* — "But seek ye first the kingdom of God, and his righteousness" (Matthew 6:33).

Temporary Togetherness

Let both grow together until the harvest: and in the time of harvest I will say to the reapers, Gather ye together first the tares, and bind them in bundles to burn them: but gather the wheat into my barn. Matthew 13:30

A responsible, hard-working farmer sowed good seed in his field. But while he slept, his enemy slipped in and sowed tares among the wheat. This presented a challenging problem. For when the blades sprang up, then appeared the tares also. His workers asked permission to go into the field and gather up the foul plants. But the wise farmer, willing to put up with the vicious vexation for the sake of the valuable vantage, said, "No, lest while you gather up the tares, you root up also the wheat with them. Let both grow together until harvest and then gather the tares and burn them, but gather the wheat into my barn."

This is the greatest story ever told on the topic of tolerance. It was related by Jesus. It was one of His parables and was narrated to illustrate how His people should behave in His kingdom. "Let both grow together until the harvest" — this sums up tolerance in a peaceful, practical manner.

Of all things, religion should not be a monstrous freak that breathes out of one lung the spirit of tolerance and out the other the spirit of persecution.

We are not asked for a toleration that throws God's Bible at the Devil's feet. That's not toleration. That's compromise. Truth is not negotiable, but we can still behave as a civilized people.

He Needs a Funnybone

Ye blind guides, which strain at a gnat, and swallow a camel. Matthew 23:24

This is humor in its purest sense. It may shock some always-somber-never-smile people to learn that it came from Jesus Christ. Think what a cartoonist could do with the idea. Portray a person straining a gnat and then drinking down a camel. It is so ridiculous that it is funny.

In discussing Brother Sober Face, one man suggested that he was direly in need of special surgery.

"How's that?"

"He needs a funnybone implanted up his sleeve," was the answer.

Certainly, there are times when we need to be somber. But just as certainly, there are times when we need to laugh. "A time to weep, and a time to laugh" comes from a better psychologist than any of us — Solomon (Ecclesiastes 3:4).

Humor is a relaxer for the mind, an antidote for depression, a load-lightener for burdened hearts and a road to serenity.

Abraham Lincoln — the great President of Civil War days — said, "With the fearful strain that is on me night and day, if I did not laugh I should die."

Thus it is readily seen why the person of humor never has to want for an audience. This vexed world is looking for something to dry a tear and spread a smile. Laugh and the world does more than laugh with you — it gathers around you.

Think of what America would be like, if there were no humor; our country would be just one big cemetery.

A Common Bug

Let no man deceive you with vain words. Ephesians 5:6

Two college freshmen thought one day that they would play a joke on their science professor. They caught a grasshopper, a beetle, a butterfly and a centipede, and from these creatures they made a strange, composite insect. They took the centipede's body, the butterfly's wings, the beetle's head and the grasshopper's legs, and they glued them together carefully. Next, with their new bug in a box, they knocked at the professor's office door.

"We caught this bug in a field," they said. "Can you tell us, doctor, what kind it is?"

The scientist looked at the bug and then looked at the students. He smiled slightly.

"Did it hum when you caught it?" he asked.

"Yes," they answered, nudging one another.

"Then," said the professor, "it is a humbug."

One of the common bugs afflicting our society is *humbug.* Its bite is painful and humiliating. Humbuggery is never good for anybody. Not for the humbugger — at first it is sweet bread but later it is gravel in the mouth. Neither is it good for the deceived — it is annoyingly painful to feel that you have been taken.

Here is some Biblical and ever-timely advice: "Take heed that ye be not deceived." To keep from being deceived, never make spur of the moment decisions, investigate, compare, turn it over and take a look from the bottom side, be not swayed by inconsequential matters, seek counsel, and remember — not all's gold that glitters.

Love of Home

And they went unto their own home. I Samuel 2:20

Be it ever so humble, there's no place like home; for it is there that the great are small and the small are great. Some of the world's most famous men and women have risen from the humblest origins. It is fitting, therefore, that we remember the words of Daniel Webster:

"It is only shallow-minded pretenders who make . . . obscure origin a matter of personal reproach.

"It did not happen to me to be born in a log-cabin; but my elder brothers and sisters were born in a log-cabin, raised among the snowdrifts of New Hampshire. When the smoke first rose from its rude chimney, there was no similar evidence of a white man's habitation between it and the settlements on the rivers of Canada.

"Its remains still exist; I make it an annual visit. I carry my children to it, to teach them the hardships endured by the operations which have gone before them. I love to dwell on the tender recollections, the kindred ties, the early affections and the touching narratives and incidents which mingle with all I know of this primitive family abode.

"I weep to think that none of those who inhabited it are now among the living; and if ever I am ashamed of it, or if ever I fail in affectionate veneration for him who reared it and defended it against savage violence and destruction, cherished all the domestic virtues beneath its roof, and, through the fire and blood of seven years' revolutionary war, shrank from no danger, no toil, no sacrifice, to serve his country and to raise his children to a condition better than his own, may my name and the name of my posterity be blotted forever from the memory of mankind!"

Leave the World Better Than You Found It

For the children ought not to lay up for the parents, but the parents for the children. II Corinthians 12:14

Each generation should lay up and do for the next. Whatever parents do for their children, those children should do for their own children. It makes for society's improvement. This constructive principle has been tenderly and graphically expressed in the popular poem:

THE BRIDGE BUILDER

An old man going a lone highway
Came at evening, cold and gray,
To a chasm vast and wide and steep,
With waters rolling cold and deep.

The old man crossed in the twilight dim,
The sullen stream had no fears for him;
But he turned when safe on the other side,
And built a bridge to span the tide.

"Old man," said a fellow pilgrim near,
"You are wasting your strength with building here.
You've crossed the chasm, deep and wide,
Why build you this bridge at eventide?"

The builder lifted his old gray head.
"Good friend, in the path I have come," he said,
"There followeth after me today
A youth whose feet must pass this way.

"The chasm that was as nought to me,
To that fair-haired youth may a pitfall be;
He, too, must cross in the twilight dim —
Good friend, I am building this bridge for him."

If all followed this philosophy, the world could never get worse. It would always get better.

Think about the bridges you can build. Even small ones help.

Man's Birthright

And God blessed them, and God said unto them, Be fruitful, and multiply, and replenish the earth, and subdue it: and have dominion over the fish of the sea, and over the fowl of the air, and over every living thing that moveth upon the earth. And God said, Behold, I have given you every herb bearing seed, which is upon the face of all the earth, and every tree, in the which is the fruit of a tree yielding seed; to you it shall be for meat. And to every beast of the earth, and to every fowl of the air, and to every thing that creepeth upon the earth, wherein there is life, I have given every green herb for meat: and it was so. And God saw everything that he had made, and, behold, it was very good. Genesis 1:28-31.

The passage makes known the fitting birthright that was given man in that early day by his Creator. It is man's charter for the possession of the earth.

It is God's commission for man to utilize for his necessities, comfort and enjoyment the immense resources of the earth, by agriculture productions, by mining operations, by scientific discoveries, by mechanical inventions and by manufacturing aids. The whole earth with all its boundless opportunities is the heritage of man. It is his right to use the earth and to be blessed by it.

And as the Scripture says, it is something God looked upon as being *good*. And what God calls *good*, no man should call *bad*. Of course, any good thing can be perverted and misused, but this does not indict the constitutional goodness of it.

Material Duty

But if any provide not for his own, and specially for those of his own house, he hath denied the faith, and is worse than an infidel. I Timothy 5:8

That's God's brief on material duty. Very stern! But very right! So there is something worse than infidelity — financial irresponsibility. The God of all justice will not join hands with the freeloader. He rather says, "If any would not work, neither should he eat" (II Thessalonians 3:10). Of course, this Scripture does not apply to the old, the decrepit and the sickly.

God meant for able-bodied people to work. His economic rule is: *No work, no eat.* An application of the Scripture would reduce the unemployment figure in a hurry.

In the light of the two above Scriptures, it is obvious that a praying tongue and irresponsible hands look a little ridiculous on the same human form. A true view of God never blinds a person to his obligation to care for his family. For it is every man's divinely given duty.

Fulfilling this duty, however, is not the whole of life. There are also spiritual duties. Jesus stated, "Man shall not live by bread alone, but by every word that proceedeth out of the mouth of God" (Matthew 4:4). However, *the passage does suggest that man does live by bread but not by bread only —* that's the point. Thus man has two needs — physical and spiritual — and one does not take the place of the other.

Work to Have

Let him labor . . . that he may have. Ephesians 4:28

Henry Ford said, "There will never be a system invented which will do away with the necessity of work."

God's plan *to get* is to *get with it* — work. The text states God's uniform and immutable condition for man to obtain material benefits — "let him labor."

Every handiwork of God bears the impress of the law of labor. The earth, the air and the water teem with laborious life. Life of every sort is busy working out the problem of its own existence. Nature never quits. Age after age it unceasingly pursues its course, which is a perpetual lesson on industry to man. The song of labor rings out from earth's thousand voices, saying *WORK*.

Therefore, let us not accuse nature. She is doing her job. Now it is our turn.

The very tenor of the Bible is that of work and industry. It is a workaday world we see in the Bible — not an idlers' circus. Of all books, lazy people ought not to go to the Bible for comfort. To the contrary, it strongly acclaims work and uncompromisingly holds idleness up to scorn.

> *This is the gospel of labor — ring it*
> *Ye bells of the kirk —*
> *The Lord of love came down from above*
> *to live with the men who work.*
> *This is the rose that he planted, here in*
> *the thorn-cursed soil;*
> *Heaven is blest with perfect rest, but*
> *the blessing of earth is toil.*

Henry Van Dyke

Honorable Sweat — and Essential

In the sweat of thy face shalt thou eat bread, till thou return unto the ground; for out of it wast thou taken: for dust thou art, and unto dust shall thou return. Genesis 3:19

A young man went into a business in Los Angeles and applied for a job; however, he really wanted a position instead of a job. The owner said, "Sorry, but I don't have enough work to keep another fellow busy."

"Sir," said the applicant, "I'm sure you have. You don't know what little work it takes to keep me busy."

That attitude was one of the causes of his down-and-out position. On the other hand, I saw an energetic man become affluent by starting out at the lowly task of seining and selling minnows. Lake Texoma had just been built and was attracting lots of fishermen. He went to the streams and seined minnows and sold them. It was so profitable that he built his own minnow farm of many acres of ponds and began raising them. His becoming well-to-do was no accident. It was the productivity of sound thinking and honorable sweat.

Life grants nothing to man except through hard work. All self-made people are hard workers. This is nature's way — and god is the creator of nature — and nature has the last say, which, in the language of God, proclaims: "The soul of the sluggard desireth, and hath nothing: but the soul of the diligent shall be made fat" (Proverbs 13:4).

The world is filled with opportunities, but the handle on every one of them is *work*, and there is no way to grab it unless you take hold of the handle.

An Explanation of Earth's Drudgery

Be strong, all ye people of the land, saith the Lord, and work:
for I am with you, saith the Lord of hosts. Haggai 2:4

The thought that lights up life's drudgery is that it has been appointed by God's wise providence. The discipline of drudgery can prepare us for greater and more responsible activities. This is seen in Joseph's going from the cruelties of the prison to the glories of the palace. If he had evaded the galling prison life, he would not have come in contact with Pharoah's servants who made it possible for him to become the second highest official in the nation.

While living through the harshness of drudgery, we cannot tell why God is exposing us to it. But perhaps there is a beneficial reason. It may be our schooling for better things ahead.

One thing sure, the faithful performance of unpleasant duties tends to form a nobler character. All that God wants of anyone is faithfulness. Not brilliance, not glamour, not publicity, but the careful and regular performance of common duties. To be "faithful in that which is least" will be rewarded as richly as to be "faithful in that which is much."

Furthermore, in every honest work, no matter how laborious and commonplace, we are fellow workers with God. It is for God to cause the golden grain to grow, but man must plant it, thresh it, grind it into flour, make the loaves and distribute them. Only in this manner can the people have their prayer answered when they cry, "Give us this day our daily bread."

As we go forth day by day to what might appear to be common work, it is inspiring to realize that God is our fellow worker. Hence, let us take up our work, fully aware of its importance and its possibilities for greater things.

The Diligent Hand

He becometh poor that dealeth with a slackhand: but the hand of the diligent maketh rich. Proverbs 10:4

Financial prosperity is the fruit of a diligent hand, a courageous heart and a persevering backbone. It is attained in spite of the call of the shade tree, the lure of loafing, and the temptation to take the easy road.

Like the kite, the person of self-made wealth has risen against the wind — not with it. As the kite is lifted by a little resistance, so is the gritty person. Yes, *success is valiant*, dauntless and at times almost lionhearted. *It's positive* — possesses a forward drive. *It's energetic* — knows the sweat of honest toil. *It's persevering* — refuses to quit.

The prosperous person picks the road lined with plenty instead of the one littered with penury.

He knows:

— *God gives the milk but not the bucket.*

— *Self do, self have.*

— *God helps them that help themselves.*

So he raises his hat to the past, takes off his coat to the present, and rolls up his sleeves to the future.

Diligence and hard work are entitled to greater rewards. Here is a just standard of remuneration: "The laborer is worthy of his hire" (Luke 10:7). More labor, more hire; less labor, less hire. No pains, no gains. This motive works well. And why shouldn't it? For it is Biblical. It is stimulating. It is fair.

Does Godliness Pay?

*Godliness is profitable unto all things, having promise of the life
that now is, and of that which is to come.* I Timothy 4:8

Religion is an appeal to common sense. It comes to us and asks us to accept it on the ground of self-interest, though it has other and higher grounds. Will it pay? It asks us to get our account books, to study the prices, to question the probabilities of profit and loss—what is gained and what is lost—and decide whether it will pay to buy it.

• *First, let us consider the question from the standpoint of this life.* Is godliness profitable for the present? Or does sin pay more? Unquestionably, sin has turned some once-fine people into poor, wretched wrecks. It has cost them character, happiness, love, a father's sleepless hours, a mother's broken heart, and their own broken dreams. Did it pay? "The way of the transgressor is hard."

But how about godliness? It is well established that it pays from a business standpoint. It makes a person honest, industrious and earnest. And these are three of the highest qualities for temporal advancement. Godliness enables a person to decide and to be firm. It gives him the conviction to say *yes* when he ought to say *yes*, and to say *no* when he ought to say *no*, and to mean it. As a general rule, godly homes are more pleasant and constructive than those that are not. Usually, the children are better fed, better protected, better trained, and even better loved.

It pays in joy. "That your joy may be full." Also, in peace of mind. "My peace give I unto you."

• *In the second place, it pays in the life which is to come.* He "shall reap life everlasting." There has to be *another life to give sense to* this one, or else the Creator's work would end in failure. Nothing permanent would be gained.

Vexations

Therefore I hated life; because the work that is wrought under the sun is grievous unto me: for all is vanity and vexation of spirit. Ecclesiastes 2:17

Grievous matters. Vexation of spirit.

The story has been told of some campers in Louisiana who were beseiged and tormented day and night by mosquitoes with electric drills and gnats with super wings. Finally, one of the campers with patience worn thin cried out in despair, "Lord, deliver us from these buzzing mosquitoes and dreadful gnats; we will take care of the alligators and wolves, ourselves."

We often find that we need more help for the little annoying trifles than for the knock-down problems.

Life is filled with irritations which try our serenity. The washing maching failed to drain. The garbage disposal won't work. The sewer stopped up. The vacuum cleaner threw dust and trash all over the floor. You stumbled into a table and knocked off a lamp and broke it. Your cherished antique plate fell and broke. Your car won't start. You had a flat tire. The paper boy continues to throw the paper in the flower bed. The boss changes your vacation time. You were overcharged on your groceries. The neighbor's dog gets in your yard and now you have fleas. Etc. Etc.

But you can live with it: For it's not the end of the world. Be determined to keep calm and unvexed. Pray — many victories are won in prayer. Read the Bible — God brings peace to tattered nerves. Realize it could have been worse. Count how much more you're blessed than battered. Smile — smiling people don't lose control.

Bible Rules of Business Success

*Beloved, I wish above all things that thou mayest prosper and
be in health, even as thy soul prospereth.* III John 2

• *Believe you can* — "I can" (Philippians 4:13). Your ship
won't come in unless you have the faith to send it out.

• *Work* — "In the sweat of thy face shalt thou eat bread,
till thou return unto the ground" (Genesis 3:19). No amount
of inspiration will succeed unless it is accompanied by
perspiration.

• *Be thrifty* — "Gather up the fragments that remain, that
nothing be lost" (John 6:12). There is no way to have by
wasting and destroying.

• *Be visionary* — "Where there is no vision, the people
perish" (Proverbs 29:18). This is essential to business survival
and growth. See the opportunity. Look ahead of the other
fellow.

• *Use wisdom* — "Be ye therefore wise as serpents, and
harmless as doves" (Matthew 10:16). To get ahead, use your
head. Think. Be analytical.

• *Be enthusiastic* — "Whatsoever thy hand findeth to do, do
it with thy might" (Ecclesiastes 9:10). Enthusiasm keeps you
charged.

• *Count the cost* — "For which of you, intending to build
a tower, sitteth not down first and counteth the cost, whether
he have sufficient to finish it" (Luke 14:28-30). Watch the
figures.

• *Watch the timing* — "Go to the ant . . . consider her ways
. . . provideth her meat in the summer, and gathereth her food
in the harvest" (Proverbs 6:6-8). Time is important.

When Success Turns to Failure

And he said, I will hide my face from them, I will see what their end shall be: for they are a very forward generation, children in whom is no faith. Deuteronomy 32:30

It's not how you begin life but how you end it that counts. Success can be appraised only backward; but life must be lived forward.

It has been reported that a group of the world's most successful financiers and industrialists met at a Chicago hotel in 1923. Those present were: The president of the New York Stock Exchange. The president of the Bank of International Settlement. The president of the largest independent steel company. A member of the President's Cabinet. The greatest wheat speculator. The head of the world's greatest monopoly.

Collectively, these wizard magnates controlled more wealth than the United States treasury had. For years magazines and newspapers printed thrilling stories of their success. They were held up as examples for youth to follow. Let's take a look twenty-five years later and see what had happened to them.

The president of the New York Stock Exchange, Richard Whitney, had been recently released from Sing Sing. The president of the Bank of International Settlement, Leon Fraser, had committed suicide. The president of the largest independent steel company, Charles Schwab, died penniless. The member of the President's Cabinet, Albert Fall, had been pardoned from prison so he could die at home. The greatest wheat speculator, Arthur Cutten, died abroad in poverty. The head of the world's greatest monopoly, Ivar Kreuger, committed suicide.

These men were able to make money for awhile, but they never learned how to live. So *Success* turned to failure.

If It Hadn't Helped

And now, brethren, I commend you to God, and to the word
of his grace, which is able to build you up, and to give you an
inheritance among all them which are sanctified.   Acts 20:32

An atheist who had been in a shipwreck was washed ashore
on an island of former cannibals. Walking inland, he came
across a native reading the Bible. "Why are you reading that
book?" snapped the atheist. "I guess the missionaries have
deceived you. Get rid of it. The Bible never did anyone any
good."

The humble native calmly replied, "If it hadn't, you'd be in
my kettle right now."

Its dynamic and revolutionary qualities make it an influence
of good. It is:

A light that drives out darkness. He who would fault the
Bible would fault light.

A sword that cuts and pricks rebellious hearts. This is a
power for good.

Seed that produces a crop of good. This cannot be called
bad.

A deterrent against sin—when hidden in the heart. This must
be appreciated.

Man's hope in what otherwise would be a dismal and mean-
ingless world. That which gives hope must not be devalued.

It is granted that our land is marred with disregard of man,
dishonesty, irresponsibility, violence, crime, unhappiness and
despair. However, this is not the fault of the Bible. Rather, it
is due to an insufficient reading of it, and even more—a failure
to practice it.

Proved

*Whereby are given unto us exceeding great and precious
promises.* II Peter 1:4

The story is told of an old man who was visited by his
minister. His rheumatism was so bad he was unable to get out
of his chair. His open Bible lay on his lap. The preacher picked
up the Bible, turned a few pages, and noticed that the word
"proved" was written in the margin beside many Scriptures:

*The Lord . . . will be with thee, he will not fail thee, neither
forsake thee.* Deuteronomy 31:8

*The eternal God is thy refuge, and underneath are the
everlasting arms.* Deuteronomy 33:27

*Blessed be the Lord . . . there hath not failed one word of
all his good promise.* I Kings 8:56

The Lord is my shepherd; I shall not want. Psalms 23:1

God is our refuge and strength, a very present help in trouble.
Psalms 46:1

Cast thy burden upon the Lord, and he shall sustain thee.
Psalms 55:22

The dear old man had taken God's book and written his
own experience on the margin — "Proved."

A neighbor who had walked in and observed said, "But
what will you do if you get worse?"

Then the old man turned to Psalms 41:3 and said, "In that
case I shall depend on this verse: 'The Lord will strengthen him
upon the bed of languishing: thou wilt make all his bed in his
sickness.' "

I Drew My Circle Again

Therefore thou art inexcusable, O man, whosoever thou art that judget: for wherein thou judget another, thou condemnest thyself; for thou that judget doest the same things. Romans 2:1

This is the explanation of a man's loneliness:

"When I first became a member of the church, my circle was very large and I was delighted to be in the group. For it included all, like myself, who had accepted the faith. I rejoiced that there were so many excellent, believing people.

"But with my keen, observant mind I soon learned that I had been hasty in my conclusions. Many in my fellowship were erring. Being conscientious, I could not tolerate any people who were not right on all points of doctrine and practice. So there was nothing I could do but draw my circle again and leave them out.

"There in the smaller circle I was happy for awhile with those I presumed to be sound and righteous. Later I observed that many of them were not the highest type. They were blind, stubborn, proud, unwilling to listen to me, even though they were not half as smart as I am. So there was no alternative but to draw my circle again and exclude them.

"We were fewer but happier and stronger. Those publicans and sinners would defile any holy church. But once again my eagerness to accept people had gone too far. It was not long until I heard ugly rumors about the worldliness of some of them; that some were drinking coffee instead of tea, as I was drinking. So I had to draw my circle again.

"This shrank my circle to include only myself and my family. I had a good family, but to my shock they disagreed with me. I was always right. So in complete support of right, I drew my circle again, *leaving me all alone.*"

Aim at Your Goal

One thing have I desired of the Lord, that will I seek after; that I may dwell in the house of the Lord all the days of my life, to behold the beauty of the Lord, and to inquire in his temple. Psalms 27:4

Having some aims in life is a most vital prerequisite of success. An elderly man who had not gotten along very well in life explained his failure: "I aimed at nothing and hit it everytime."

A national marksman while passing through a countryside saw evidences of expert shooting. There it was on barns, walls, trees and fences. Each showed a bullet hole in the exact center of the bull's eye. This was too much for his curiosity to stand. "I've never seen shooting like this before," stated the astounded man. "How did you do it?"

"Not hard at all," replied the local marksman. "I shot first and drew the circle later."

This is one of the tragic mistakes of many people. They have a fast draw. They shoot first and then try to draw a circle around it. They have no formulated aims. This is why they run in circles.

Sometimes we sing, "I'm a pilgrim." It's definition is much different from a vagrant. The latter is only a stroller. But the pilgrim has a fixed purpose and a compelling goal. Which are we?

What are our aims? In family, business, social and religious life? At what are we aiming in youth, middle life and old age? Furthermore, what are we doing to reach those goals? Columbus didn't reach America by merely drifting. Remember the word *goal* has as its first two letters *GO*.

Investigate Before You Follow

Let them alone: they be blind leaders of the blind. And if the blind lead the blind, both shall fall into the ditch.

Matthew 15:14

There is this original inscription on a tombstone:

Remember, friend when passing by,
As you are now, so once was I.
As I am now, you soon will be,
Prepare for death and follow me.

Evidently some man considered it, for he wisely added these two lines:

To follow you I'm not content,
Until I know which way you went.

Jesus knew the value of such caution, for He warned against following unseeing leaders. He said, "If the blind lead the blind, both shall fall into the ditch."

All along humanity's trodden highways, the ditches are strewn with people who did not heed this advice. The warning should be applied to all areas of life: religion, business, finance, education, associates, politics and government. Before you enter, find out where the trail ends.

The leader who promises the most could be exploiting you. In politics, he could be offering you in advance the fruits of your children's labors. Be wary of the person who would mortgage them to get your support. In religion, be circumspect of those who offer special bargains and cut rate prices in a competitive appeal to draw a crowd. It's better to take God's word straight and pay the divinely stipulated price.

God bless us with leaders of vision — who see as God sees.

If God Let Us Alone

*Humble yourselves therefore under the mighty hand of God
. . . Casting all your care upon him; for he careth for you.*
I Peter 5:6,7

I read a little anecdote the other day which illustrates our blindness to God's care and providence. The story goes that a farmer was showing his picturesque, springing crop of oats to his cousin from the city. It had great promise.

The cousin remarked, "That is as fine oats as I have ever seen."

The farmer replied, "Yes, if God Almighty will only let it alone, it will make a fine harvest."

And, so the story continues, the crop stopped where it was. God Almighty let it alone. This is a parable to us. Many people are proposing that God leave us alone, that He stay out of our personal business and national affairs. They are suggesting that individuals and nations carry on without God, without even thought of God, that if He withholds Himself we shall prosper.

But if God should let us alone, we would perish. If he should withhold the growing of crops, we would have no food. If He should hold back the rains, there would be no water to drink. If He should stop the earth, there would be no place to put a foot. Whether we like it or not, we are dependent on a power outside of ourselves.

It is true that the God of love and mercy sometimes disciplines us. This, too, is for our good. He has said, "As many as I love, I rebuke and chasten" (Revelation 3:19). I have known fathers to talk and talk vainly to heedless sons. It took a little discipline to get their attention.

The Criticized Preacher

And he said unto them, Go ye into all the world, and preach the gospel to every creature. Mark 16:15

"If he's young, he lacks experience; if his hair is gray, he's too old.

"If he speaks from notes, he has canned sermons; if he is extemporaneous, he wanders.

"If he spends time in his study, he neglects the people; if he visits, he's a gadabout.

"If he is attentive to the poor, he's playing to the grandstand; if to the wealthy, he's trying to butter his bread.

"If he suggests improvements, he's a dictator; if he doesn't, he's short of vision.

"If he condemns wrong, he's cranky and intolerant; if he doesn't, he is a compromiser.

"If he preaches thirty-five minutes, he's windy; if less, he's lazy.

"If he preaches the truth, he's offensive; if not, he's a hypocrite.

"If he fails to please everyone, he's hurting the church; if he does, he has no convictions.

"If he preaches on giving, he's a money grabber; if he doesn't, he's not developing the people.

"And some folk think the preacher has an easy time."

Author Unknown

But — you can make it easier for him and happier for yourself by exercising a little more tolerance.

The Melting Pot

There is neither Jew nor Greek, there is neither bond nor free,
there is neither male nor female: for ye are all one in Christ
Jesus. Galatians 3:28

Soon after my first arrival in New York City, I took a tour which included going to the Statue of Liberty. What it symbolizes should be held gratefully and uncompromisingly in American hearts. Liberty — its price has been too dear and its benefits are too large to let it slip away. May what She stands for still be as strong as ever. May the commitment to be free never be blemished by selfishness and crumbled by indifference.

As I stood there, a tingling sensation ran down my spine as I read this inscription:

> *Give me your tired, your poor,*
> *Your huddled masses yearning*
> *   to breathe free,*
> *The wretched refuse of your teeming shore,*
> *Send these, the homeless, tempest-tossed,*
> *   to me:*
> *I lift my lamp beside the golden door.*

This grace has been the great equalizer — melting pot — in our nation, the true and kind philosophical touch which has transported humanity from every corner of the earth into the world's most powerful nation — America.

Then I thought of a greater sanctuary for all races and classes of people in every station, condition and circumstance of life — Christ. He holds out a divine light and says, "Come unto me, all ye that labor and are heavy laden, and I will give you rest" (Matthew 11:28). All! The tired! The poor! The masses yearning to be free! The wretched! The homeless! The tempest-tossed! All! No condition or status excepted!

Sheep or Goats?

And before him shall be gathered all nations: and he shall separate them one from another, as a shepherd divideth his sheep from the goats. Matthew 25:32

Well, in my judgment, they have not accomplished anything! A group of scientists in Cambridge, England, have produced a cross between a sheep and a goat. You guessed it — they named this poor creature "Geep." It looks like a goat with long hair, cannot reproduce itself, and mingles and hobnobs with both sheep and goats. Being a cross, it doesn't know where it belongs.

What an unfortunate predicament!

Many people in the world, however, should be quite pleased with this freak, because it represents exactly their view of religion. Not all out for God and not all out for Satan. A cross between the two. They want to be "geeps," half goat and half sheep.

But Jesus made a clear distinction between goats and sheep. He said, "My sheep hear my voice, and I know them, and they follow me" (John 10:27). Not the goats. This line of recognition and separation will become even more pronounced at the judgment. "And he shall set the sheep on his right hand, but the goats on the left" (Matthew 25:33).

The very nature of serving God does not permit a divided allegiance. "He that is not with me is against me." These words ring in our ears and put us in one camp or the other. Of course, all are subject to temptation and sometimes yield (Peter did), but the general behavior is such that we are as distinguishable as light, salt and sheep. Definitely, there can be no "geep" servant of God.

Stay Out of the Way

Alexander the coppersmith did me much evil: the Lord reward him according to his works. II Timothy 4:14

Alexander not only refused to help in God's plan for the betterment of man, he got in the way. Even worse, he opposed it intentionally.

A teacher asked her first-graders what they did to help at home. One by one, each gave such an answer as "feed the dog," "feed the cat," "dry dishes," "get the paper," and "make my bed." Fred hadn't said a word, so she asked him what he did.

He hesitated a moment and replied, "Mostly, I stay out of the way."

I wish all adults could say that.

If we're not willing to push the church, school, business, brotherhood of man, family, moral uplift, law enforcement, and a stronger nation, at least we should get out of the way of those who would.

If we're not lifting a fallen person to get upright, stay out of his way as he struggles to get on his feet.

If we're not helping to reclaim an alcoholic, don't stand in his way. Don't offer him a drink as he strives to muster the will to leave it alone.

Furthermore, if we don't want to go to church, the least we can do is stay out of the way of those who would. Don't make them have to climb over us to get there.

Just staying out of the way is not the biggest accomplishment, but it is some attainment.

Now Swim

Is not my help in me? And is wisdom driven quite from me?
Job 6:13

When I was eight or nine years old I couldn't swim. As you would expect, my father and uncle thought I should know how. They decided it was time to give me my first lesson on swimming. I was all for it, not knowing just how it would be given. They took me to a pond and had me to undress. Standing there on a little bluff, my father took me by the hands and Uncle Roy took me by the feet. Then they began to swing me and at the high point they let go and my father yelled, "Now swim"!

That came about the nearest of being perpetual motion any person ever saw. My arms and legs started flapping and kicking. I knocked and splashed water like a drunken whale — and I swallowed quite a lot of it. But I stayed afloat. I swam. I have been able to swim ever since, and with experience a little more gracefully.

My father was a strong believer in the School of Experience, the School of Hard Knocks, and the School of Self-reliance. He believed that you learn to do by doing. To him there was no substitute for individual effort and struggle.

In the intervening years there have been times when threatening waters have risen around me, or the current was against me, or I was in over my head. Each time my father's words would ring in my heart, "Now swim"! They have meant so much to me. They have kept me from going under. A person must be self-reliant or he will sink.

How encouraging it is to know that every person can be a fish in his own ocean, if there is a real need for it.

Thinking Puts You Ahead

I thought on my ways, and turned my feet unto thy testimonies. Psalms 119:59

"I thought . . . and turned." There was no turning until first there was thinking. Indeed, each turns his own world by thinking.

A little girl was asked to define "drawing," and she did it with such an accuracy and clarity that a philosopher could not have done better. She said, "Drawing is thinking and then marking round the think." Don't you like that?

Every achievement must first begin with a thought.

God was surely smiling on man when He endowed him with the ability to think.

The greatest human power to make wealth is thinking. A Morse thinks of telegraphic communication, and it results in hundreds of millions of value in telegraph stock. A Stevenson thinks of locomotive traction, and it materializes in thousands of millions in railroads. A Bell thinks of speaking by wire, and from it springs billions in telephones.

Thinking does more, however, than add wealth. It enables a person to reach the potential for which he was created. It increases farming, adds to industry, opens new developments in medicine, broadens education and inspires art. It has empowered man to go to the moon. And it will let me get my feet off the ground.

Think big! For big results!

> *Greatly begin! Though you have time*
> *But for a line, be that sublime,*
> *Not failure, but low aim, is crime.*

The Singing Heart

Singing and making melody in your heart to the Lord.
Ephesians 5:19

About seven in the morning a man walked into the big lobby of a big hospital singing, "What a Friend We Have in Jesus." Everybody stopped, looked and listened. Then one man inquired, "Who is that?"

The answer: "Oh, that is one of the greatest surgeons in town." He was my doctor and a close friend.

Singing is one of the assets of mankind. It gives peace and joy. We are thrilled with its power. It is not necessary to have a trained voice to have a singing heart. In describing a beautiful and powerful inner life, Paul said, "Singing and making melody in your heart to the Lord."

Singing explains one of the reasons for the bravery and peace of early Christians who faced bitter and cruel persecutions. It saved them from drooping spirits and lifted them to ecstacy when the going was rough. When Paul and Silas were wrongfully held in jail, they "sang praises unto God: and the prisoners heard them" (Acts 16:25).

Life would be hard today if we did not have the singing heart which soothes us, summons us, strengthens us, day by day. Workers have it as they face their tasks. Parents feel it as they anxiously think upon the welfare of their children. The sick lisp a melody in the night watches, and its music serves them as they launch into the river of death. And over on the other side the song of the heart becomes the song of the redeemed.

The Law of Compensation

Give, and it shall be given unto you; good measure, pressed down, and shaken together, and running over, shall men give into your bosom. For with the same measure that ye mete withal it shall be measured to you again. Luke 6:38

Ours is a world of compensation. We reap what we sow; if not today, then later. Under a just God it cannot be any other way.

The world operates on the basis of paying each person in his own kind, and generally speaking it varies very little from this rule. If we smile, it smiles back at us. If we frown, it frowns at us. If we sing, we will be invited to the chorus. If we think, our advice will be sought by the troubled. If we love mankind, we will be surrounded by loving friends. On the other hand if we criticize, censure and hate, we will suffer the same from our fellow men. Every seed produces after its kind. The law of compensation.

Because of the rule of compensation life has much more balance than we think. We obtain one thing at the price of giving up something else. The poor man cannot always have meat, and the rich man cannot always digest it.

Even all our toils, sufferings and sorrows can have their compensations, depending upon our reactions. A man who had been hospitalized for several days later stated that it had taught him to have a greater concern for the ill. His suffering had contributed to a finer person. The law of compensation.

Outside the Door

For where your treasure is, there will your heart be also.
Matthew 6:21

Years ago Robert Southwell said, "Not where I breathe, but where I love, I live." No poised, successful person lives merely where his body occupies space. A person's family may be scattered, but if he loves them, that is where he lives.

Man — the exalted creature — is the only being or thing in all the world that can live outside himself or itself. We can become so absorbed in an outside interest that we live in it instead of ourselves.

A mother said, "The happiest days of my life were when my children were little. They needed me to do things for them they could not do for themselves. I lived for my children." Her life was outside the door of self.

You can find health-invigorating happiness and deep satisfaction just outside the door of yourself. The self-centered person tries to leap on happiness; but when he lands, it is not there. The reason — every leap is within himself. Spring outside yourself, and there just outside the door you will find happiness.

> *Who seeks within for happiness*
> *Will find it not.*
> *It stands a guest unheeded at thy very door today,*
> *Open thine eyes to see,*
> *Thine ears to hear,*
> *Thy heart to feel,*
> *The call for touch of human sympathy;*
> *In answering this there is*
> *And close outside thee sits*
> *The guest thou soughtest in vain within.*

Adapted, Caroline S. Woodruff

What Is the Cause?

Behold, I am he whom ye seek: what is the cause wherefore ye are come? Acts 10:21

I once read the story of a man who experienced a little trembling in the night. Thinking he was taking a chill, he got up and took a cold tablet. Then he went back to bed and slept through the night. The next morning when he picked up the paper there was this headline screaming at him, "Earthquake shakes city in night."

This emphasizes the need of correct diagnosis and the absolute necessity of getting to the cause of the problem.

The world of reality calls upon us to deal with the matter of cause and effect. There is no escaping it. Thus when there is an effect we need to know what the real cause is.

There is much disregard for the rights of others — what is the cause?

There is much dog-eat-dog spirit among us — what is the cause?

There is much crime in the land — what is the cause?

There is much restlessness and nervousness among the people — what is the cause?

There is much absenteeism at church — what is the cause?

It appears to me that the basic cause of our woes is a failure to live up to God's bottom-rock requirements of man. Here they are simply and concretely stated:

He hath showed thee, O man, what is good; and what doth the Lord require of thee, but to do justly, and to love mercy, and to walk humbly with thy God? Micah 6:8

Tie a Knot and Hang on

Paul purposed . . . to go to Jerusalem, saying, After I have been there, I must also see Rome.   Acts 19:21

Paul was determined to see Rome. And he did. Moreover, there he made saints in Caesar's household — the household of Nero, the brutal enemy of Christianity. This was the fruit of determination. Paul had the unyielding spirit.

When I was a student in college it was my privilege to know a student whose limbs, upper and lower, were twisted and drawn, making it very difficult for him to even wobbly walk. His head was bent to an angle and his mouth was contorted. His irregular speech came very laboriously and was hard to understand. He was a stumbling fellow physically, but he was tops in friendliness and mentality.

He was admired and loved by all who knew him. No one had dared to ask him what dealt him this fate. But one day a special pal inquired of his trouble.

"Infantile paralysis," was the short reply.

Then the friend said, "With a blow like that, how can you face the world so confidently and lovingly, free from bitterness?"

The young man answered in broken speech, "It never touched my head or heart."

He received a BA degree. Really, don't you think he could have been given a DD — Doctor of Determination?

He proved that a person can be a submitter to circumstances or a master of fate. Sheer determination changed his life. So — when you get to the end of your rope there's still a chance — tie a knot and hang on.

Another Life

This mortal must put on immortality . . . then . . . death is swallowed up in victory. I Corinthians 15:53,54

In Philadelphia I went to the grave of the famous Benjamin Franklin, printer, writer, statesman and patriot. It was thought-provoking to stand there and read the epitaph Franklin himself had written:

THE BODY OF B. FRANKLIN
PRINTER

Like the cover of an old book
  Its contents torn out
And stript of its lettering and gilding
  Lies here food for worms.
But the work shall not be wholly lost
  For it will, as he believes, appear once more
In a new and more perfect edition
  Corrected and amended
By the author.

I was struck with this great American's intellect, wisdom and faith in immortality. He was walking in good company when he cherished another life and wrote of it. For the Apostle Paul pays recognition to those "who by patient continuance in well doing seek for glory and honor and immortality, eternal life" (Romans 2:7).

The chief hope of humanity has been and is another life in a fairer land. This one is too short and too burdened with problems to satisfy us mortals. The Indian dreamed of the Happy Hunting Ground; and the Christian, the Ivory Palaces.

Man is the only creature filled with such longings. Surely God would not have created him with this distinctive ability just to have it come to naught.

A Story About a President

Not forsaking the assembling of ourselves together, as the manner of some is. Hebrews 10:25

An interesting story is told of President Garfield's first Sunday in Washington after his inauguration. A member of the cabinet requested that the President call a cabinet meeting at 10:00 A.M. the next day (Sunday) to deal with a matter that could lead to a national crisis. Garfield refused on the ground that he had another appointment. The perturbed cabinet member insisted that the national interest was so involved, the President should break his engagement.

Garfield politely refused. Then the cabinet member remarked, "I would like to know with whom you have an engagement so important that it cannot be broken."

The President replied, "I will be as frank as you are. My appointment is with the Lord to meet Him at His house at 10:30 tomorrow, and I shall be there."

He was there. The threatening crisis passed. The nation survived. And the President got to meet with a greater ruler — the Prince of Peace — who had promised, "For where two or three are gathered together in my name, there am I in the midst of them" (Matthew 18:20). Garfield had done considerable preaching. His reaction was as natural as breathing.

You will recall that President Garfield was assassinated while in office. As family members and friends gathered round the flower-decked casket to bid him good-bye, what do you think gave them the most comfort? Not that he had made it to the white House, but rather that he had made his plans to dwell in a mansion made by the Lord.

He Is No Playful Kitten

Be sober, be vigilant; because your adversary the devil, as a roaring lion, walketh about, seeking whom he may devour.
I Peter 5:8

Perhaps you will enjoy listening to the conversation of two boys as they walked home from Sunday Bible class. The teacher had given a stirring lesson on the Devil. Being disturbed, one of them asked, "What do you think of the idea that there's a Devil?"

"He's just like Santa Claus. He's your daddy," replied the other one.

Most people believe in the existence of an all powerful, all good Spirit — God. By the same token, it's easy to believe in an all sinister spirit that seeks to harm man. For the world that contains so much good also contains so much evil. You can't see with the physical eye either spirit for spirit is invisible, but you can see the works of both.

There is no way you can drive to town and back and not be convinced there is a Devil. The outrageous, vile, dastard things you see could not have accidentally happened. They had to have some help from a wicked source. Evil has now become so bold that kittens prey where lions once dared to roar.

Satan is the great deceiver. He offers one thing and gives something else. If you take Satan into your boat, he will steer you into the rapids and waterfalls. Keep the church building filled. For it's mighty easy for Satan to come in, if the building is nearly empty. If it is, maybe he has already been there.

The most comforting thought is: "Resist the devil, and he will flee from you. Draw nigh to God, and he will draw nigh to you" (James 4:7,8).

This World Is Not My Home

They were strangers and pilgrims on the earth. For they that say such things declare plainly that they seek a country . . . a better country, that is, a heavenly. Hebrews 11:13-16

We need to bear in mind that we are sojourners. This world is not our home. Unless we are mindful of this obvious fact, we may become so attached to this world that we lose sight of the distant land to which our pilgrimage is going.

Thus it is fitting that we consider some facts of our pilgrimage:

• *First, there is no inheritance in the land we now occupy.* Then why should we fix our affections on earthly things? They are unsatisfactory and must be left behind.

• *Furthermore, this pilgrimage is short and fleeting.* We are passing through for a purpose to reach a certain destination. There is work to do. Failures to sadden. Victories to gladden. Pleasantries to enjoy. Sufferings to endure. But time is short for either. The pilgrimage will soon end.

• *Moreover, distance now separates us* from many friends and loved ones who have gone on ahead. There are still many fellow pilgrims at our side, but so many others have already made it to the Fatherland.

• *Accordingly, let us be faithful* to the duties involved in the journey. We are passing through this life but once — we shall not pass this way again — therefore we should be true and helpful along the way.

• *Also, let us be content.* It is too much to expect all the comforts and joys here that are to be found over there. As we now face a few hardships, let us remember that in the land beyond we shall rest from our labors and no heart shall ever ache and no tear shall ever be shed.

The Word Is Now

For now we live, if ye stand fast in the Lord.
I Thessalonians 3:8

The knowledge we possess today is an accumulation of yesterday's lessons. This being true, we are smarter now than we have ever been in our life. Being more experienced and wiser, we should be able to do more.

Now is the time for life to be used, lived and enjoyed. Much precious time is wasted by using the *now* to get ready to live tomorrow. But this is still true — "Whereas ye know not what shall be on the morrow."

Now is the watchword of the wise. The foolish, however, say that they will do this or that tomorrow. This takes no working of the brain, no activity of the hands, no moving of the feet — just a little wagging of the tongue.

Sometimes it is *now or never* for two reasons: First, time may run out and there are no more "nows." Second, tomorrow you may no longer have the desire. Good intentions don't always linger. Quench them enough times and they will die.

NOW

Never mind about tomorrow —
It always is today;
Yesterday has vanished.
Wherever none can say.

Each minute must be guarded —
Made worth the while somehow;
There are no other moments;
It's always, Just Now.

Then never mind tomorrow —
'Tis today you must enjoy
With all that's true and noble;
And the time for this is —
NOW.

A Good Today and a Better Tomorrow

For thou knowest not what a day may bring forth.
Hebrews 10:25

There was an elderly brother who often prayed at church: "Forgetting the things which are behind, give us strength and wisdom to press onward to a brighter future. May we be a progressive, improving people. May our tomorrow — if there be a tomorrow — be a little better than today and a lot better than yesterday."

How do you like that? Elderly. But not too old to dream.

Your future is laid on your own door step; and it is brighter, if God is the keeper at the door.

While the Book of Fate is hidden from the present, you have much to do with what is written in it. No person can tell what the future holds, but there are many things you can forecast with considerable accuracy.

For instance, if you want your house—literally and spiritually—to stand the ravages of time, be thoughtful and visionary enough to build it on the rock. It doesn't go up as fast, but it lasts longer.

Furthermore, if you would drink pure water from your well tomorrow, don't throw garbage into it today. And if you would have a harvest in the fall, don't eat the seed corn in the winter. If you want a high credit rating in the future, pay your present bills.

Moreover, don't waste your bread today, if you're going to have an appetite tomorrow. Don't be ugly to people now, if you would have them as helping friends in time to come. Don't sow wild oats in the spring, if you would have a better harvest in the fall.

Laws Were Made for Man

And he said unto them, The sabbath was made for man, and not man for the sabbath. Mark 2:27

Jesus and His disciples went through some corn fields on the Sabbath. The disciples plucked some of the ears and this irritated the Pharisees. Then these more-concerned-with-law-than-people Pharisees charged the disciples with violating the Sabbath. But the very Lord of the Sabbath came to their defense, and thus gave the above passage.

The Sabbath law was made to bless man; but if a circumstance should arise whereby the keeping of it would produce the opposite effect, then its observance would counteract the very purpose for which it was given. Jesus thought that in this case man's welfare comes first. This proves that the Lord really, really loves man. Man is very special to the heart of God. The wonders and benefits of nature, the laws in the Bible regulating man's conduct, his relationship to each other and to God — all — are for the good of man.

Every law God ever gave was for the welfare of man. He never gave a single commandment just to "boss" man but to bless man. The highest motive prompted it.

Moreover, God's laws have always applied equally to all people. Even the law on tithing applied to all alike. God never eased this requirement for some to put a heavier burden on others. For laws to be fair they must treat everybody the same way. Fairness is so important in legislation, and God is one to be copied.

Another point — man has passed thousands and thousands of laws, but he has never improved on the Ten Commandments.

Make Hay While the Sun Shines

To every thing there is a season, and a time to every purpose under the heaven: a time to be born, and a time to die; a time to plant, and a time to pluck up that which is planted.
Ecclesiastes 3:1,2

My father operated a general merchandise store in a little village. Much of my early life was spent working in it. Growing up in a village store, observing and listening to the people, was a whole education within itself. I learned of their loves, their hates, their prejudices, their philosophies, and their personalities. I learned people and what makes them tick.

Bright and early one morning a farmer rushed in and bought some binder wire to use in binding hay. He commented, "I've got to make hay while the sun shines." He needed to take care of his duty before the rains came.

What he said is more than efficient farming; it's sound philosophy.

In every success story, timing has had a vital part. There is a time to act; to delay means failure. People who get ahead are always on top of things at the right time.

By procrastinating, one can lose the opportunity. Some people are too slow. It takes them two and a half hours just to see "60 Minutes." Their hay will rot in the fields.

God's best gift to us is not things but opportunities and the time to seize them. So let us make hay while the sun shines.

The Fox and the Crow

A man that flattereth his neighbor spreadeth a net for his feet. Proverbs 29:5

There is a valuable lesson in an old fable about a crow that took a piece of cheese out of a cottage window and flew up into a high tree. There she planned to eat the cheese.

Then an observing fox came and sat underneath the tree, and began to flatter the crow. He said, "I never observed it before, but your feathers are whiter and more delicate than I have ever seen on any crow in my life. What a fine shape and graceful turn of body you have. And your voice is so melodious and sweet. There is no bird anywhere that can stand in competition with you."

The blarney tickled the crow and she nestled and wriggled about. The honeyed words prompted her to sing, and that very instant the cheese dropped from her mouth. This being what the fox wanted, he snapped it up and trotted away, laughing at how credulous the crow was.

The love of praise is quite common among us. There are very few who do not enjoy hearing themselves complimented — even from people whose opinions don't usually count.

This proneness to fall for flattery makes a person vulnerable to exploitation by self-seeking people. We must watch, therefore, to see that compliments come free; they could come with a dear price tag.

'Tis an old maxim in the schools,
That flattery is the food of fools;
Yet now and then your men of wit
Will condescend to take a bit.

Who Am I?

Who hath woe? who hath sorrow? who hath contentions? who hath babbling? who hath wounds without cause? who hath redness of eyes? . . . At the last it biteth like a serpent, and stingeth like an adder. Proverbs 23:29-32

I get man to take me, and then I take the man. I enter lives and chase wisdom out. I am a chief destroyer of homes — have made countless numbers of orphans. I am the greatest murderer — have killed more people than all the wars of the world.

I have done more to destroy the human brain than anything else. I produce hangovers and decrease efficiency. I am the undertaker's round-up of business. I have knocked a world of people from the peak, but have never lifted any up. I have turned ambitious, industrious youths into irresponsible bums.

I weaken the strong and destroy the weak. I have made unconscionable brutes out of sensitive, high-grade people. I bleed the hearts of parents whose child likes me so much. I have bankrupted thousands of businesses. I dull the senses of people and give them a don't-care attitude.

I have put many people to work, especially officers of the law. If I were not around, many law enforcement personnel would be out of a job. I am to many people a god they daily worship.

I am something the Bible permits for medicinal purposes (I Timothy 5:23). I am also something of which the Bible severely warns (Proverbs 20:1).

I am *ALCOHOL!*

The Mouse

It is a land that eateth up the inhabitants . . . and there we saw
the giants . . . and we were in our own sight as grasshoppers,
and so we were in their sight. Numbers 13:32,33

An exaggeration!

In a more modern time and in another country the mountains echoed with strange and inexplainable noises. The residents of the area, much alarmed, gathered to learn what was causing the peculiar sounds. After waiting a while in anxious wonder, out crept a mouse.

The moral is: Do not make much ado about nothing.

This story is an old and well known fable, which approaches the closeness of a proverb. It reproves those who frighten easily, who see nothing but danger and defeat in every kind of challenge and pleasant event.

Fear is one of the most devastating adversaries of man — one he himself feeds and nurtures. The most frightening agonies of mankind come from the dread of trouble rather than from the actual presence of trouble. It will cause people to think the noise of a mouse is underground rumblings soon to erupt. It exaggerates every danger and every trouble. It makes mountains out of ant hills. Fear kills man's expectancy of better days, breaks down his defense, and unfits him for triumphant living.

The problem, however, is not one of the mouse, the mountains, the land, the other fellow, but is a matter of the heart of the fearful. More faith and trust in God will arm us with a more fearless spirit. Truly —

For God hath not given us the spirit of fear; but of power, and
of love, and of a sound mind. II Timothy 1:7

The Victor's Strength

They go from strength to strength, every one of them in Zion appeareth before God. Psalms 84:7

The Indian's view is that when a man kills an enemy the strength of the slain foe passes into the victor's body. In that weird fancy lies a truth concerning man and his struggles. Each conquest makes us stronger for the next combat, but each defeat leaves us weaker for the next battle. Truly, victory heralds victory, and defeat follows defeat.

Victory gives confidence, which is a most needed quality in facing opposition. This was exemplified in David's courage. He had tangled with the lion and the bear and had slain them. This gave him confidence to go up against the giant.

Victory, however, can undo you; and will if it gives you an over-confidence that causes you to drop your guard.

Anybody can win if there is no opposition. Moreover, anybody can act bravely when there is no combatant to lift a dagger, or when the opponent has fallen. When the brave lion is dead, even the scared donkeys switch to theatrical bravery and come out and kick him.

It's the hard fought victories that prove our heroic nature. Battles easily won add little to glory.

Hard fought battles leave us bruised, scarred and hurt, but it's not so painful when we win.

No group can struggle, endure and take the blows like those who fight out of conviction. Mercenaries never do as well in the pulpit, in the classroom, in medicine, in business, in the factory, or on the field of battle as those who are energized by a commitment that says, "Keep up the fight."

The Ghost of Might-Have-Been

How shall we escape, if we neglect so great salvation?
Hebrews 2:3

NEGLECT

Miss Meant-to has a comrade
And her name is Didn't-do.
Have you ever chanced to meet them,
Did they ever call on you?
These two girls now live together
In the house of Never-win,
And I'm told that it is haunted
By the ghost of Might-have-been.

The Sunday School Journal

Last year it was my thought-provoking experience to pass by an old cemetery in the country that had suffered the ravages of neglect. Weeds and bushes were as high as a man's head. Some monuments had fallen. Others with cherished epitaphs were leaning, including one which said, "Gone But Not Forgotten." Not forgotten? It appears that all the dead there have been erased from today's memory.

The dead who once slept beneath fragrant flowers, watered by the briny tears of weeping mourners, are no longer subject to this world's negligence. But what about the living? Indeed, many of them with a short view of today's ease tie their fortune to a tragic post — postponement.

On the way back to town I passed an old farm house that was falling apart, leaning and tumbling to the ground. It was a crumbling reminder of the havoc wrought by negligence. The old house had perhaps been a sacred place to a happy family. There diligence had seen dreams fulfilled and hopes realized. Now negligence, creeping in like the hand of death, is the mocker of dreams and the dasher of hopes. It is now the ghost of Might-have-been.

Sin at the Door

If thou doest well, shalt thou not be accepted? and if thou doest not well, sin lieth at the door. Genesis 4:7

Sin is sin no matter what we call it — error, mistake, thoughtlessness or bad judgment. There is the constant appearance of all kinds of ways to sin — no end to them. Sin comes clothed in a new garb everyday.

One thing the human family has in common is sin. "For all have sinned, and come short of the glory of God" (Romans 3:23). It's the attitude we have toward it that differentiates us. "Fools make a mock at sin" (Proverbs 14:9). "But a prudent man foreseeth the evil, and hideth himself" (Proverbs 22:3)

Because of our own vulnerabilty to sin we should be merciful toward those who have succumbed to this common foe of man. Jesus said to the accusers of the sinful woman, "He that is without sin among you, let him first cast a stone at her" (John 8:7).

One of the damaging effects of sin is that it hardens sinners and leaves them with an insensitive conscience. Commit a sin a few times and you will think it is permissable.

Much of the history of the world has been written in the annals called *Sin,* and it is not pretty. Of course, it promised something beautiful. Unquestionably, sin is the great deceiver of all time. The Bible speaks of "the deceitfulness of sin."

The philosopher and patriot Benjamin Franklin said:

Sin is not hurtful because it is forbidden, but it is forbidden because it is hurtful.

Since "the wages of sin is death," it behooves every person to get his sins rubbed out before payday comes. Thank God for Jesus who makes it possible.

Call the Doctor

But when Jesus heard that, he said unto him, They that be whole need not a physician, but they that are sick. Matthew 9:12

What about the health of your soul? It is a matter of great concern to the Great Physician. This is His wish: "I wish above all things that thou mayest prosper and be in health, even as thy soul prospereth" (III John 2). It is important that we be able to read our soul's spiritual condition.

Note these signs and features of good health of the soul: (1) Humble conduct. (2) Delight in hearing the Word. (3) A growing commitment to take the gospel to others. (4) Joy derived from meeting at the house of the Lord. (5) Growth in sacrifice. (6) A lessening bondage to the world.

Now let us think upon some of the illnesses of the soul to which we are subject: (1) *Eye trouble.* Vision is bad. Can't see very far — only self. (2) Another is *heart trouble.* The heart is the source of all conduct. When it is wrong, everything goes wrong. (3) Then there is *consumption.* Inwardly you get weaker and weaker. You scarcely feel it. You do not know it. You think all is right and that you will be better tomorrow. (4) And there is *creeping paralysis.* It leaves you with no religious feelings at all. You feel neither happiness nor unhappiness. Your vital power is passing away. But you neither know nor care. (5) Or to the contrary there is *fever.* There are different degrees of it. In the lesser degrees there is foolish and wild talk. Words are extravagant and difficult to restrain. In higher degrees there is explosive conduct and uncontrollable behavior. (6) Finally, there is *mortification.* No pain now. This is death!

There is a remedy. Call the doctor — the Great Physician.

Burning Hearts

And they said one to another, Did not our heart burn within us,
while he talked with us by the way, and while he opened to us
the Scriptures? Luke 24:32

The two traveling disciples did not at first recognize the resurrected Jesus who walked with them. Our own experiences at times may be very similar. How often we fail to recognize His presence. He walks with us in both severe trials and in blessed occurrences.

His talking with them and opening the Scriptures for them caused their hearts to burn. This is understandable, for the word of God is spoken of as a fire. "But his word was in mine heart as a burning fire" (Jeremiah 20:9). It melts the coldness of indifference and worldliness, burns up the dross of selfishness, and manifests itself in warm words and actions.

Devoid of burning hearts, we can assemble to worship without worshiping, can say our prayers without praying, can sing a hymn without making melody in the heart, can be exposed to a sermon without hearing it, and can give money without giving ourselves.

We need glowing hearts — burning hearts — to give us power. Why do we have still hands, silent tongues and leaden feet? Why should one sermon on the day of Pentecost convert three thousand souls while today it takes almost three thousand sermons to convert one soul? Certainly one answer is a lack of burning hearts.

Can you imagine how much warmer and better the church and the world would be if every person would read just one Scripture a day? If just placing your hand on the Bible when taking an oath has some bearing on telling the truth, just think what it will do to put a little of it in the heart everyday.

Influencing Future Generations

When I call to remembrance the unfeigned faith that is in thee,
which dwelt first in thy grandmother Lois, and thy mother
Eunice; and I am persuaded that in thee also. II Timothy 1:5

As seen in the above Scripture, we affect our children — for good or bad — and they in turn affect their children, and on it goes generation after generation.

It has been revealed that an investigator of New York prisons ran across the Jukes family. Max Jukes, a Dutch settler in New York, had two sons. Each chose disreputable characters for wives. These homes had no regard for religion and the Bible. Their genealogical stream was traced five generations. Of the 709 descendants investigated this is the findings: One-fifth of them were criminals, having spent a total of 140 years in prison — a number of them murderers. Nearly one-fourth had been paupers. One out of six of the women was a prostitute. My only point in giving these sickening facts is to present an eye opener that shows what a lack of religious and moral influence can do to hundreds yet unborn.

But now look at Jonathan Edwards. He spent the most of his life preaching in and serving the little New England village of Northampton. In morals he was very strict; he stood four-square for the higher things of life. His descendants include 265 college graduates, 12 college presidents, 65 college professors, 60 physicians, 100 ministers, 75 army officers, 60 prominent authors, 100 lawyers, 30 judges, 80 public officers (such as governors, state officials and mayors), 3 congressmen, 2 U.S. senators, and 1 vice-president of the United States.

We are now! now! shaping the destinies of unborn generations!

Stairs of Opportunity

And truly, if they had been mindful of that country from whence they came out, they might have had opportunity to have returned. Hebrews 11:15

Stairs of opportunity — just before you reach them you have to pass through a closed gate that is marked "Push." No pull. All push. Then you will enter a path of many stones, which will bruise your feet or be steppingstones, depending on you. It is a one way passage marked "Go." No opportunities are behind — they are all ahead. When you arrive, be not deceived into thinking opportunities are not there just because they are in the form of struggle, hard work, sweat and tears. Don't wait for fortune to knock at your door, the stairs are there — just start climbing.

> The stairs of opportunity
> Are sometimes hard to climb;
> And that can only be well done
> By one step at a time.
>
> But he who would go to the top
> Ne'er sits down and despairs;
> Instead of staring up the steps
> He just steps up the stairs.

Precious opportunities come to all. The trouble is — many people don't recognize them when they see them. Opportunity seldom comes labeled.

We must live with the fact that every opportunity implies an obligation. When chance smiles, don't frown. Grab it.

As the apple reddens on the high limb, the apple pickers passed it by — no, not that they didn't see it, but they couldn't reach it. When opportunity shows and we are not tall enough, build a ladder and then our opportunities shall pay off.

Helping Another

For we are unto God a sweet savor of Christ, in them that are saved . . . the savor of life unto life. II Corinthians 2:15,16

After paying the fees to enter the engineering school of a university, I attended a revival meeting for a few nights. The preacher was also a scientist and the head of the chemistry department in a Christian college. I was converted, and subsequently packed my bags and went back with him to his college. Four months later I preached my first sermon.

Some years passed and this time I was in physical trouble. I had undergone a tonsillectomy. Down deep where the needles had been injected an infection set up. My fever was high. My perspiration was a constant outpouring. Nature was doing its best but was losing the battle. The doctor told my family that I was going to die. But the Great Physician always has the last say. He wasn't ready for my work to end. He was sending a cure for my recovery.

A doctor of chemistry came to Fort Worth and spoke to the physicians about the amazing new sulfa drug and its ability to kill infection. My doctor was present. (What if he had not been there?) After the meeting my doctor asked the chemist for some of this medicine, explaining that he had a man dying, and went straight to the hospital and started giving it to me. It worked. My life was saved.

The almost unbelievable circumstance is that the very man who helped to save my soul had a small but significant part in developing this new drug.

One person can make a world of difference for you. One person can do so much to aid mankind. And that person can be you — you to receive and you to give.

They Gave Up

And this is the victory that overcometh the world, even our faith. I John 5:4

This is the report given by a man who applied for a job with our company: He stated that he had prepared himself to preach, but when he got in the field he met many discouraging situations. So he decided to get another job. He said that he had preached for a church the Sunday before and learned they had drained the baptistry and filled it with chairs. Not people. Empty chairs. Their reason was that they seldom ever baptized anyone and never used the chairs. With this attitude, they won't need the pews they are using very long. Might as well hang a crepe on the door. Death is upon them.

They sort of remind me of the person who blew out the candle because it was dark. Just got darker.

Faith that overcomes, gives victory, leaves no room for pessimism. How can you be pessimistic when you believe that somehow you are going to come out on top? Maybe not today, but eventually at the proper time. God's timing is better than ours.

Regardless of circumstances, keep your chin up and a forward look. Don't let yourself get down in the mouth and sing the blues.

The one place where you should never, never find pessimism is in the church. For God has said, "So shall my word be that goeth forth out of my mouth: it shall not return unto me void, but it shall accomplish that which I please, and it shall prosper in the thing whereto I sent it" (Isaiah 55:11).

The Wrong Cue

Let no man deceive himself. I Corinthians 3:18

The master of ceremonies had been informed by the speaker that his subject would be, "Shadrach, Meshach and Abednego." The M.C., however, had found it difficult to remember those unfamiliar names. Not wanting to hold notes, he devised a unique way to receive a little prompting. He wrote those three names — Shadrach, Meshach and Abednego — on a slip of paper and pinned it inside the lapel of his coat. He planned at the proper time in the introduction to make a grand gesture, open his coat, and take a look.

And that's what he did. At the height of his enthusiastic eloquence, he said, "Our intelligent and scholarly speaker will discuss the three brave and courageous Hebrew children: (then he glimpsed) Hart, Schaffner and Marx."

The wrong cue is very deceiving and bewildering. As you see, this can happen to a speaker. Similarly, the football player can be given the wrong signal. Confusion results. Correspondingly, a church audience can be given an uncertain sound. It takes its toll. "For if the trumpet give an uncertain sound, who shall prepare himself to the battle?" (I Corinthians 14:8).

In semblance, a farmer can fall victim to hurtful advice. Then failure is his harvest. Likewise, the stock buyer can be exploited with misleading tips. Bankruptcy ensues. In parallel, the voter may be fed vote-getting, vote-buying promises. Disappointment follows.

Therefore, closely examine everything that affects you and weigh it carefully. Be not deceived; and above all, deceive not yourself.

Blest Be the Tie That Binds

And they continued steadfastly in the apostles' doctrine and fellowship, and in breaking of bread, and in prayers. Acts 2:42

John Fawcett, the minister of a poor country church at Wainsgate, Yorkshire, received such a meager salary that it barely supported his family. Hence, he accepted a call to a London church, with a substantial compensation.

The day came for the wagons to be loaded with family goods and furniture. Soon the house was surrounded by sorrowing, weeping people, who begged their beloved preacher to remain. Mrs. Fawcett, overcome by the outpouring of grief, called to her husband, "Oh, John, we cannot go!"

"No," he replied, "we cannot go; we will stay." He then gave the orders to take everything back into the house.

The story goes that the gifted Dr. John Fawcett stayed with the country church — poor but rich — on $125.00 a year support and the devotion and attachment of its members. In celebration of the event, he wrote the hymn which accentuates human closeness and fellowship, three of its verses we note:

> Blest be the tie that binds
>   Our hearts in Christian love;
> The fellowship of kindred minds
>   Is like to that above.
>
> Before our Father's throne
>   We pour our ardent prayers;
> Our fears, our hopes, our aims are one,
> Our comforts and our cares.
>
> We share each other's views,
>   Each other's burdens bear;
> And often for each other flows
>   The sympathizing tear.

Feed Them

Jesus saith unto him, Feed my sheep. John 21:17

The local minister called a meeting to discuss the subject, "How to Get People to Attend Church." A representation of various occupations attended . . . with their advice.

The manager of the Little Theater suggested, "The church needs to be more theatrical."

"Drop some of the spiritual activities and introduce athletics. In season we play a game every Friday night and every pew is filled," recommended the football coach.

The psychologist said, "If we could just find some way to call everybody's name — people like attention." A very novel idea came from the head of a thrift association: "It will be appealing to have some free services, take no collections on certain Sundays."

A young man, fresh out of a school of modernism, stated, "I have learned that the church has become too churchy. Let's use some word other than *church*. Using another word will appeal to those who don't want to be too churchy."

"Giving double stamps for Sunday attendance will work miracles" was the advice of a business-conscious merchant.

But it was the old farmer who came up with some very practical advice we sometimes don't like to acknowledge. He stated, "Last week I was at a farmer's convention. I never heard a single address on how to get cattle to come to the rack. We spent our time discussing the best kind of feed."

Christ's solemn command to Peter in the beginnng Scripture is still relevant. It will still do more to increase attendance than all other things combined.

Seek Wise Counsel

Where no counsel is, the people fall: but in the multitude of counselors there is safety. Proverbs 11:14

I recall the amusing story of the cowboy, tormented with a rash, who ran and jumped into a cactus plant. Later his classic explanation was, "Well, at the time it seemed like it was the thing to do."

We laugh at the cowboy because actually we are laughing at ourselves. For most of us at times have jumped too fast.

It is, therefore, a mark of wisdom to seek counsel. However, unless the counselors are wise and knowledgeable, one is no better off — maybe worse. It is easy to get the wrong advice, especially up and down the streets. So do not listen to failures, or near failures, or mediocre achievers.

After consulting counselors, in the last analysis you will have to make the decision. So think it through. Personally, I like to sleep on a proposition; it may have a different look in the morning. This gives me a little more time before I leap.

You certainly need a little more time before answering those who call and say, "You have been selected . . ." More than half the time you had better run the other way as fast as you can. I can say this because I have been *selected*. More than once.

Now as we press onward, having been bumped here and there along the way, may we always remember that man is not the creature of circumstances but instead the circumstances are the creatures of man.

Gossiper or Gossipee?

A talebearer revealeth secrets: but he that is of a faithful spirit concealeth the matter. Proverbs 11:13

A college freshman class was asked to define gossip. One said, "It's quietly going after a person behind his back." Another answered, "It's an effort to build one up by lowering another." A third replied, "It's a secretive pastime for some that others have to pay for." A fourth stated, "It's telling something bad on another that usually begins with, 'They say,' or 'Have you heard?' or 'Don't tell I told you, but.'" Those freshmen were doing some thinking.

The crowd of talebearers is large in numbers but short on respectability. Nobody trusts them; for if they will gossip to you, they will gossip about you.

The talebearer, having overrated his importance but with no more talent than the ordinary, with a temperament unrefined by grace, has gone underground with his activities and whispers in hush-hush tones that build up, reverberate and become roaring thunders.

Just being an observant in talkative society has taught me that gossip is mischievous, juicy and easy to swallow, easy to share, but grievous to bare. It spreads on vulture's wings and feeds on the death it carries. Even after the victim is buried in clean earth, beneath fragrant flowers, some who like the stench of death and hunger for the decomposing mass will dig him up and feed on him again.

There are two classes of people in the world: *gossipers and gossipees.* As much as I dislike being talked about, God help me to belong to this class instead of the other.

Just Be Glad

*Why art thou cast down, O my soul? And why art thou dis-
quieted within me? hope thou in God: for I shall yet praise him,
who is the health of my countenance, and my God.*

Psalms 42:11

Longfellow has told of going out into his garden after a
devastating storm. He saw a bird's nest ripped from the tree
and scattered on the ground. As he beheld the wreckage and
thought of all the apparently wasted labor, he felt sorry for
the little birds. But at that moment he heard a chattering
overhead and then looked up and saw that the birds, far from
being discouraged, had already begun to build another nest.
They could sing and work and try again when things went
wrong.

The bravest and strongest have their bad and sad days. But
God can drive out dismay and make us glad.

JUST BE GLAD

Oh, heart of mine, we shouldn't
  Worry so!
What we've missed of calm we couldn't
Have, you know!
What we've met of stormy pain,
And of sorrow's driving rain,
We can better meet again
  If it blow.

For we know, not every morrow
  Can be sad;
So forgetting all the sorrow
  We have had,
Let us fold away our fears,
And put by our foolish tears,
And through all the coming years
  Just be glad.

James Whitcomb Riley

What Did You Do With the Ship?

Give none offense, neither to the Jews, nor to the Gentiles, nor to the church of God. I Corinthians 10:32

Shortly after World War II a magician was entertaining in a ship that was sailing in the Atlantic not far from the English coast. The passengers were astounded by his feats of taking eggs from ears, pickles from noses, rabbits from hats, and his sawing through a box containing a woman. Also, there was a haughty parrot in on the show. Each time the parrot would squawk, "Faker, faker." And the people would roar.

Finally the magician promised that he would do a trick that not even Houdini had ever been able to perform. The parrot blabbed, "Faker, faker." The sleight-of-hand artist sprinkled some hocus-pocus dust and waved his wand. At that very moment the ship hit a floating mine and was blown to pieces.

When dawn came there was the parrot sitting on one end of a make-shift raft and the magician sitting on the other end. After a little pause, the parrot hopped over and said, "O.K. Smarty, you win, but what did you do with the ship?"

Often we refer to the church as "The Ship of Zion." It, too, has suffered from — shall we say — "Fakers?" At least, from incompatible behavior.

It has been blasted with compromise; torpedoed with infiltration of uncommitted members; mined with lukewarmness; gunned with worldliness; shelled with humanism; bombed with ritualism; and missiled with commercialism.

All of this has been hurtful, so injurious that religion has been on the decline. If it continues, we may be asking, "What did you do with the ship?"

Ima Mess

The prudent man foreseeth the evil, and hideth himself; but the simple pass on, and are punished. Proverbs 27:12

A woman made this startling statement: "If they had named me in keeping with the life I've lived, my given name would be *Ima* and my last name would be *Mess.*"

We get ourselves in so many messes our status quo can be defined as the mess we're in. Come to think of it, that isn't a bad description of a big portion of our population.

We fail to figure our expenses versus our income — especially the probability of the unknown arising — and then we have debts that smother us. This puts us in another bind, as Solomon said, "The borrower is servant to the lender."

Sometimes we talk when we should listen. This gets us in difficulty. Alienates friends or expels strangers who might have become friends. At other times we get in a mixup by signing notes and becoming the surety for another person's debts.

The most heartbreaking messes, however, come from getting caught up in a web of sin and evil. People don't plan to go very far down the downward path, but it's hard to stop anything going down hill. At the bottom is the crash. Nevertheless, this caution can spare one the first step which ends in the smashup: "Abstain from all appearance of evil."

No matter what mess we're in, we caused it. Maybe some others helped, but in the last analysis we made the decision that put us there. Man's problems are man-made, but take heart — they can be God-solved, and He is saying, "Your iniquities will I remember no more."

Cut Wood and Let the Chips Fly

For do I now persuade men, or God? or do I seek to please men?
for if I yet pleased men, I should not be the servant of
Christ. Galatians 1:10

When I was a boy we burned wood. Those cold winters required a lot of it. I, with the help of a hired hand, had to cut it from standing trees. My helper was an old man, wise and overflowing with practicality. His name was Fred.

One day as we were getting ready to fell a tree, Fred said, "You see that tree. You see that axe. Just cut wood and let the chips fly."

That's what I did that day, and that's what I've tried to do ever since — "cut wood and let the chips fly."

This philosophy requires one to preach the gospel, or do his job whatever it is, or speak the truth, or uphold the right, and let the consequences take care of themselves. It requires fearlessness, forthrightness and uncompromise. And these qualities are essential if one would have the respect of the people. For the world is not going to follow the person who is not seen in this light. Wishy-washy people are never esteemed. Nobody can lead others while riding a merry-go-round, for he has no convictions on where he wants to go.

In making decisions, we should not be moved by what is popular but by what is right. In keeping with this spirit, Henry Clay said, "Sir, I would rather be right than President." And the Apostle Paul requested the Ephesians to pray for him to "speak boldy, as I ought to speak" (Ephesians 6:18-20).

Seeing Our Own Faults

*And why beholdest thou the mote that is in thy brother's eye,
but perceivest not the beam that is in thine own eye?*

Luke 6:41

A very unique story has come out of a village in Scotland where a half-witted man lived. He had a most curious coat that provoked conversation among all who saw it. All down the front it was covered with patches of various sizes, mostly large. When asked why his coat was patched in such an uncommon way, he would answer that the patches represented the short-comings of his neighbors. He would point to each patch, and relate the sin of some neighbor, then on to another until he had rehearsed the sins of all in the village.

On the back of his coat there was a small gray patch about the size of a penny. When asked what it represented, he would reply, "That's my sin and I can't see it."

This is a fair picture of many today, though they wouldn't want to make and wear such a coat.

Hence, what can we do to overcome this common problem of man:

1) *Recognize our faults.* "I do remember my faults this day" (Genesis 41:9).

2) *Overcome evil with good.* "Be not overcome of evil, but overcome evil with good" (Romans 12:21).

3) *Watch.* "Be vigilant" (I Peter 5:8).

4) *Pray.* "Watch and pray, that ye enter not into tempta-tion: the spirit indeed is willing, but the flesh is weak" (Matthew 26:41).

> *Somewhere, some way, sometime each day,*
> *I'll turn aside, and stop and pray.*
> *My own sins, dear Lord, let me see,*
> *And that will be a victory.*

Unexpected Trouble

Whereas ye know not what shall be on the morrow.
James 4:14

A tombstone with the human touch had this unique inscription, "I expected this, but not just yet."

When Job was enjoying health, happiness and prosperity, he did not expect his children to be slain, his property to be taken, his body to be afflicted with boils from head to foot, and his friends to deride him.

Today, we know illness will come, but we don't expect it to strike when it does. We are susceptible to accidents, but we're not looking for them when they arrive. The dismissal slip comes. When it does you suddenly belong to the unemployed. This catches you unaware.

Burglars strip your house. Precious valuables are gone. You had not planned to cope with this loss. A storm rips off your roof. Much damage is done. You weren't expecting this. Some of your supposed friends misjudge you and it hurts. You never thought it would happen. The death angel visits your family and kisses to sleep a dear one. And your heart aches and bleeds and breaks. The shock is severe. You hadn't counted on it.

What, oh what, can we do to handle unexpected trouble?

First, learn from Job who maintained his faith and trust in God. He said, "Though he slay me, yet will I trust in him" (Job 13:15). Leave it to Him.

Second, meet the problem with grit. You have strength you don't know you have. When the occasion comes you can draw on it.

Longing to Run Away

Oh that I had in the wilderness a lodging place of wayfaring men;
that I might leave my people, and go from them. Jeremiah 9:2

When we suffer demoralizing disappointment or bitter sorrow or agonizing failure, we are struck with the thought to flee and to seek refuge in a new place.

This was the mood of Jeremiah, as penned in the above Scripture. His tremendous sensitivity subjected him to the despondency that often goes with such a responsive temperament. And certainly the conduct of his people was enough to distress him — or any other impressionable person. In this gloom, he longed to get away from the burden of responsibility. He desired escape. He thought he could find relief in running away. Most people at some time or other feel much the same as Jeremiah did. This occurs because they experience defeat, disappointment, sorrow, humiliation, pessimism or some other suffering.

Running away, however, is no solution to the distress. It is not the heroic thing to do. Neither does it nurture self-respect nor personal strength. It rather weakens a person to run again when the next struggle gets rough. This is why some people have spent most of their life on the run. Too pessimistic or too frightened or too much in love with ease, they ran, and every run weakened them more and more for the next chase.

Understandably, fleeing is not the right thing to do. For it is our role to be stewards and a necessary duty of a steward is to be faithful and responsible. Also, it is our calling to be soldiers — not deserters. We honor God, family, friends and self when we trust on, hold on and fight on. Not in some distant place but where the conflict needs us most.

Betrayed but Not Beaten

The Lord Jesus, the same night in which he was betrayed, took bread: And when he had given thanks he broke it.

I Corinthians 11:23.24

Betrayed!

No one ever faced the world's sin and sacrilege, sorrow and suffering, scoff and snicker, as Jesus did. Yet throughout it all He was unchanged and undaunted, hopeful and heroic.

Jeusus was prepared to deal with the unfair and hateful treatment of a wishy-washy, degenerate, traitorous people. He knew all about them, their weaknesses, passions and prejudices. He understood the cowardice of His friends and the hate of His foes. He knew the weakness of Peter and the treason of Judas. Notwithstanding, He continued with His plans. Every step took Him closer to a cross on which a bloodthirsty mob would nail Him. Yet he did not refuse His destiny in a terribly evil world.

But how did all this affect His spirit and outlook? His feelings remained the same. He continued to pray and to be thankful. "The same night in which he was betrayed," He prayed and gave thanks. In the shadow of the cross He found there was much for which to be thankful. In that trying hour, with death so close, He also spoke to the disciples about the future of the church, and additionally gave instructions about a memorial to Him. Serenity and hope — not frustration and desperation — ruled his heart. This feeling was based upon a knowledge of all the facts.

In contrast, our partial knowledge and incomplete faith make us doubt and despair. Good people often become disillusioned in their fellowmen and become down-hearted. This presents a danger to their spirit and a threat to their future. Thus for a victorious life, let us look to the Master. He is saying, "Take up your cross and follow me."

Stay in There

For as he thinketh in his heart, so is he. Proverbs 23:7

A little boy who was in a scuffle ran away. When asked if he had lost, he replied, "No, I just ran away for a while."

I like that. For there is no defeat until a person admits it. So train your mind not to accept overthrow. Stay in there.

Nine times out of ten defeat was due to the mind's raising a white flag when it should have shouted, "Charge"!

DEFEAT

If you think you are beaten, you are;
If you think you dare not, you don't;
If you'd like to win but you think you can't,
It's almost a cinch you won't.

If you think you'll lose, you're lost;
For out of the world we find
Success begins with a fellow's will,
It's all in the state of mind.

Life's battles don't always go
To stronger or faster men,
But soon or late the man who wins
Is the one who thinks he can.

Defeat is not so bad, if it does not become a vocation. Not so tragic if it's a preparation for a continued effort. In this case defeat is not defeat — just a temporary setback which gives stimulus to a new start.

To be a winner we need to be mentally prepared to face struggle, no matter how big it is. I am reminded of the minnow which — due to hallucinations — said, "Now where's that whale?"

I Don't Like Being Taken

And your father hath deceived me, and changed my wages ten times; but God suffered him not to hurt me.   Genesis 31:7

After a lady and her five little children started attending church, she appealed to me to help her. Her husband was in the state penitentiary, and she wanted me to get him released. That wasn't easy back then and especially since he was a bricklayer and was needed in the construction work going on at the prison. Feeling sorry for her and the children, I agreed to help and without charge.

After several calls to the governor and other officials, they agreed to let him out if I would get him a job. Now that's difficult — getting a job for an unseen, unknown convict. After much effort, however, I got him employment.

Still more had to be done. He needed clothes and I furnished them. He needed transportation to get to and from his job and to carry his tools. I lent him $100 (equal to $500.00 now) to make a down payment on an old car. He promised to pay me back $10.00 per week. All I ever got from him was $30.00 and that wasn't easy to get.

However, under the same circumstances I would do it again. I didn't help him, for people who fail to respond to goodness are not helped; but maybe I did help the poor wife and the even poorer children. Whether the effort helped them or not, it helped me. For God blesses givers regardless of the merit of the receivers.

A Lifetime of Learning

*And besides this, giving all diligence, add to your faith virtue;
and to virtue, knowledge.* II Peter 1:5

The haughty college senior, feeling his importance, said, "Listen, I know a few things."

The freshman confidently answered, "You don't have anything on me. I suppose I know as few things as anybody."

After the senior finished the semester and received his degree, he rushed out and shouted, "O world, you would have suffered if I had not been born. Here I am. I have an A.B."

Then the world shouted back just as loudly, "Listen son, it will take you a lifetime to learn the rest of the alphabet."

When a person is educated beyond his intelligence, the world has a way of adjusting him—lowering him from High Brow to Low Brow.

Then he gets the shock of his life when he learns that many people with so little classroom schooling know so much that he doesn't know. The reason is: Education is where you find it and they continued to find it where they were on a day-to-day basis.

God wants us to add knowledge. The Christian's calling does not include a non-studious life but rather a lifetime of increasing knowledge. And if older people have lived up to this command, they're going to know more than the younger ones — all other things being equal. "Days should speak, and multitude of years should teach wisdom" (Job 32:7).

I suppose at the bottom of every diploma it would be beneficial to add this relevant statement, "To Be Continued."

Ears That Don't Hear

They have ears, but they hear not. Psalms 115:6

Little boy Bobby got permission from his mother to play with another boy in a near-by park. The mother warned him, however, not to go to the other boy's home. She was insistent, "Don't go home with Jimmy, for I don't know how to get in touch with you."

Night was beginning to come on and Bobby hadn't returned home. Mother and father began to get frantic. He wasn't in the park. The neighbors didn't know where he was. After many calls and much searching, they located the other boy's home and there was their wandering boy.

After a few sighs of relief, hugs and kisses, the father said, "Bobby, didn't you hear your mother say that you were not to go to Jimmy's house?" "Yes, but barely," came the scarcely audible answer.

Bobby's hearing describes a world of adults. They hear, but barely. They hear, but don't heed.

A wife learned this from her husband. She asked him to carry a pot plant from the den to the backyard. He paid her no mind, just kept watching the football game. Five minutes later she asked, "Did you hear me?"

"Yes, I heard you, but didn't heed you," was the blunt reply.

Bobby's problem was he heard with the ear and not with the heart. Jesus linked both together — closed ears and hardened heart (Mark 8:17, 19). To hear, we must use more than our ears. We must also use our hearts.

The Beauty of Holiness

Favor is deceitful, and beauty is vain: but a woman that feareth the Lord, she shall be praised. Proverbs 31:30

A lady church member, known for her ugly face, was visiting the minister's wife. The preacher's boy — and children speak their feelings — blurted out, "You sure are ugly."

The mother embarrassingly scolded him.

The boy in his apology said, "I only meant if for a joke."

Too confused to think, the mother replied, "Well, dear, how much better the joke would have been had you said, 'How pretty you are.' "

Yes, some of us have a special talent for opening our mouth and sticking our foot in it.

It is said that "beauty is only skin deep." If you're speaking of physical beauty, that is right. That is why it is so short lived. And in departing, it leaves the marks that it has gone. But spiritual beauty is different; it gets more attractive as the years rapidly pass.

In a counseling session I asked a woman to write down the most beautiful and lovely qualities a person could have. She came up with this list: tolerant, forgiving, merciful, unrevengeful, courteous, polite, thankful, kind, helpful, affectionate, understanding, humble, mild, faithful, trustful, unselfish, enthusiastic, cooperative, prayerful, not self-willed, not easily provoked.

Nobody could say a person with these qualities is ugly. We can all be beautiful when we clothe ourselves with the beauty of holiness.

Provided It Is the Right Two

*And the Lord God said, It is not good that the man should
be alone.* Genesis 2:18

Last year little Jimmy went to summer camp. This was the
first time ever for him to be away from home alone. He wasn't
known for his letter writing, but one day he did write a card.
It contained only twenty-one words:

> Dear Mom and Dad,
> There are 60 boys in camp this week, but I sure wish there
> were only 59.
>
> Jimmy

As seen in Jimmy's case, one can be lonely without being
alone. The most lonely I have ever been was in the midst of
seven million people. I was in New York City and knew
nobody. Many others must have been lonesome, too. As I
walked down the Great Illuminated Way, I saw the stamp of
loneliness on the faces of the mass of humanity. So it takes
more than people to save you from the empty lonely feeling.
You need people you know and enjoy and with whom you
have a communion of spirits.

Of course, there is one comforting thing about loneliness —
it is better to be alone than to be in bad company.

However, there are ways to prevent loneliness even though
you're separated from people: When you're with a book that
is pleasant and helpful, you're not alone. When you're engaged
in prayer, you're not alone. When you permit God's Holy
Word to speak to your heart, you're not alone.

Nevertheless, this is still true: "Two are better than one" (Ecclesiastes 4:9) — provided it is the right two.

Horse Sense

Let your yea be yea; and your nay, nay. James 5:12

A boy at dinner asked his father, "Dad, what does it mean when they say a fellow has horse sense?"

"He can say, *Nay*," replied the father.

It's horse sense to learn to say, "No." Not easy. But power for daily living and success demand it. We face a barrage of requests — hit from every side — that require us to say *Yes* or *No*. It's easy to say *Yes*. It's the *No* that is harder to speak.

Mankind has suffered immeasurably because frail humans found it difficult to say *No*. And this trail of tears leads all the way back to Adam and Eve. Eve couldn't say *No* to the serpent. Adam couldn't say *No* to Eve.

Many a failure and predicament has come because *No* was too hard to utter. The alcoholic, the dope addict, the playboy, the criminal, the idler, the beguiled, the holder of bad debts, the school dropout, the compromiser, all failed to say No.

Today a world that groans in misery says, "My unhappiness is the unhappiness of not saying *No*."

But many *Yeses* are needed in life. No person should be all negative. So my definition of *greatness* is the courage to speak *Yes* and *No*, and the discernment to know when to speak each.

Playing on One String

Thus saith the Lord; Refrain thy voice from weeping, and thine eyes from tears: for thy work shall be rewarded . . . and there is hope . . . Jeremiah 31:16,17

The story goes that a distraught man was all set to jump from the Brooklyn Bridge. But a kindhearted policeman laid hand on him and pulled him back. The man, bent on suicide, protested: "I'm so miserable. My life is so hopeless. Please let me go."

"I will make you this proposition," stated the officer, "you take five minutes and give your reasons why life is not worth living, and I will take five minutes and give my reasons why life is worth living. Then if you still feel like jumping I shall not stop you."

At the end of the ten minutes they joined hands and both leaped.

As to whether this is true or not, I don't know. But this I do know — hope is the "anchor of the soul" (Hebrews 4:19). Without it a person is free to drift, or jump or give up. When hope is gone, there is nothing left.

There is a lesson in Frederic Watt's famous painting of "Hope." A young woman is sitting on a globe, head bowed, eyes bandaged, a figure of dejection; in her hand is a harp with only one string — all others are broken — and she is playing it, thumping out the music she can produce on that one string.

When everything is broken, gone, and the harp of life is left with only one string and it pressed to the breaking point, hope plays on it a sweet melody. When fortune is gone, health broken, opportunity fled, then hope takes up life's harp and plays on the one remaining string.

Laugh It Off

God hath made me to laugh, so that all that hear will laugh with me. Genesis 21:6

One of the very effective resources of creative people is their sense of humor, adaptability and playfulness. Their comments on unexpected ideas is entertaining to them and to others. Laughter comes easily to such people, like the bubbling waters of a flowing well. Anything is to them the starter for a bit of wit.

Care drives nails in our coffin, but laughter pulls them out.

> *Care to our coffin adds a nail, no doubt;*
> *And every grin, so merry, draws one out.*
>
> John Wolcot

The person who has not cultivated a sense of humor is to be pitied. For laughter is one of those blessings, like music and flowers, that God has given to relieve the tensions of life.

The day we can laugh at ourselves is the day we have grown up. And when we do, there is little chance that we shall be proud and pompous.

When we are faced with serious, difficult, and trying situations, we can clear our burdened heads and think better if we can laugh a bit.

> *Does your work get into kinks?*
> *Laugh it off.*
> *Are you near all sorts of brinks?*
> *Laugh it off.*
> *If it's sanity you're after,*
> *There's no strategy like laughter —*
> *Laugh it off.*
>
> Henry Ellis

Louder

But there be some that trouble you. Galatians 1:7

Grandfather held a revival in a community where some profane men decided to break up his meeting. In his first sermon, one of the men stood up and shouted, "Louder!" Accordingly, there being no public address system, grandpa raised his voice. A little later the man stood and yelled again, "Louder!" And louder grandpa got until surely everybody could hear. But shortly the man stood again and roared, "Louder!"

It was then that grandpa stopped his sermon and said, "Ladies and gentlemen, the day will come when this old world will quit turning, the sun will cease to shine, the stars will fall and explode, and Gabriel will blow the trumpet so loud that it will be heard around the world; and at that time I'm sure one in this crowd will stand up and holler, 'Louder!' "

One doesn't have to be able to make a speech to interrupt one. Nor does one have to be talented to stir up strife. Neither does a person have to be a seamstress to needle somebody. Being human, you are more sensitive than a piece of cloth; and smarter, so don't let the pricks show.

Be calm. Keep cool. Keep your head, for if it gets to be a battle of wits, you will need it.

You have no control over frustraters, hecklers, needlers and agitators, but you can control yourself and refuse to allow bitterness to spring up within you and trouble you even more than what some person does and says.

Life Is Not a Hundred Yard Dash

The thoughts of the diligent tend only to plenteousness; but of every one that is hasty only to want. Proverbs 21:5

Solomon states that haste leads to want. Yes, to many wants. Hurry wreaks its damage in stress, strain and unproductivity. It leaves many victims along the way of life.

Some people hurry sitting down doing nothing. When sitting down, waiting for a plane, they hurry; of course, it doesn't hurry the plane. Waiting for their meal at the restaurant, they hurry; but their steaming doesn't cook the meal any quicker. They feel hurried because they have had their foot on the accelerator of their nervous system so long.

We must wait for some things to run their course. For this reason some who live in a frenzied hurry would not make good obstetricians or midwives.

We should not allow external things and situations to set our tempo in life. For each individual is different and must set his own pace. The great Finnish runner, Paavo Nurmi, illustrated this principle. He always carried a watch with him in his races. He referred to it, not to the other runners. He ran his own race, kept his own tempo, regardless of competition.

Life is not a hundred yard dash, but is more in the nature of a cross-country run. Since it is not a short dash, victory does not always go to the swift but rather to the persevering.

My Country 'Tis of Thee

Then the chief captain came, and said unto him, Tell me, art thou a Roman? He said, Yea. And the chief captain answered, With a great sum obtained I this freedom. And Paul said, But I was free-born. Acts 22:27,28

The Apostle Paul was thankful for his Roman citizenship.

There is no perfect country; and to speak out against what you believe is wrong in a nation does not mean that you are any less patriotic than the citizen who tolerates wrong. The true patriot takes this view: "My country right, to keep it right; if wrong, to set it right." We want America always to be a country that kindles the pride of patriotism and makes us want to sing:

> AMERICA
> My country, 'tis of thee,
> Sweet land of liberty,
>   Of thee I sing;
> Land where my fathers died,
> Land of the pilgrims' pride;
> From every mountain side,
>   Let freedom ring.
>
> My native country thee,
> Land of the noble free,
>   Thy name I love;
> I love thy rocks and rills,
> Thy woods and templed hills;
> My heart with rapture thrills
>   Like that above.
>
> Our father's God! to Thee,
> Author of liberty,
>   To thee we sing;
> Long may our land be bright
> With freedom's holy light;
> Protect us by Thy might,
>   Great God, our King!

Remember the Goal

The Lord had called us for to preach the gospel unto them.
Acts 16:10

A young preacher went to an older preacher and asked him what to do to draw a crowd and to make a congregation grow. He said, "I have tried philosophy, history, book reviews and even politics, but the people won't come. What shall I do?"

The old man kindly responded, "Now suppose you try the gospel."

In writing, pick up the pen or touch the typewriter. In farming, plant the seed. In merchandising, sell. In sheep ranching, shepherd the sheep. In mechanics, wield the wrench. In transportation, move. In banking, get money in and lend it out. In social work, help somebody. In baseball, hit the ball. In education, teach. In building and maintaining a church, preach the gospel.

The point is — no matter what the cherished reason for a group's existence is and the major goal they have, unless they are watchful they may get diverted and bogged down in so many other matters that they lose sight of the original intent. This is one of the reasons people fail in various endeavors. It was said of a man whose business failed. "He got so involved in other interests that he let up on what supported his business." If a school gets so entangled in new projects that it gives only minor attention to the basic three R's, then a new crop of students will come forth who can barely read, write and figure. And if a church (which is a spiritual body) gets so absorbed in material matters that it assigns the gospel only to a back pew, then in time the other pews shall go empty.

Lose or Use Opportunity

And after the reading of the law and the prophets, the rulers of the synagogue sent unto them, saying, Ye men and brethren, if ye have any word of exhortation for the people, say on. Then Paul stood up, and beckoning with his hand said, Men of Israel, and ye that fear God, give audience. Acts 13:15,16

The name of William Jennings Bryan has gone down in the annals of time as one of the greatest orators that ever graced a platform. A few years before his death a friend was riding with him across Chicago. They passed close to the coliseum where he made a most forceful speech at the Democratic Convention, 1896, the very speech which catapulted him to become the presidential nominee of his party in three elections. It was the speech in which Bryan concluded by saying, "You shall not press down upon the brow of labor this crown of thorns. You shall not crucify mankind upon a cross of gold."

The friend said, "Mr. Bryan, I suppose many times before you had made just as able a speech as that, and it was never heard of."

"Yes," he replied, "I suppose so. But that convention was my opportunity, and I made the most of it." Then after a moment of silence he said, "And that's about all we do in this world — lose or use our opportunity."

Grabbed opportunity is the key that opens the door of success. Seized occasion is the ladder by which men and women climb to usefulness and achievement. The answered call is the victory over slumber. He who seizes the right moment becomes the man of the hour.

So — "strike while the iron is hot." This is what the Apostle Paul did when he went into the synagogue.

Open House for Friends

And Julius courteously entreated Paul, and gave him liberty to
go unto his friends to refresh himself. Acts 27:3

Always keep an open heart and open house for friends. Also, open hands and open time. George W. Childs has said, "Do not keep the alabaster box of your love and tenderness sealed up until your friends are dead. Speak approving, cheering words while their ears can hear them. The kind things you mean to say when they are gone, say before they go. The flowers you mean to send for their coffin, send to brighten and sweeten their homes before they leave them.

"Let us learn to anoint our friends while they are yet among the living. Post-mortem kindness does not cheer the burdened heart; flowers on the coffin cast no fragrance backward over the weary way."

Of what shall a person make room in his house, if he has not room for friends? And of what shall he have time, if he has not time for friends?

True, helpful and beautiful friendships consist of knit souls like "the soul of Jonathan was knit with the soul of David" (I Samuel 18:1). This demands more than the shaking of hands and nodding of heads.

> *We just shake hands at meeting*
> *With many that come nigh;*
> *We nod the head in greeting*
> *To many that go by—*
>
> *But welcome through the gateway*
> *Our few old friends and true;*
> *Then hearts leap up, and straightway*
> *There's open house for you,*
> *Old friends,*
> *There's open house for you.*
>
> Gerald Massey

Live Expectantly

*For our sakes, no doubt, this is written: that he that ploweth
should plow in hope; and he that thresheth in hope should be
partaker of his hope.* I Corinthians 9:10

Call it the whispers of fancy if you wish, but I prefer to call
it the whispers of hope — and to listen to them. Hope is an
energizing voice. When you would drop dead in your tracks
it keeps you taking another step.

Living expectantly changes the tune of life. It makes the
night less dark, the solitude less lonely, the hurt less painful,
and the fear less acute. It gives broad dimensions to life.

But for many people this charming and winsome trait — the
zest of life — is gone. Instead of a growing expectancy and
excitement as the years go by, their lives have shrunk into dull
routines and dumb acceptances of the status quo. Here they
are in a big, wonderful world with just one try at it, and they
are allowing their days to be little more than the ticks of the
ever moving hands of time. It could be their world of adventure, savor, enjoyment and expectation. It should be.

Why do they live with no dream of the future? One reason
is they are asleep. Yes, asleep and satisfied. They are satisfied
to eat three meals a day, read the evening paper, watch a
favorite TV program, sleep eight hours, go to work and start
the same type of day all over again. No expectancy!

Another reason is they have practiced caution and timidity
so long that anything different would be disconcerting. It
would break into their routine of habits. Might make them
temporarily uncomfortable. Might threaten their safety. They
don't care to take the risks.

For these reasons they assign themselves to the humdrums
of life.

Go Apart With God

And when he had sent the multitudes away, he went up into a mountain apart to pray: and when the evening was come, he was there alone. Matthew 14:23

While God saw that it is not good for man permanently to live alone, His own Son saw that sometimes it was a great relief. Since Jesus felt the need to seek relief from the strain and stress of life, then how much more should that feeling sometimes exist in us. If He could find needed relief in solace and prayer, so can we.

Gaius Glenn Atkins has aptly stated: "Twice in each twenty-four hours the tides of the ocean — soiled and discolored through contact with our shores — withdraw themselves into the bosom of the deep to be cleansed and rebaptized in the clean and salt immensity of the sea. There they hear again the call of the sun, the moon and the stars, and come back cleansed with a blessed power upon the coasts which are unlovely without them and are kept sweet only by their healing contact.

"Life is like that. For we too are much stained through our contact with occupation or pleasure through all the coast of reality. The withdrawing tides of our souls need to be gathered again into the clean, the vast, and the unfailing; there to be rebaptized in goodness and vision; there to hear the voice of the eternal, to answer to the compulsion of the Unseen.

"Out of such a communion as this we shall return again to our duties and our relationships — healed and recollected — to achieve some vaster advance, some new victory and to release some deepened measure of love and power."

Every person needs sometime each day to be alone for a while, but not to stay.

The Bridge Not Crossed

The earth is full of the goodness of the Lord. Psalms 33:5

After a bachelor who was a recluse had passed this life some interesting pieces of paper were found in his cheap room, destitute of comforts. On those papers were written estimates of how long his money would last if he spent $50.00 a week; and how much longer if he could squeeze by on $40.00, including rent. The startling news is he could have lived another sixty years on the first figures.

The story arouses more sympathy than humor. He was haunted by fear; apprehensive of a future of forebodings. He pulled around him a cloud of gloom and lived on the basis that he might never make another penny, that his present pile might never earn a cent, and that his miserable, paltry existence might extend many more years than the normal span. While he denied himself peace of mind and necessities of body, his gold only cankered. He spent a life in building a bridge he never crossed.

This is an illustration of many people who are torn by needless worry. The utter futility and folly of this wretched lifestyle is most obvious. Truly a most serious barrier to happiness and efficiency is this tendency to brook over imaginary problems. It sets one up to become the prey of his own cheerless thoughts, which enfeeble him. Anxiety about some imaginary difficulty makes us less able to meet today's actualities. It is weakening to build bridges you will never cross. So —

> *Distinguish gold from dross;*
> *Waste neither time nor thought about*
> *The bridge you'll never cross.*

Confounding Speech

Go to, let us go down, and there confound their language, that
they may not understand one another's speech. Genesis 11:7

A man received a letter from an out-of-town attorney. But he didn't understand it; so he went to his own local lawyer with it, who said, "Go ahead and read it to me."

This is it: "Your uncle James, having come to advanced years, having suffered reverses, being debilitated by the encroachment of senility, in a moment of temporary dementia, perpetrated his own demise."

The lawyer said, "You want to know what it means? Well, in simple language it means this: Your uncle James grew old, lost his wad, went nuts, and bumped himself off."

I don't know that we have to speak this plainly, but we do learn from it the value of speaking with simplicity. Using speech hard to comprehend makes communications difficult.

The major consideration in speaking is not to use the biggest and most uncommon words but rather the words easiest understood. As an example in communication, we keep going back to Jesus. He used simple words and common examples. To shed light on His thoughts, He talked about a vine and its branches, a shepherd and the sheep, a watchman, light, salt, leaven and a sower. He used ordinary matters to teach the deepest and most profound lessons. An extraordinary point can be expressed in ordinary words.

No one is blessed by what he does not understand. Our speech is to communicate; if it doesn't, we have failed.

Pluck Makes Its Own Luck

Be of good courage, and he shall strengthen your heart, all ye that hope in the Lord.   Psalms 31:24

Fortune favors the brave. The bells of success toll for the gritty. The person with pluck definitely has better luck than the person without it.

Pluck is the bulldog spirit of bravery and tenacity one exemplifies in facing opposition or an adverse circumstance. All of us at times are called upon to wrestle with failure, disappointment, miscalculation and outright opposition. The question is: Do we have the grit to bravely meet the threat and to triumph over it? If we have, there is a good chance our pluck will turn to luck.

> *For any struggle to be won,*
> *Must be determined, dared and done.*

And also in that same spirit,

> *No problem has a wrench that will fit,*
> *Unless appl'd by a person of grit.*

A person's grit, however, is never fully known until he's fully tested. Then the hidden heroic quality has a chance to come out. What is thought to be ordinary people rise to extraordinary heights when the challenge comes. A common cat can prove to have a lion's heart when backed into a corner. How much more this valiant spirit is seen in man . . . and in the simple, ordinary affairs of life, as in the case of a man's having a sick wife, three kids and a mortgage.

The harder the match, the greater the victory; and the more strenuous the struggle, the more satisfaction in winning.

Logical Deduction

He answered them, I have told you already, and ye did not hear: wherefore would you hear it again? will ye also be his disciples? John 9:27

A logical deduction!

Some of the clearest and most irrefutable logic I have ever heard was expressed many years ago by an old farmer. It was down-to-earth logic from a man of the soil. He said that he had learned from experience (now get this — had learned from experience) that when cholera breaks out among his hogs and one takes it and lingers on and on and on that it has a much better chance of getting well than one that takes it and dies right straight.

I never did question his logic.

Jesus made an appeal to logic in teaching a lesson on the wise and foolish builders (Matthew 7:24-27). Actually, it is a story of the logical thinker in contrast with the illogical one. The wise man built his house on the rock and it withstood the storms. But the foolish man built his house on the sand and the storms swept it away. In his defiance of logic and common sense he tried a short cut. His logic went to pieces and so did his house.

The lives that stand are the workmanship of sound logical thinking. The fallen lives that lie in heaps of wreckage along the pathway of life are the ill results of unsound reasoning. They thought they could get without giving, play with fire and not be burned, could sow one thing and reap something else. They couldn't!

It's tragic to disregard facts or to try to suppress them. Thus we should never abdicate logic and common sense.

Shall We Soak the Other Fellow?

They that received tribute money (taxes) came to Peter, and said,
Doth not your master pay tribute? He saith, Yes.
Matthew 17:24,25

While eating breakfast in a local restaurant a very interesting and revealing conversation occurred. Three men at a table close by were discussing Federal income taxes. It was their unanimous view that *all* loopholes should be closed. Yes, *all*. They thought some taxpayers were getting breaks. Their views were definite, ardent and almost vehement.

After some introductions I joined in their discussion. I said, "You say you don't want any loopholes. Well, let's look at some. You get a tax deduction for you, your wife and your children. Do you want that loophole closed? You have another loophole on the deduction of interest you pay on your home and other debts. You want this ended? You get a deduction on contributions to church and charitable institutions. You want this loophole closed?"

They responded, "Certainly not," to all the questions. Then came the revealing answer: "What we meant is to close the loopholes for the rich."

That seems to be the consensus of a fair tax — one that taxes the other fellow. God commanded the tithe — 10%. This was a flat rate and God's view of fairness. The more one made the more he gave, but the rate was the same. Jesus paid taxes and surely it was not out of His abundance.

As citizens we enjoy the benefits of government, and thus have a fair and divine obligation to "Render therefore unto Caesar the things which are Caesar's" (Matthew 22:21).

Thanksgiving

Giving thanks always for all things unto God and the Father in the name of our Lord Jesus Christ. Ephesians 5:20

Our forefathers' desire to have a special day of thanksgiving is indeed a laudable quality. While they were poor in many respects, they were rich in thanks. We are blessed to be the descendants of such robust, grateful, high-type people. We are the privileged children of a glorious heritage.

It is not what a person gets that makes him truly great — it is what he is thankful for. This shows the nobler side of his soul.

Thanks are justly due for favors and blessings bestowed. And the person who feels no compulsion to say "Thanks" for the courtesies, considerations and blessings given him is unworthy to receive more.

Even a dog will wag his tail at the person who gives him a bone.

So don't expect happiness if you live below the level of a dog. Indeed, our degree of happiness depends much upon the depth of our gratitude. Have you ever noticed that a grateful mind is a joyful mind?

If life is sweet, give thanks; if bitter, give thanks — that you still have life, which gives you another chance.

> *My God, I thank Thee who hast made*
> *The earth so bright,*
> *So full of splendor and of joy,*
> *Beauty and light;*
> *So many glorious things are here,*
> *Noble and right.*

Adelaide A. Procter

Be Thankful

Know ye that the Lord he is God: it is he that hath made us, and not we ourselves; we are his people, and the sheep of his pasture. Enter into his gates with thanksgiving, and into his courts with praise: be thankful unto him, and bless his name. Psalms 100:3, 4

"Every good gift and every perfect gift is from above, and cometh down from the Father of lights, with whom is no variableness, neither shadow of turning" (James 1:17). This is visibly evident in His supplying the needs of His creatures. Year by year earth's inhabitants are fed, watered, clothed and warmed. Generations come and go, nations rise and fall, yet God continues to live and keeps this old earth turning and the sun shining, and sends seedtime and harvest, day and night.

"My cup runneth over" (Psalms 23:5).

At this national Thanksgiving season may we recognize the God from whom all blessings flow—either directly or indirectly—and offer Him the praise of our lips, the love of our hearts and the consecration of our lives.

Such gratitude can deepen character and spark personality. One of the chief requisites for making an optimist is a grateful memory. Yet, how often we forget! And how devastating it is to personality and outlook on life! The person who constantly complains that nothing goes right, that everything is against him, invariably has a good "forgettery," rather than a good memory. But the optimist—the winner—sees his blessings and counts them with appreciation. It centers his days on the positives of life.

"It is a good thing to give thanks unto the Lord" (Psalms 92:1).

A Great Person Is Thankful

And be ye thankful. Colossians 3:15

A Sunday School teacher began her class by stating that everyone has been blessed and should be thankful. Then she asked one little boy for what he was especially thankful.

"My glasses," he replied.

That seemed strange.

He explained, "They keep the boys from hitting me and the girls from kissing me."

In time he will outgrow the latter cause for thankfulness, but he will never, never outgrow — no matter how old he becomes, or how much he amasses, or how much he accomplishes — the many other reasons for gratitude that are visited upon all people in every nation and circumstance of life. Whether all are thankful or not, there are a thousand reasons to be.

You can be thankful for the earth that gives a place to stand, for the sun that gives you warmth and light, for the tree that gives you shade, for the air that lets you breathe, for the animals in your subjection, for the sprouting seeds that give you food, for friends who walk by your side and hold your hand, for the God who loves you, for the Bible that gives you direction and hope, for the fellowship of the church that gives you strength, for the hope of immortality that takes tragedy out of death, and for countless other blessings.

You will never outgrow the reasons to be thankful. For you are a dependent being, and that dependency will last a lifetime.

Read to Your Little Children

Blessed is he that readeth, and they that hear . . .
Revelation 1:3

I know some parents who are always buying books to read to their children. Their favorites are Bible story books: books with high morals that shape the mind and mold the character. They would gladly sacrifice food for their own stomachs to have books (mental food) for their children. Every purchase is a matter of priority, and they place the cultivation of the mind at the top.

Napoleon said, "Show me a family of readers, and I will show you the people who move the world."

Reading will open up new worlds for your child, real and imaginary. Read for information, read for character formation, read for inspiration, and read for pleasure.

By reading to your child you write on his or her heart. Moreover, you write what water and soap can't wash away. Many things you do for your child may change with the shifting sands of time, but reading to him or her engraves on the heart a record that time changes not. Actually, the child becomes a book himself, known and read of others.

If you want your child to have a scholastic and wholesome mind, start shaping it when it is young. In so doing, you give that precious one the richest riches. Here are the closing lines from one of my favorite poems, *The Reading Mother*, by Strickland Gillilan:

> *You may have tangible wealth untold;*
> *Caskets of jewels and coffers of gold.*
> *Richer than I you can never be —*
> *I had a mother who read to me.*

Keep an Open Mind

What need we any further witnesses? Mark 14:63

The judge's decision left them astonished and bewildered. One morning as he was shaving, dressing, getting ready to go to his court, his wife was very insistent that he meet her on a certain street corner at 11:00 o'clock. At first he refused. But, after reconsidering, he decided it would not take too long to hear the case, so he agreed.

After the trial got underway, it was evident that it would take longer than he had thought. As it got near the critical time for him to leave, lo and behold, the two opposing attorneys asked for one hour each to argue the case further. The judge ruled: "Requests granted. But I promised to meet my wife at 11:00 o'clock, and when you get through arguing, you will find my decision in this little drawer. I wrote it out last night before I went to bed."

The judge's mind was in a strait-jacket.

Too many decisions are made on no truths, or half truths, or one-sided presentations, or preconceived ideas.

Prejudice is a slave to error, a lid on open-mindedness, and an obstacle in the road of progress. May we keep an unbiased mind. Hear a matter fully, investigate, compare and analyze. Hear both sides. Factual decisions can't be made without all the facts.

One of the most noble examples of the open mind is the Bereans who "received the word with all readiness of mind, and searched the Scriptures daily, whether those things were so" (Acts 17:11).

Ambition Pursues High Goals

There remaineth yet very much land to be possessed.
Joshua 13:1

Edward Gibbon's epic, *The Decline and Fall of the Roman Empire,* is a classic example of a pursuing ambition. The author began this work at Rome on October 11, 1764. Twenty-three years later on June 27, 1787 at Lausanne he wrote the last line of the last page. The price had been great: it had absorbed his attention; he had given up much of his freedom; he had sacrificed many calls and joys of life; though old age was coming on, the astounding work was accomplished. His fame was secure. He had aimed high. He had "hitched his wagon to a star," as Ralph Waldo Emerson has suggested that man should do.

The urge to go forward, to attain, to succeed, to improve, and to master is a fundamental law of human nature and Christianity. It is a law of growth and development.

The Apostle Paul is a great example. He counted not himself to have apprehended, but reached forth to the things that are before — and that showed him to be a great Christian.

Frederick Watts is also a noteworthy pattern. At eighty he felt that his best pictures were yet to be painted. No wonder he became historic.

Joshua is another glorious example of high seeking. At the age of a hundred and ten he went down to death with these words of the Lord ringing in his ears, "There remaineth yet very much land to be possessed" (Joshua 13:1).

He who shoots at the stars will shoot higher than he who aims at a bird's nest. Ambition is a necessary condition of success. It has no substitute.

If We Knew Each Other

Then hear thou in heaven thy dwelling place, and forgive, and do, and give to every man according to his ways, whose heart thou knowest; (for thou, even thou only, knowest the hearts of all the children of men). I Kings 8:39

While some of us claim to have an open mind we have a tendency to shut it to people we don't like and to their failures. This could be because we don't really know them.

If we understood the causes of one's failures, we would be less critical of him or her. Let us, therefore, be more eager to find an explanation of one's faults.

If we knew each other better, we would love each other more; we would be more tolerant, more forgiving, and more helpful. There are so many hidden causes we don't know. All we see are the effects. It is easy to jump to conclusions; but before you do, try jumping into his shoes and walk awhile. Oh, how those shoes might pinch. You just might turn out to be the limpingest fellow on the street.

TO KNOW ALL IS TO FORGIVE ALL

If I knew you and you knew me,
As each one knows his own self, we
Could look each other in the face
And see therein a truer grace.
Life has so many hidden woes,
So many thorns for every rose;
The "why" of things our hearts would see,
If I knew you and you knew me.

Nixon Waterman

Fatigued From Fanning

Seeing then that we have such hope, we use great plainness of speech. II Corinthians 3:12

"When you deal with something, don't mince words" was the view of Grandfather, an unusual preacher.

At a preachers' conference that was held to discuss the merits or demerits of preaching on hell, the chairman pointed him out and asked, "Do you preach on hell very often?"

"No, not often."

"Why not?" inquired the chairman. "Is it because you feel that you are not effective on this topic?"

"No, because it disrupts the service."

"How's that?" continued the chairman.

"It's like this," explained Grandpa, "the audience becomes so fatigued fanning that I have to declare a recess about every five minutes."

Being fully plain gives one a chance to be recognized as a sharp intellectual — or as a blundering fool. On the other hand, speech that hides one's views is to no purpose — unless that purpose is to be political and to ride the fence, and that's no feather in any person's cap.

Speaking plainly is the safeguard of democracy in government and orthodoxy in religion. When people don't speak up they get exploited.

As we speak forthrightly, however, let us follow the common decency of courtesy, consideration, kindness and helpfulness. Then we shall be welcomed as people worthy of an audience, whether it be one person or a million.

Free the Slaves

*Stand fast therefore in the liberty wherewith Christ hath made
us free, and be not entangled again with the yoke of bondage.*
Galatians 5:1

The cruelest and most rigorous slavery is self-enslavement.
We put ourselves in a harsh bondage by picking and serving
the wrong masters. In doing this we become:

• *Enslaved to self-satisfaction.* This takes away the freedom
to advance and make progress. This slavery is usually ra-
tionalized by saying, "Oh, I'm holding my own." But the world
is bigger than hold-your-own perimeters. There are still rivers
to cross, plains to traverse, and mountains to climb. Where
there is no ambition there can be no climb.

• *Enslaved to hate.* Love opens the whole world to you, but
hate is very restricting. Hate can always build a fence around
the hated one. The trouble is: when the fence is completed the
hated one is not within it — only the builder.

• *Enslaved to vengeance.* Whosoever digs a pit shall fall
therein. And he that rolls a stone shall be hit by it. A crip-
pled, imprisoned slave. The better way is, "If thine enemy
hunger, feed him; if he thirst, give him drink."

• *Enslaved to restlessness.* Our world is surely a troubled
one. Every newspaper we pick up screams scary headlines at
us. There is so much disorder to unsettle our nerves and trouble our brow. Confusion in government, in world politics, in
military matters, in business, in labor, in education, yes, and
even in religion. Why do we have a frenzied, frustrated people who can't handle their lives and resort to quackery and
even suicide? It may sound simplistic but the basic reason is:
They have gotten away from Him who said, "Come unto me,
and I will give you rest."

What a Friend We Have in Jesus

If ye shall ask any thing in my name, I will do it. John 14:14

This popular hymn was written by Joseph Scriven, who was born in Ireland, 1820. He immigrated to Canada at age twenty-five, where life was hard and trying. His heart was big, and he freely helped the poor and needy, giving away most of his own clothes.

Though Scriven was kind and sympathetic, he was a lonely man. His only link with his family in his native land was the slow traveling mail. His mother became ill in 1857. Besides illness, there was her sorrow of Joseph's being away. He would write and comfort her as best he could. On one occasion he wrote and sent to her this renowned hymn to dispel her fears and give her courage.

What a friend we have in Jesus,
All our sins and griefs to bear!
What a privilege to carry
Everything to God in prayer!
Oh, what peace we often forfeit,
Oh, what needless pain we bear,
All because we do not carry
Everything to God in prayer!

Have we trials and temptations?
Is there trouble anywhere?
We should never be discouraged,
Take it to the Lord in prayer:
Can we find a friend so faithful
Who will all our sorrows share?
Jesus knows our every weakness,
Take it to the Lord in prayer.

Changing Circumstances Require Adjustments

Thou knowest not what a day may bring forth.   Proverbs 27:1

Changing situations demand adjustments. This is the way life must be lived. Confucius stated it this way, "The grass must bend when the wind blows across it."

We are forced to react to such changes as ill health, loss of job, financial reverses, coming of a baby, misunderstandings, misplaced confidence, new assignments, a move into a strange city, marriage of a child, and even death.

Let me tell you about a good woman's adjustment to death. After years of happy marriage her husband passed this life. They had been together so long. A love couple was cut half in two and it seemed that half of her had died. A big change had come. A big adaptation had to be made. And she heroically and hopefully made it. She resigned herself to the unchanging fact that her lover had been taken, that she was left behind, and that life for her would have to continue. There was no bitterness, no resentment. She sought no sympathy. She rather quoted, "The Lord gave, and the Lord hath taken away; blessed be the name of the Lord" (Job 1:21). She knew she could not roll the calendar back. She would have to start a new life from where she was.

She found these words of David who lost his son a healing balm for an ache she once thought would never end: "Wherefore should I fast? can I bring him back again? I shall go to him, but he shall not return to me" (II Samuel 12:23). Such a fixed purpose gave her a triple blessing: hope, direction and courage.

If she at her age could make such a major adjustment, don't you think you, the younger, can make the more minor adjustments you are called upon to make?

What an Honor to Be Called "Chicken"

Thou shalt not follow a multitude to do evil. Exodus 23:2

If one refuses to go along with the crowd, he is apt to be called "chicken." However, those who do conform certainly have nothing to crow about.

The word is used to slur and belittle the person who refuses to fall in line with the group. Unquestionably, it takes real strength and iron will to stand for convictions against the crowd. When one brave soul of convictions was told that the whole crowd was against him, he simply replied, "Then I'm against the whole crowd."

If the slur "chicken" causes you to give up your persuasion and become a conformist, it is then that you actually become "chicken," a weakling so weak that you can be scared and handled like a chicken.

All truly great people have learned to be different from the run-of-the-mill type of humanity. It takes much more courage to stand alone than it does to run with the crowd.

Pilate, the governor that tried Jesus, let the crowd infamously control him. He had some conviction but not enough. During the trial his wife sent a message to him, warning him not to listen to the multitude's clamor. He was afraid, however, the mob would say, "Pilate chicken"; so he decided with the crowd. His wife tried to get him to hear another voice — the voice of right. Nearly everybody has someone that is trying to get him or her to hear the voice of right.

The major concern should not be the smear from the smearers but the possibility of becoming one of them.

"My son, if sinners entice thee, consent thou not" (Proverbs 1:10).

Godliness Makes for Prosperity

And the Lord was with Jehoshaphat because he walked in the first ways of his father David, and sought not unto Baalim . . . Therefore the Lord stablished the kingdom in his hand . . . and he had riches and honor in abundance. II Chronicles 17:3-5

Jehoshaphat began his reign as king of Judah when he was thirty-five, and reigned twenty-five years. Since it was one of the most prosperous reigns, it gives insight to the true way of prosperity. He was a peaceful king. Godly. He was a teacher, sending out princes and priests to instruct the people in the Scriptures. God honored him because he honored God.

Being on God's side is the best way to avoid the pitfalls of evil and to secure our footing. Those on sinking sand or questionable ground are the most vulnerable to attack. Moreover, they are unhappy, and unhappiness invites the assaults of temptation.

There is a great uplift of heart in the consciousness of doing right. It lifts one above discouragements, doubts, and temptations toward an unworthy life. This sort of elevation and self-image gives courage, hope and cheer.

Thus piety is the best friend to prosperity. The Bible states this, "Godliness is profitable unto all things" — even for "the life that now is" as well as for "that which is to come" (I Timothy 4:8). It pays here and now to do right.

No kingdom or government is on a solid and lasting foundation that does not make room for the law of the Lord.

"Righteousness exalteth a nation: but sin is a reproach to any people" (Proverbs 14:34). A fact of life!

A Tribute to a Dog

Moreover the dogs came and licked his sores. Luke 16:21

One of the most beautiful tributes ever paid a dumb animal came from the lips of George Graham Vest. The occasion was a court trial pertaining to the killing of a boy's dog, which was held in a Missouri town. He said:

"Gentlemen of the Jury . . . the one absolutely unselfish friend that man can have in this selfish world, the one that never deserts him, the one that never proves ungrateful or treacherous is his dog. A man's dog stands by him in prosperity and in poverty, in health and in sickness. He will sleep on the cold ground, where the wintry winds blow and the snow drives fiercely, if only he may be near his master's side.

"He will kiss the hand that has no food to offer; he will lick the wounds and sores that come in encounter with the roughness of the world. He guards the sleep of his pauper master as if he were a prince. When all other friends desert, he remains. When riches take wings, and reputation falls to pieces, he is as constant in his love as the sun in its journey through the heavens.

"If fortune drives the master forth an outcast in the world, friendless and homeless, the faithful dog asks no higher privilege than that of accompanying him, to guard him against danger, to fight against his enemies. And when the last scene of all comes, and death takes his master in its embrace and his body is laid away in the cold ground, no matter if all other friends pursue their way, there by the graveside will the noble dog be found, his head between his paws, his eyes sad, but open in alert watchfulness, faithful and true even in death."

When he concluded there were but few dry eyes in the audience. The jury promptly returned a verdict for the plaintiff.

Sixty Years Ago

I remember the days of old.   Psalms 143:5

How lasting is a precious memory; and, as Alexander Pope stated, "How vast a memory has love." Moreover, it gives the heart something to feed on.

By playing on the heart strings of memory there comes the swelling of a sweet and precious melody.

Reliving the happy past can put zest in the present. We need a memory that does more than take us backward, that also turns us around and pushes us forward with hope.

Memory — Oh! how many days and worlds you encompass! Within that one word lies the quickened poetry of humanity's emotions.

> I've wandered to the village, Tom,
>   I've sat beneath the tree
> Upon the school house playground
>   That sheltered you and me;
> But none was there to greet me, Tom,
>   And few were left to know
> Who played with us upon the green,
>   Just sixty years ago.
>
> Well, some are in the churchyard laid,
>   Some sleep beneath the sea,
> But none is left of our old class,
>   Excepting you and me;
> And when our time shall come, Tom,
>   And we are called to go,
> I hope we'll meet with those we loved
>   Some sixty years ago.

Overcome Evil With Good

Be not overcome of evil, but overcome evil with good.
Romans 12:21

There is a fascinating story about a wealthy but miserly farmer. A poor man whose house had burned and had no provisions came to him for help. The farmer, moved with compassion, decided that he would be generous and give the man a ham from his smoke-house. On the way to get it, the tempter whispered to him, "Give him the smallest." The farmer struggled whether he would give a large or small ham, but finally he took down the largest one.

"You are a fool," the tempter said.

"If you don't keep still," the farmer replied, "I will give him every ham I have."

It seems that when a person gets set to do something good, he is always struck with a satanic thought to prevent it or to lessen it.

This conclusion is fully borne out in the following verse: "Now there was a day when the sons of God came to present themselves before the Lord, and Satan came also among them" (Job 1:6). Not to aid! But to hinder! A little shocking, but isn't that a logical place for him to work?

When your good intentions are bombarded with selfish, evil and diverting thoughts, there is not but one thing to do: answer with a big emphatic *NO*. This is the tactic used by Jesus, who said, "Get thee behind me, Satan: thou art an offense unto me" (Matthew 16:23).

If the temptation persists, you must go all out and threaten to do even better and more. You can overcome evil with good. Never by succumbing!

Lying Lips Are Not Becoming

The lip of truth shall be established for ever: but a lying tongue is but for a moment. Proverbs 12:19

Mrs. Jones got an awful shock when she learned that little junior had told a lie, at least a fib. In her confrontation with him and discipline of him she hammered away at the ugliness, vileness and danger of telling a lie.

She said, "A big mean man, looking like an ape, with long scrawny fingers, with blood-shot eyes, and a horn growing out of each side of his head, grabs little boys who tell lies and stuffs them in a big bag and carries them off to the dark side of the moon and makes them work in a coal mine and gives them nothing to live on but bread and water. Now," satisfied with her graphic presentation she gave it the final punch, "you won't ever tell another lie, will you, sweetie pie?"

"No mom," answered junior, "you tell bigger ones."

It's easy to tell a lie, but it's not easy to tell just one lie.

But we hear it said, "Maybe it's not so bad to tell white lies." It's not long, however, until the tellers become color blind.

Again it is said, "This world would be a boresomely dull place, if all we had was truth." Wait a moment, I don't take that view of another habitation where liars shall not dwell — heaven.

Another thing — most people don't have a memory good enough to be a liar. And still another thing — the liar because he is a liar believes nobody.

"Lying lips are abomination to the Lord: but they that deal truly are his delight" (Proverbs 12:22).

Each Complements the Other

And the rib, which the Lord God had taken from man, made
he a woman, and brought her unto the man. Genesis 2:22

Years ago I was asked the question, "Why was man made before woman?"

I jokingly replied, "I don't know unless it was to give him some time to think up the answers to her first questions."

Really, we can't fault the answer too much because the Apostle Paul has said, "And if they will learn anything, let them ask their husbands at home" (I Corinthians 14:35). This does put appreciable responsibility on the man. Why not? For if he's going to be the head, he needs to come up with some answers.

A long time ago God made the couple. Each was made to complement the other. Eve was indebted to Adam for life; and Adam to Eve for making life worth living. Today we still have couples: some good, some not so good, some bad. Therefore, it is appropriate that we consider:

THE MEASURE OF A COUPLE

Not — how shall they die?
    But — how shall they live?
Not — what do they gain?
    But — what do they give?

These are the standards
    To measure their worth,
A man and woman
    Regardless of birth.

Was It a Compliment?

Woe unto you, when all men shall speak well of you! for so did their fathers to the false prophets. Luke 6:26

Recently I attended a funeral in which the minister said of the deceased, "No one ever spoke an ill word of our beloved." He meant that sentence as a compliment, but was it?

This could not be said of the Apostle Paul. He was called a babbler and a troublemaker. Finally he was led outside the gates of Rome and beheaded because of his unyielding faith and uncompromising convictions.

Neither could this compliment be paid to Jesus. He was accused of working in conjunction with Beelzebub, the prince of the devils. Public favor so turned against Him that He was crucified.

When a person has the praise of all people (there are many kinds), he has been so flexible and so wiggly as to bend out of true form. As seen in the above passage, it places a person under the condemnation of the Bible and tags him as one we should avoid.

Paul knew enough about people to know that his expressed belief could precipitate ruffled feelings and strong opposition; nevertheless he spoke out. He did, however, temper his message by asking, "Am I become your enemy because I tell you the truth?" (Galatians 4:16).

When no one ever speaks a harmful word against you, it indicates that: You haven't done much. Or you have no convictions. Or you are afraid to speak up. In any case, it is not complimentary.

Sheep Thief

Ye have put off the old man with his deeds; and have put on the new man. Colossians 3:9,10

It has been reported that two brothers were once convicted as sheep thieves. In keeping with their crime, their recognizable and humiliating punishment consisted of branding on the forehead the letters *ST*, which meant "Sheep Thief."

One of the brothers was unable to bear the brand of shame; so he ran away and buried himself among strangers in a foreign land. But still he was asked the meaning of the letters, which agonized him to flee from land to land. At last, he died embittered and friendless, and was buried in a forgotten grave.

But the other brother, penitent of his mistake, decided to stay at home and stick it out. He told himself: "I can't run away from the truth that in a time of weakness I gave way to temptation and stole sheep. Running away won't change the fact. Whether the people know it or not, I shall know it. So I will remain here until I win back the respect and good will of the people." As the years passed, he gained a reputation for respectability, integrity, dependability, helpfulness and godliness. No one questioned his living on the highest plane. He had established himself.

One day a stranger in the little town saw the old man with the letters *ST* on his forehead and curiously asked a villager what they indicated.

After thinking a little while the neighbor replied, "It happened a long time ago, and I have forgotten just what occurred; but I think the letters are an abbreviation of *Saint.*"

Tragedy of Believing Something False

And for this cause God shall send them strong delusion, that they should believe a lie: That they all might be damned who believed not the truth, but had pleasure in unrighteousness.
                                                            II Thessalonians 2:11,12

In the western part of our county a lady was faced with a very perplexing problem. Her husband went to the battlefields of World War I. She lived in fear that he would not survive, and in this concern she herself died a thousand deaths. Finally the dreaded letter from the War Department came, stating that he had died in battle. Believing the report, she grieved immeasurably. With the passing of time, however, a broken heart began to heal and she married again. More time passed and one day her first husband appeared on the scene. He was alive. Her believing a false report did not make it true. Her believing he was dead did not make him dead.

In all the affairs of life — government, business, marriage, war, religion — the belief of a proposition does not guarantee the truthfulness or safety of it. Many a bad move has been made by legislators who believed they were doing right. Many a person has lost money by believing a fraudulent investment was sound. Many a battle has been lost because the commanders believed a lie. Many a person has blindly followed man instead of God because he did not investigate.

Thus it is incumbent upon us that we look before we leap, think before we move, and investigate before we align. John commanded this wise course in religion: "Beloved, believe not every spirit [every person who claims to be under the influence of the Holy Spirit], but try [prove] the spirits whether they are of God: because many false prophets are gone out into the world" (I John 4:1).

More Faith and Less Worry

Which of you by taking thought can add one cubit unto his stature? Matthew 6:27

I remember seeing my grandmother in her old rocking chair. I can still hear the profound bits of philosophy that came from it. One was, "Worry is like a rocking chair; it gives you something to do, but it doesn't get you anywhere."

There is a world of difference between worry and concern. A worried person fretfully sees a problem, even though it's not there; and the concerned person calmly solves the problem. The worried person crosses rivers before he gets there, and if it's not there he makes one; but the concerned person goes ahead and when he gets to a river, he detours, or swims it, or takes a ferry, or builds a bridge.

Worry is the payment of a debt before it is due, which in most cases is never due. Most of our worries are over troubles that never happen. Life requires thought, planning, arrangement, re-arrangement, adjustment, re-adjustment; but you can do it without worrying about it.

More faith in God's care prevents fretful anxiety. Worry can't get started, if you believe that everything will work out all right, someway, somehow.

> Said the robin to the sparrow,
> "I should really like to know
> Why these anxious human beings
> Rush about and worry so."
>
> Said the sparrow to the robin,
> "I think that it must be
> They have no Heavenly Father
> Such as cares for you and me."

The Last Token

There is no fear in love; but perfect love casteth out fear.
I John 4:18

There is a very impressive painting by Max Gabriel which tells a touching love story. It is called "The Last Token." The original is in Paris, but copies of it are found in many galleries.

It portrays a scene when Christians were the objects of fierce persecution and ghastly martyrdom. It pictures a beautiful and slender maiden about to be gnashed and torn to pieces by wild animals. She is standing on the ground of the amphitheater, crowded with a cruel mob ready to make sport while she dies. The iron grating to the cage has been lifted, and an enraged tiger has crept out of his steel confines, and, with the glaring eyes of an instinctive killer, faces his helpless victim.

The maiden is clothed in white, except the dark mantle covering her head and shoulders. Only a few feet from the opening out of which the tiger is coming, she heeds him not, but rather seems to be caught up in another thought. At her feet lies a white rose, thrown into the arena by some lover or relative or friend, who isn't afraid to be loyal to the very end. Her upturned eyes eagerly scan the crowd for the face of him who cast the rose.

One single rose with one loving, unfailing heart behind it has changed the whole spectacle. She is oblivious to the hungry beasts and jeering mob — all that matters is a white rose and triumphant love. Perfect love has cast out fear.

Knowing that God and others love us, plus our reciprocal love for them, casts out fear. It is impossible to be brave, if we love no one and think no one loves us. Love gives the assurance that we do not stand alone, and this braves the heart.

Every Life Needs a Center

When Christ, who is our life, shall appear, then shall ye also appear with him in glory. Colossians 3:4

There is an interesting story concerning Rear Admiral Richard E. Byrd's first expedition to the South Pole. He left his small isolated hut one day for a brief trip of exploration, and then in a sudden storm became hopelessly lost. In that barren whiteness there was nothing to give him any sense of direction. If he had struck out blindly to find his hut and had failed, the chances are he would have become lost in the storm and would have perished.

He had a long pole which he always carried to feel if there were holes in the ice; so he stuck it in the snow and tied a scarf to it. He said, "That was my center. If I failed to find my hut, I could return to the center and try again. Three times I tried and failed, but each time I returned to my center, without which I would have been lost and would have died. In the fourth attempt, I stumbled upon my hut."

Every life, to be safe, must have a center, a point of reference, a point of return. Everything must have a center around which it revolves. In mathematics it is established in the decimal point. In literature it is set up in the basic rules of grammar. In Christianity it is found in Christ. He is the center. Our standards come from Him. "To live is Christ" (Philippians 1:21).

If we should lose our bearings when life's storms beat upon us, we can return to our center and start all over again. This assures us that we shall not lose our directions for long. Indeed, it is a comforting thought to live in the Land of Beginning Again where all our mistakes and all our heartaches can be left behind.

Do It Now

Behold, now is the accepted time; behold, now is the day of
salvation. II Corinthians 6:2

Whatever you need to be saved from — sin, dismay, disillusionment, fear, boresomeness and hopelessness — behold, now is the time.

Whatever you need to do for God, country, others and self, now is the time. If all postponed intentions were given normal caskets and buried, this old world would be crowded for space. And in burying those good but never-performed intentions, the procrastinators buried their might-have-beens.

What greater grief than to look back on the wasted past? One *Now* is worth a hundred *Laters*. There is no better philosophy than *Live Today*. He who doesn't get full value from today's living is not apt to get a better bargain tomorrow. Concerning real living, it almost boils down to this—*now or never*. Some exceptions. But not many.

NOW

If you have hard work to do,
  Do it now.
Today the skies are clear and blue,
Tomorrow clouds may come in view,
Yesterday is not for you;
  Do it now.

If you have kind words to say,
  Say them now.
Tomorrow may not come your way,
Do a kindness while you may;
Loved ones will not always stay;
  Say them now.

The Harder Fence to Pull Down

Love your enemies, bless them that curse you, do good to them that hate you, and pray for them which despitefully use you, and persecute you. Matthew 5:44

Two farmers became bitter enemies because of a fence which separated their farms. That fence of posts and wire could be pulled down easily. But there was another fence between them much harder to remove than one made of wood and metal — the barrier of hate. At first it harrassed their peace of mind. Then it upset their production. Next, it sickened their bodies.

Finally one of them called in his minister and spoke of the fence and his neighbor. After awhile the preacher said, "You don't like him . . ."

"Like him!" he stormed out. "He's a stinkin' skunk with no principles."

The minister proceeded, "George, that fence out there on the farm is really not very important, but that one in your heart is. Unless you overcome this animosity it is going to destroy your living, peace of mind, health and soul. You should pray for your neighbor every night and for yourself. Ask God to bless him and his farm. Ask God to help you to rid yourself of hate."

Naturally he objected. But after much reasoning he agreed that he would try. That night he prayed, "Dear God, I promised the preacher I would pray for that dirty excuse of a man. You know I have mixed feelings, that I want him to be blessed and I don't want him to be blessed; but if you think it's best, go ahead and bless him."

The next night it was easier; and the next, still easier. In time they became the best of friends and a new life opened up for them.

Can't Stop to Chase Off Every Dog

Ye shall observe to do therefore as the Lord your God hath commanded you: ye shall not turn aside to the right hand or to the left. Deuteronomy 5:32

When I was a boy we had one possession that not every family had. It was our pride and joy — an automobile, a Model T Ford. Values are a relative matter.

Occasionally we made the trip into town in that Model T. It was a luxurious, pleasurable ride. It certainly beat walking or riding in a buggy or a wagon. The ride was slow, over a narrow, bumpy, dirt road.

Our slow travel subjected us to the harrassment of all the dogs along the way. They would run out and bark at us; however, their bark was much worse than their bite. I shall never forget my father's philosophy on this point. He said, "If we stop to run off all the dogs that bark at us, we never will get there."

That principle, learned at an early age, has stuck with me. I have tried to live by it. If I had stopped every time somebody barked at me, I never would have accomplished anything.

There are many things to divert our attention. Pulls from every source and every direction.

Therefore, to reach our goal:

- *Look ahead.*
- *Go.*
- *Keep going.*

You may not completely reach it, but there's one thing sure: you will get closer and put on muscle for the effort.

Go One Way

And they . . . did eat their meat with gladness and singleness of heart. Acts 2:46

Singleness of heart. Go one way.

A farmer, while driving down a street in a Texas town, was loudly warned by a pedestrian, "This is a one way street!"

He yelled back, "I'm going only one way!"

Though it was unintentional, the farmer expressed a very profound and essential principle of life, singleness of direction, go one way. It would prevent a world of frustration, nervousness, unhappiness and defeat.

One Sunday afternoon, a greatly distraught woman came to our house, seeking help. She was an unhappy bundle of raw nerves, thinking she couldn't wait until Monday for consultation. She said, "I'm pulled to pieces. It's killing me. I haven't had a peaceful day in three years." She was trying to travel in opposite directions — north, south, east and west — at the same time. The conflict was tearing her to bits.

Our peace of mind is dependent upon one-directional living. The reason we cannot have peace of mind is because we have too many minds. Those opposing minds need to be unified into a singleness of mind.

The Apostle Paul, as great as he was, also had to deal personally with the opposing pulls of life. He said, "I find then a law, that, when I would do good, evil is present with me" (Romans 7:21). He, as all successful and happy persons, got himself organized into a sufficient pattern of life to travel one direction. He could say, "This one thing I do" (Philippians 3:13). It gave him peace and satisfaction. This is what every life wants.

As Brooks Make Rivers

And he came to Nazareth where he had been brought up: and, as his custom was, he went into the synagogue on the Sabbath day, and stood up for to read. Luke 4:16

Years ago a rural mail carrier who drove a buggy stated that his horse would go the right way because of habit. The horse had gone over the route so many times he needed no guidance. When they came to a crossroad, there was no need to pull on either rein. That horse knew which turn to take. Habit had prepared him for the trip.

Thus it's a matter of horse sense that we develop habits that guide us aright. Life's up-hill-down-hill road has its turns and crossroads, and is much easier to traverse if habit just spontaneously keeps us on the right course.

Habit begins so small and becomes so big.

Ill habits gather by unseen degrees —
As brooks make rivers, rivers run to seas.

John Dryden

Habits — both good and bad — have a powerful hold on the human family. Habit is first just a cobweb, but when cultivated it becomes a cable — hard to break. We have the first say — we make the habits; but the habits have the last say — they make us. We cannot sow bad habits and reap a good life. You don't pick sweets from bitter weeds.

When evil habits make their play,
Give it no ear nor glance its way,
Touch not, taste not, when it first nears,
Stop the slavery when it appears.

Since habit is such a dominating power, then it should be made to work for us. All we have to do is develop the right kinds.

Protective Power of "No"

My son, if sinners entice thee, consent thou not.   Proverbs 1:10

In other words, give the enticement negative treatment. Say *No*.

As long as there is breath there must be the everlasting *Yes* and the everlasting *No*. This is because each person is caught between truth and error, right and wrong, love and hate, accomplishment and failure, sin and sanctification.

The courts, the jails, the penitentiaries, the clinics, the unemployment lines, the territory of the unhappy, and the heaped up pile of failures are filled with people who could not say *No*.

No is a little word, but it takes big people to speak it and stay with it. It is so easy to grant requests and to move along with the crowd.

There is aggressive power in positive thinking, but there is also protective power in negative thinking. In our society the former has been lauded and the latter lambasted. But both are needed. Both are essential to a successful life.

Even in the Ten Commandments eight are in negative form: *no, no, no, no, no, no, no, no,* and two in the positive: *yes, yes*. If you don't want to be putty in the hands of a world that would mold you into its shape, then you must say *No* when the hurtful call comes.

When we say *Yes* to God, we must say *No* to the world. Furthermore, our *No* must be stronger than the exploiters', the tempers', and the sinners' *Yes*.

Indeed, the person who hasn't a *No* in his vocabulary and a loud voice to speak it will be *Yessed* to death.

What Makes Achievers

They went forth to go into the land of Canaan; and into the land of Canaan they came. Genesis 12:5

This Scripture is a favorite among pursuers and achievers. It is well suited to all who have ambition, drive, determination and perseverance.

There are two qualifications for success in life:

• *Have a goal to which we start* — "They went forth to go into the land of Canaan." They knew where they wanted to go. You can't start going unless you have a goal; you wouldn't know which direction to go. A limousine is no better than an oxcart if a person doesn't know where he wants to go. So ask yourself: What do I want from the world? What do I want to contribute to the world?

The problem some people have is setting goals too low. This is what makes ordinary people ordinary — they need to raise their sights. Of all the goals we may have, let's be sure we include these: walk with God, enjoy life to the fullest, serve our fellowmen, and leave the world better than we found it.

As we act on our goals, they act on us: grip our attention and keep us happy, moreover — keep us young.

The words of Napoleon are very appropriate:

Great ambition is the passion of a great character.

• *Get going and continue.* A person needs to know what he or she wants to do with life, and then want that something so much that the goal is fully and tirelessly pursued. Move! And keep moving! No turning back! No letting up! After ambition is headed in the right direction, then it must become mobile.

Benefits From the Christmas Season

And suddenly there was with the angel a multitude of the heavenly host praising God, and saying, Glory to God in the highest, and on earth peace, good will toward men. Luke 2:13,14

At this season of the year when our minds are slanted toward peace and good will toward men, it is an excellent time for personal improvement:

• *Think first of someone else.* Be kind. Be gentle. Gladden the lives of others. Appreciate your friends and what they do for you. Express gratitude for all favors.

• *Examine your demands of others.* Think more about giving than receiving, and serving rather than being served.

• *If trouble has come between you and another, mend it.* Overcome malice. Replace suspicion with trust. Give a soft answer. Dismiss a grudge. Forgive a wrong. Flee envy. Listen. Try to understand. Apologize if you are wrong.

• *Contact a friend you have not seen or heard from for a long time.* Live again some of the joys you have had with that one in the past.

• *Be a friend to strangers.* Do something for the down-and-out.

• *Stretch your hand out to little children, to youth and to the aged.* All three groups are in special need of attention.

• *Enjoy the wonder and beauty of the earth.* Lift up your eyes to the heavens and see the glory of God.

These are but a few of the large number of helpful things we can do. They are simple. They are old but ever relevant. Their influence is immeasurable.

The Spirit of Christmas Recaptured

Remember the days of old, consider the years of many generatons: ask thy father, and he will show thee; thy elders, and they will tell thee. Deuteronomy 32:7

By rewinding the past, we can gain momentum for the future. As this occurs at Christmas time, we find ourselves joyously rejuvenated.

Eleanor Arnett Nash has stated: "Yesterday I wasn't a woman at all, but a little girl with a plump face and fat round black curls, a red sash tied about my cozy tummy, and a crisp white dress. For I've captured the spirit of Christmas. You see, I've recaptured it through the memory of Christmases of my childhood . . .

"*The sights of Christmases gone by:* Tinsel. Icicles. Red ribbon and white tissue. Flaming candles on a full branched tree. My mother, unbelievably beautiful for seven o'clock on Christmas morning. My father, a six-foot-two with the reddest hair, pretending to feel no emotion over our excitement . . . Broken candies you can't get nowadays, hanging from bough tips. Red bound volumes of St. Nicholas magazine. Toys — and the wax angel with the silver trumpet, topping the tree.

"*The smell of Christmas:* Cedar. Pine cones. Oranges. The crisp unmistakable odor of snow. Wood smoke from the huge open fire.

"*The taste of Christmas:* Peppermint. Maple sugar. Raisins. Yams all sugary . . . .

"As I remember I wonder.

"Are all the children of today being given memories to store up and bring out in much later years?"

One Solitary Life

For unto you is born this day in the city of David a Saviour,
which is Christ the Lord. Luke 2:11

An anonymous writer once penned this classic summation of the life of Christ:

"Here is a young man who was born in an obscure village, the child of a peasant woman. He grew up in another village. He worked in a carpenter shop until he was thirty, and then for three years he was an itinerant preacher. He never wrote a book. He never held an office. He never owned a home. He never had a family.

"He never went to college. He never put his foot inside a big city. He never traveled 200 miles from the place where he was born. He never did one of the things that usually accompany greatness. He had no credentials but himself.

"While he was still a young man the tide of public opinion turned against him. His friends ran away. He was turned over to his enemies. He went through the mockery of a trial.

"He was nailed to the cross between two thieves. While he was dying, his executioners gambled for the only piece of property he had on earth, and that was his coat.

"When he was dead he was laid in a borrowed grave through the pity of a friend. Nineteen centuries wide have come and gone, and today he is the central figure of the human race and the leader of the column of progress.

"All the armies that ever marched and all the navies that ever sailed, and all the parliaments that ever sat, and all the kings that ever reigned, put together, have not affected the life of man upon this earth as has that one solitary life."

The Man in the Mirror

*And herein do I exercise myself, to have always a conscience void
of offense toward God, and toward men.* Acts 24:16

When I first began to shave it was a first class comedy. If
Hollywood had known about it, I'm sure they would have paid
a big price just for the film rights.

As you can guess, there wasn't much to shave — just a little peach fuzz. Maybe three or four longer whiskers. By the
time I finished I was nicked, cut and sliced like I had been
through a storm of flying glass.

My father said, "Son, it's not the whiskers you see, but the
man in the mirror that counts."

Through the years I have remembered those words. He was
right. Let others think and say and do as they please, it's the
man that looks back at me in the mirror that makes the difference. If I have his respect and approval, I have the friendship of the one person on earth who can help me most, except God.

> *When you get what you want in your struggle for self,*
> *And the world makes you king for a day,*
> *Just go to a mirror and look at yourself,*
> *And see what that man has to say.*
>
> *He's the fellow to please, never mind all the rest,*
> *For he's with you clear up to the end.*
> *And you've passed your most dangerous, difficult test,*
> *If the guy in the glass is your friend.*
>
> *You may fool the whole world down the pathway of years,*
> *And get pats on the back as you pass.*
> *But your final reward will be heartaches and tears.*
> *If you've cheated the man in the glass.*

Mockery Changes Nothing

*Let them be turned back for a reward of their shame that say,
Aha, aha.* Psalms 70:3

Derision is a shameful thing. And useless. It changes nothing.

The grasshopper mocks the ant, but it alters neither the fortune of the grasshopper nor the ant. Winter will find them out, and then the little ant that stuck with his job all summer can say:

> *Where be your gibes now?*
> William Shakespeare

What difference does it make if the owl hoots at the dog's bark. The dog still has his job to protect the house and his bark continues to sound the warning. Neither does the parrot's mockery change the sweet melody of the canary.

When reason is against a person, he or she may resort to ridicule. It is a low, backhanded stroke that flattens nobody who is willing to stand up to it and go about his or her business. God made us, so let us be determined that mockers shall not unmake us. Mockery should be regarded as only an unkind sport that mocks the mocker and feeds on itself. So sneerers must be content to live on their own dish.

The important thing is for us to live as we should and leave the reaction to others, whether it be applause or mockery. It is ours to act, theirs to react. So let us stick to our purpose, do the best we can, and say in the relevant words of Job: "Suffer me that I may speak; and after that I have spoken, mock on" (Job 21:3).

Does No Good to Grumble

And when the people complained, it displeased the Lord.
Numbers 11:1

Constant grumblers are not appreciated. For the public knows the worst wheel of the cart creaks the most. So, say what you wish, nagging isn't horse sense. It is so useless.

> *Grumble? No, what's the good?*
> *If it availed, I would.*
> *But it doesn't a bit,*
> *Not it.*
>
> *Laugh? Yes, why not?*
> *'Tis better than crying a lot;*
> *We were made to be glad,*
> *Not sad.*
>
> *Sing? Why, yes to be sure;*
> *We shall better endure,*
> *If the heart's full of song*
> *All day long.*

Not everything can always go your way. Sometimes it's your fault. Sometimes it's the fault of others. Regardless of the cause, handle the aggravation in a way that spares your friends the fire and smoke of the occasion. It's wise to consume your own smoke lest friends annoyed by the fumes and soot of your complaints. When you feel wronged, file your complaint with the proper one in a gentle tone of voice. Hold your temper. Don't make enemies. A general rule is — be nice and nice will come back to you.

Making a just complaint is different from being an indefatigable grumbler. The latter comes so naturally with some people that they would grumble about their halo, if they had one.

Not Living in Vain

For I was ahungered and ye gave me meat: I was thirsty, and ye gave me drink: I was a stranger, and ye took me in.
Matthew 25:35

This means we do not have to live in vain.

If I can stop one heart from breaking,
I shall not live in vain.
If I can ease one life the aching,
Or cool one pain,
Or help one fainting Robin
Into his nest again,
I shall not live in vain.

Emily Dickinson

If I give a cup of cold water to a thirsty wayfarer, my life is not in vain. If I lift up a child who has stumped his toe and dry a tear, my life is not for nought. If I am only one tiny flickering light in a world of darkness, my life is not a failure. If I weep with one that weeps and rejoice with another that rejoices, my life is not purposeless.

If I guide and mold a child into honorable manhood or womanhood, my life is not useless. If I cast a ray of sunshine wherever I go, my life is not unimportant. If I set in motion one little bit of influence for good, my life is not futile.

If I bear the burden of a friend weighted down, my life is not unavailing. If I lift up one fallen person, my life is not ineffectual. If I read one Scripture to a soul that hungers and thirsts for righteousness, my life is not unfruitful. For God's word shall not return unto Him void (Isaiah 55:11).

I Shall Not Be Moved

They that trust in the Lord shall be as mount Zion, which cannot be removed, but abideth for ever.   Psalms 125:1

The ancient people of God beheld mount Zion as stable and unmovable. But they saw more than the mount and did more than relate to it. They perceived that trust in God would give them a fixed purpose and an unmovableness like the mount in the distance. It stood as a symbol of complete stability. This everyday scene, always there, always unchanged, conveyed a message to them — one that all humanity needs to heed. Stability! Solidity!

Indeed, trust in God provides the firm foundation that prevents us from slipping and tottering. It gives the fixed heart which brings the whole man into the effort, uniting and co-ordinating all his labors, and thus raises up a mountain of stability within him. On the other hand, distrust changes the solid mountain into the quicksands where the soul sinks lower and lower. However, when our trust in Him is full and undivided, we stand as unmovably as the mountain and can confidently declare, "The Lord is my rock . . . in whom I will trust" (Psalms 18:2).

I SHALL NOT BE MOVED

Though the tempest rage round me,
  Through the storm, my Lord, I see;
Standing like a mountain holy,
  I shall not be moved from Thee.
  I shall not be moved,
  Anchored to the Rock of Ages,
  I shall not be moved.

Alfred H. Ackley

Praise the Lord

*Praise ye the Lord . . . let every thing that hath breath praise
the Lord. Praise ye the Lord.* Psalms 150:1-6

Praise the Lord is chosen as the last devotional and guide
in this series of 365. In making this decision, I am following
the example of the Psalmist. For in the last five Psalms (containing 150) each begins and ends with praise — "Praise ye the
Lord." This was the fitting ending to the wondrous and superb
Book of Psalms. It is also appropriate that this volume ends
with an expressive laudation of the majesty of God.

As pilgrims, we have kept up the march, we have come to
the end of another year. Our days have been beset with trials,
temptations, conflicts, disappointments, sufferings, troubles,
defeats, sorrows and tears; but we also have had steps of faith,
climbs to greater heights, glorious victories, abundant blessings,
overflowing joys, renewals of confidence and beckoning hopes.
All of these vicissitudes have accompanied our chequered lives
as we have traveled to another marker in life's eventful
journey. The experiences, we hope, have made us smarter,
stronger, better, kinder, more helpful and more dependent
upon God and each other. Thus it is fitting that we exclaim,
"Praise the Lord!"

> *Praise the Lord, ye heavens adore Him!*
> *Praise him, angels, in the height;*
> *Sun and moon rejoice before him;*
> *Praise Him, all ye stars of light.*
> *Praise the Lord, for He is glorious;*
> *Never shall His promises fail;*
> *God hath made His saints victorious:*
> *Sin and death shall not prevail.*

Lowell Mason